TEACHING IN AMERICA

Teaching in America

A Cross-Cultural Guide for International Teachers and Their Employers

by

CHARLES B. HUTCHISON
University of North Carolina at Charlotte, NC, U.S.A.

 Springer

A C.I.P. Catalogue record for this book is available from the Library of Congress.

ISBN-10 1-4020-3771-6 (HB)
ISBN-13 978-1-4020-3771-9 (HB)
ISBN-10 1-4020-3772-4 (e-book)
ISBN-13 978-1-4020-3772-6 (e-book)

Published by Springer,
P.O. Box 17, 3300 AA Dordrecht, The Netherlands.

www.springeronline.com

Printed on acid-free paper

Printed in the Netherlands.

Dedication

To my wife Sandra—a mother to our children, a teacher and inspiration to our children and me, a global trauma consultant, an author in her own right, and the true intellectual in our family.

To Aba and Nana—our young children who sometimes insisted on offering slightly too much help during this project—our dream and pride.

To my late parents, Charles Bartels Hutchison and Regina Hutchison (also known as Nana Ekua Akyere II, Queen Mother of Abodo, Jukwa, and Obaatan Edziekyir of Twidan Ebusua of Cape Coast, Ghana), and Maame Sarah Aggrey, my late great grandmother: An encomium to all of you, for sowing the seeds of graciousness, worthy of emulation.

Acknowledgments

This book has become a reality only through the toil and tedium of many. I first thank God for the providence of the ambition to pursue and finish this project.

I am especially grateful to Mike Laspina for formatting this book, reproducing the diagrams, and reading through the whole manuscript to offer insightful editorial advice.

Thanks also go to Stephanie Phillips for reading through the manuscript, offering useful editorial advice, and helping with the indexing. This book would have taken much longer time to finish, were it not for the willing help of Mike and Stephanie.

I wish to thank the following for being instrumental in my life, and, ultimately the realization of this book: Mr. I.B. Eshun, an official at the Ministry of Finance and Economic Planning in Ghana; Harold and Tomalene Hutchison of Vici, Oklahoma, my godparents; and Professor (Emeritus) Jack Hassard of Georgia State University, my professional mentor. All these people helped to chart the course of my life, and I am grateful to them.

Hearty thanks go to the international teachers who participated in the study leading to this book. Without their voices, this book would not have been possible.

Thanks to Tamara Welschot and Astrid Noordermeer of Springer Publications, and also to my editors, who saw the potential of this book to help cross-cultural educators and provided constructive critiques for making it more useful to the readers. Thanks also go to the publishers of all the works cited in this book.

Finally, I wish to thank my family for accommodating my intermittent disappearances to work on this book. Thanks to my wife, Sandra, for being the compass in my life. Thanks to my daughter Aba and son Nana, for making it worth investing in this project. Together, these people always bring me down to earth, so that I might inhale, and I cherish them for it!

About the Author

Charles Hutchison, Ph.D., is Assistant Professor of Education at The University of North Carolina at Charlotte, and a consultant in international education, cross-cultural pedagogy, and instructional strategies for teaching diverse learners. He previously taught science in Ghana, and did research work in immuno-genetics in Hungary. In the United States, he has taught high school for nine years, and supervised a large science education program in a research university. He has been featured on national television and several international magazines. In 1990, he was awarded Key to the City of Boston and a Certificate of Recognition for his work in the greater Boston community.

Contents

INTRODUCTION

Scenario One
Imagine a teacher walking into a classroom. The students stood up to greet the teacher on his or her entrance through the door, and remained standing until they were beckoned to sit down. The students then sat down, with their eyes fixed on the teacher, waiting for instructions on what to do next. The teacher was in absolute control, knew exactly what was going on, and what to expect from the students. On their part, the students knew exactly what to expect from the teacher; standing up to greet the teacher on his or her entrance into the classroom was normal. In fact, it was cultural. They had therefore not done anything extraordinary. The teacher proceeded to have a very good class period. Nothing different was expected; this was a normal day.

Scenario Two
Imagine the same teacher, with the same expectations as in *Scenario One*, walking into a different classroom. The students did not stand up to greet him or her; they did not know about such a tradition, nor was it a part of their culture. In fact, some were standing and chatting with friends as he or she entered the classroom. The teacher became surprised, apprehensive, and wondered: Did some stand up as a sign of respect for me while the others sat? If they so respectfully stood up, then why were they still chatting with their friends? Should I "instruct"—forget that word!—plead with those sitting to stand up for me, or beckon those standing and chatting to take their seats? The teacher managed somehow to get those standing to sit down. They sat down, but with their eyes wandering, and so the teacher tried to find another strategy to keep the students' attention. The rest of the class period is better left to one's imagination.

The teacher knew exactly what to do if this scenario were changed to *Scenario One* above. However, in this new situation, he or she did not know what to expect from the students, and vice-versa. Needless to mention, the whole class period therefore became a grand stage for the exhibition of the teacher's frustration—and possibly the students' as well. The class period was therefore not so much for instruction as it was for experimentation with classroom management strategies.

Scenario Two can easily depict the world of teachers who move across cultural or international borders to teach in an American school. Indeed, many of the more than 10,000 international teachers currently in the United States (U.S.) are experiencing different levels of difficulty. International, cross-cultural education has been documented in the literature as a challenging experience (Atwater & Riley, 1993; Fortuijn, 2002; He, 2002; Kuhn, 1996; Shatz, 2002). Even if teachers are experienced and very successful in their own native countries, it is still very possible to be inept in a different teaching context. This book defines some possible new contexts for international teachers, and provides suggestions for making instructional success more attainable.

PARTICIPANTS IN, AND CONTENTS OF THIS BOOK

This book is laced with "case studies," making it an original, research-based analysis of the issues pertaining to international teachers. Perhaps a little unconventional for its content combination (and intentionally so), the conceptual view of this book is that international teachers, though intellectuals, are also concerned with real life issues in education. Yet, their academic selves yearn for theoretical frameworks for what others think and proffer. For this reason, there is a chapter included which discusses theories of interest for cross-cultural educators. There are also chapters devoted to some of the current best practices in teaching and learning that even veteran teachers may find refreshing. School administrators and employers will also find certain chapters especially useful for understanding and addressing the needs of cross-cultural educators.

Case studies, as a research method, can be useful in conveying the unadulterated voices of the participants. Coming through in the first person, the direct narration of the teachers' experiences (and therefore voices) are provided in the hope that such true-to-life stories will make the book more readable and more directly instructional. As readers travel through the contents of this book, they will hopefully be fully immersed in the realities of the lives of these international teachers. Commentaries on issues are provided, and research insights are consulted, in the hope that potential problems are recognized and resolved before they happen.

Although more fully introduced later, it may be useful to be briefly acquainted with the international teachers featured in this book. Each person in this book, by American standards, may be seen as successful teachers for several reasons. They were respected in their schools (located in southeastern part of America), very confident, professionally knowledgeable and effective, and could easily secure a teaching position in any school of their choice.

Mary was a middle-aged British woman who had lived and taught in several countries before coming to teach in America. Joe was a middle-aged British man who had also previously lived and taught in several countries. Kofi was a middle-aged, Ghanaian man who had taught in two African countries and traveled to a few other countries before deciding to teach in America. He began teaching after having lived several years, and obtained two graduate degrees in America. Inga was a German woman in her late twenties who did not have as much teaching or traveling experiences as the others. She had had less than two full years of teaching in Germany before coming to teach in America. Finally, I, the author am an African who lived and taught in Ghana, and lived in Hungary, before coming to teach in a U.S. high school for nine years. I am currently teaching in a university.

I, the author, reveal my identity and personal, true stories; facts and stories which are in harmony with those of the other teachers in this book. However, the names and other identity-revealing information have been modified in order to protect the identities of all the other research participants mentioned in this book. Although impossible to know the individuals involved in these stories, international teachers and faculty would find that these stories resonate with their own personal experiences.

AUTHOR'S PERSONAL STORY AS AN
INTERNATIONAL TEACHER

I was born and raised in Ghana, West Africa. I lived there for 28 years, during which I earned a science degree and a diploma in education. After graduating from college (which was modeled after the British system), I taught in a public high school for two years. This was a boarding school with about 600 students in Cape Coast, within a ten minutes' drive from the Atlantic Ocean. The students ranged between 13 and 21 years old, and I taught general science and advanced level biology.

The students were very respectful, mostly because that is a reflection of the African culture; a respect for elders and anyone in authority. For this reason, even before I entered the classroom, the junior-level students would run to their seats, sit up straight, be quiet and, at least, appear physically ready for instruction. If not hurrying to their seats, I could at minimum expect the upper-level students (who were just about five or six years younger than me) to be quiet and alert in all my classes, for the whole duration of the class periods. For any teacher in this or any other Ghanaian school that I knew of at the time, there was no reason to expect any less: Our students generally believed that they were in school to work toward a better future for themselves—not for the teacher. The teachers and students understood that any formal or informal instruction that transpired beyond the normal class hours were a favor to the students. Teachers generally went out of their way to help any willing students to do well in school, and the students were solicitous of teachers for extra teaching after normal class hours. What else could a teacher expect but the students' fullest cooperation, and even thankfulness and veneration?

Then I received a fellowship to study research methods in biotechnology in Szeged, Hungary. I seized the opportunity.

Life in Hungary was my grand introduction to global education and world cultures. For one thing, I needed time to get used to Hungarian foods—which were cooked quite differently from my familiar Ghanaian staples. For example, I had never seen temperately-grown apples. Ghanaian apples looked very different. Also, Hungarian was a very different language—one known to be very difficult to learn. The local people, however, were very nice and were most willing to help foreigners. They also almost took great humor to foreigners struggling to vocalize the Hungarian vocabulary. I still remember visiting a small church in the Hungarian countryside with a Baptist pastor (who thankfully spoke English), where many of the local people had never seen a dark-skinned person before! I therefore became a great specimen for them to adore. There was much hugging, kissing, feeling the texture of my hair, and so on. I had finally become popular (for about two hours)!

As a proficient English speaker in Hungary (even with my Ghanaian accent), it was interesting that I became the English teacher to my colleagues (over 30 of them from all over the world). During this whole year, we lived together in an international hostel and shared each other's culture—since no one in this international group understood or spoke Hungarian yet. We became a support-group to help each other; those who were missing home, children, spouses, and those who were sometimes frustrated with the difficulty of acquiring the basic phrases of the Hungarian language for such elementary functions as buying dinner at the market or restaurant. We cooked and ate foods from our native lands. We talked about our research, cultures, and politics. We also compared our native educational systems.

Again, as a good English speaker, I became the "local authority" of the English language within my small circles at church, work and international colleagues. People wanted to talk with me in order to improve their spoken English. I edited scientific articles meant for later publication in international journals. I also tutored a professor of pharmacology who had a lot of foreign students, and wanted to improve his English for instruction. In a way, this also helped me to have a quicker and deeper immersion into the Hungarian culture, since I was invited to numerous homes, and so was able to pick up on the language the fastest among my colleagues.

Then I got the opportunity to come to the United States in 1989. Again, I scized the opportunity. Since then, I have taught in a middle school, high school, and at three universities. In 1993, when I began full-time teaching in middle and high schools, I thought things would be easy. Having been a successful teacher in Ghana, the thought of having any difficulty teaching similar age-groups in the U.S. never occurred to me. However, on my very first day of teaching in the U.S. classroom, I realized that life was going to be different. Although I was teaching in a school where classroom discipline efforts were supported by the administration, it did not take long before I was overwhelmed with problems. There were two kinds of problems, looking back. The first problem concerned professional teacher expectations, which I found to be very different from what I was familiar with. The second problem was my lack of knowledge of contextualized, classroom management strategies, which proved to be the greater problem for me.

Looking back to those difficult days, I remember thinking to myself: "Anyone can teach African students, but very few can teach American students," and that, "In Africa, the teacher just teaches; in America, the teacher manages." Although not completely accurate statements in themselves, they still captured my sense of how things were—for me—and that was all that mattered to me at the time: that was the state of my world, and my obsession!

Although I asked a lot of questions, and had other teacher-colleagues help me, things got worse with time. The help I needed was beyond their reach; they were willing to teach me what they knew, as locally-trained teachers. They knew what worked for them, mostly by a lot of assumptions, pure intuition, and context-based training. Unfortunately, assumptions are built on knowledge—specific kinds of knowledge—a kind I did not have as an international teacher. Intuitions, like assumptions, could be seen as learned experiences which are so much a part of "natural" phenomena that they may be initially assumed, and then almost "wired" into one's nervous system. There, again, I was found wanting: I did not know what were the normal phenomena or traditions within the American teaching profession; the school systems, the nature of the students, etc. My assumptions (and therefore intuitions) and professional training were essentially Ghanaian; they did not work in America.

For the reasons above, as much as my American-trained colleagues tried to help me, there still existed a gap; an international, cross-cultural teaching issue. I was certainly operating in "survival mode," that is, doing just enough to make it through each period, knowing that I would live to pay for it the next day when I met the same students. This certainly made life very tough in and out of school. This is quite obvious; I was a struggling teacher, not in the content matter, but with mostly everything else. The students knew that too, and that is what made it worse. Naturally, after school, I would spend most of my time trying to make up for the deficiencies of the previous classes, and therefore had a rather miserable social life.

About two months to the end of the year, I was called to the principal's office. He informed me that, although I was very strong in content, I had certain peculiar difficulties, the chief of them being poor classroom management. I was therefore given about a month to show some significant improvement, or my contract would not be renewed for the next school year. (I still have the official letter he sent me.) I must confess that the principal was both nice and fair to me. I also understood that he had to be fair to his students; they needed a more effective teacher. To be sure, I became very concerned about my own future: If I was fired, how would I pay my bills? Could I get another job? What kind of job? Where? If I did not get any job, what would happen to my family? The list went on.

Of course, I knew that I had difficulties, and knew that solutions had to be found, and quickly! I resolved, and tirelessly worked out solutions to the problems. I even ended up becoming a popular teacher (with both students and parents). I was selected to become a mentor in the same school, where I taught for nine years. In the end, when I went to study for my doctoral degree, what else could I research, but the issue of international teachers' transitional issues?

In a way, I must confess that I had it easier: I had lived in the U.S. for almost four years before going to teach. I had even obtained a graduate degree (not in education) in a local university before getting back into the classroom to teach. I had also lived in a foreign country, and was familiar with some cultural issues that accompanied life as a foreigner. For these reasons, this story has not taken into account the cultural barriers I had to cross during my previous few years.

I found a way, not only to survive in the American classroom, but also to thrive. A more detailed and instructive narration is found later in this book.

Welcome to the American classroom. You too can succeed!

THE GLOBAL VILLAGE

The saying, "It's a wide, wide world" should be reserved for the days when the common means of transportation was by foot and mules. The new saying should rather be, "What a small world," describing the new, tiny "global village," and to connote our ability to have lunch in New York, and travel in a supersonic airplane to have dinner in Paris later the same day. The advents of the television and the Internet phenomenon have brought the whole world into the tiniest living room. Images of the realities in Indian and Bangladeshi villages and the largest cosmopolitan cities are now available in the small villages of Ghana, through CNN. One could pick up a cell phone on the plane and call a small village somewhere in the world; a phenomenon unthinkable just in the last decade. Hence, and thenceforth, middle school students in Zimbabwe are capable of collecting and exchanging environmental data with their American and Russian colleagues. Globalism, a kind of virtual reality, is upon us!

This shrinking world has brought about its own issues. In early 2003, when the SARS epidemic began haunting the world, airlines suffered a big dip in sales, since the Centers for Disease Control (CDC) in the U.S. made people understand that the disease was being spread rather quickly around the world, especially by air travel. Within hours, germs could be effectively spread around this small, global village. This message quickly resonated with the world, as nations took immediate measures to ensure that business- and tourism-related activities were under control.

Education has also felt the influence of this shrinking world: to some extent previously, and to a large degree nowadays. On-line, Internet, or distance education comes to mind. Teacher-, faculty-, and student-exchange programs have almost perennially been a part of education, and even more so, as the globe shrinks further. SARS, for example, interfered with several of these programs, as students and faculty either could not return home on time for fear of transmitting the disease, or had their teaching or learning experiences abbreviated, or completely eliminated. For better or for worse, this world has grown smaller, and this has inadvertently bound all cultures closer together.

INTERCONNECTIVITY: A COMMON DENOMINATOR

As this piece is being written (on October 27, 2003), 20 of the world's richest nations are meeting in Mexico, with global trade on their minds. Also making the headlines in the news lately are the concerns of various industries in the U.S. which are losing business to other countries, where labor is cheaper. Even such places as Mexico, to which American industries moved in the last decade, have begun losing their industries to nations where labor is even cheaper.

One result of this globalization process of the labor force is that education is beginning to respond to global pressures. In fact, the very idea of educational exchanges (as opposed to cultural exchanges) is inherent in the word "university," which connotes "universality." This begs the question: Universality of what? Is it the universality of curricula (the contents of subject matter in the disciplines), or universality of the contents of practice? Arguably, the tacit point could be made that educational practitioners did, long time ago, envision a smaller world abiding by a "universal" syllabus, especially at the university level. It is for this reason that, at the tertiary level, an education degree is transferable to virtually any part of the world; a kind of "one world system."

The above are just examples to help us understand how the world has become even more inter-twined, and interdependent, and that international teachers share in this experience.

THE EDUCATION CONNECTION TO GLOBALIZATION

Another interesting phenomenon is that as the world has shrunk into a global village and mobility has increased, the exchange of goods and services are taking place at several levels. These may broadly include general labor mobility, whereby people move to work in other places, and educational exchanges. Student and faculty exchanges of various kinds have been in existence for a long time. However, with the advent of such technologies as the cell phone, whereby anxious parents could reach their children immediately and vice-versa, it is conceivable that such exchanges will only increase.

The labor movement into the U.S., especially highly skilled labor, has typically included areas such as medicine and technology. The movement of teachers from mostly English-speaking world into the U.S. has expanded the flow of skilled laborers to include the area of education. Many of such teachers are coming to teach in critical shortage areas such as mathematics, science, and foreign languages. Others are coming to teach in areas where American-trained teachers prefer not to work, mostly in the urban regions and smaller towns.

The purpose of this book is to facilitate the transitions of expatriate teachers from their native countries into the American classroom. This is done by discussing some of the important issues to consider for easier transition.

Prospective employers may also find this book useful for understanding the strengths and the conceivable needs of their prospective employees. Once their needs are identified, numerous suggestions and ideas are provided for resolving them.

Chapter #1

MAKING THE DECISION
What International Teachers Need to Know Before Leaving Home

1.1 Why Foreign Teachers are Coming to Teach in America

United States (U.S.) schools have been experiencing a general shortage of teachers for several years. This is especially true in the areas of mathematics and the sciences (Orlosky, 1988; Darling-Hammond, 1999). Although Ingersoll (1997) and others have argued that this problem is only a perceived one, many schools in U.S. are indeed scrambling for teachers (National School Boards Association, 2000). In fact, the problems of demand and supply of teachers has always been a part of education (Pipho, 1988). Recently however, the shortage of teachers has become so critical that several states have changed their long-standing policies and practices for hiring teachers in order to secure enough teachers for their schools. For example, in the state of Georgia, teachers' salaries have been increased for several consecutive years so as to appeal to prospective candidates who otherwise would enter other competing professions. Other states such as Maryland and Massachusetts have offered $1,000.00 and $20,000.00 respectively as sign-up bonuses for prospective teachers willing to commit to teach in certain shortage locations (Chaddock, 1999).

Several states, including New York, Georgia, South Carolina, North Carolina, California, Chicago, Texas, and many more have been inviting experienced teachers from other countries to fill math and science positions (National School Boards Association, 2000; Cook, 2000). According to a National Education Association November 2003 report, as many as 10,000 international teachers are working in public school systems on "nonimmigrant" or cultural exchange visas. Although teachers are coming mostly from the English-speaking countries such as Canada, India, the

Philippines, and the like, there are also international teachers from many non-English speaking countries including France, Germany, Russia, and Mexico. Indeed, the issue of teacher shortages in the United States has grown in its importance as a national problem that an issue of Newsweek magazine was devoted to it with the front cover caption: "Who will teach our kids? ... Half of all teachers will retire by 2010. ... What schools and parents can do" (Kantrowitz & Wingert, 2000).

This problem has been long in coming, and was anticipated (Pipho, 1988). Orlosky noted in 1988 that, "critical problems are emerging with regard to a pervasive teacher shortage, competition with other enterprises for the most able people, ethnic and racial imbalances in the teaching profession, and a lagging response in education to developments in technology, business and industry" (p. 1). In retrospect, time has proved him right. Teacher shortages are indeed here, and the problem is real.

1.2   The Future of American Education and Foreign Teachers

The National Commission on Teaching and America's Future (NCTAF) and NCTAF State Partners (2002) state that "The high demand for teachers is not being driven by an undersupply of entering teachers, but by an excessive demand for teacher replacements that is driven by staggering teacher turnover." (p. 6). Darling-Hammond (1999), in concert with NCTAF, predicted the following in a report concerning the future of American teacher demand and supply:

> There is no doubt that demand for teachers will continue to increase over the next decade.... The most well-reasoned estimates place the total demand for new entrants to teaching at 2 million to 2.5 million between 1998 and 2008, averaging over 200,000 annually. About half of these are likely to be new teachers, and about half will be migrants or returnees from the reserve pool of teachers. (P. 6)

The trend of teacher shortages can be expected to continue for several reasons, including the following:

i)   increased student enrollment (via increased birth rates and immigration)
ii) demands of reformers for smaller-sized classes
iii) high or rising numbers of teachers retiring or leaving the profession

iv) the decline in the size of the teacher "reserve pool," and also,

v)   the decline in the current queue of teacher entrants
     (Darling-Hammond, 1999; Pipho, 1988; Grissmer & Kirby, 1997).

Beyond all this, the next ten years are set to see the first grand wave of baby-boomer retirees (Darling-Hammond, 1999). This will further aggravate an already difficult situation. It can therefore be expected that even more teachers may have to be "imported" to supplement the existing teacher workforce.

According to Hussar (1999), the median age of U.S. teachers is projected to be about 55 (in the year 2004). This implies that, all things being equal, the problem of teacher shortage is going to be even more certain, as larger numbers of U.S. educators retire each year. In fact, the next decade should see a huge wave of U.S. teachers go on retirement (ibid.).

1.3   The Open Door

To the international teacher, the shortage of teachers in the U.S. can be seen as an open door. On the one hand, it presents a real opportunity to work in the U.S., the land of opportunity. In fact, if one were to do a search on "international teachers" on the Internet, one would find several companies trying to recruit international teachers for American teaching positions. On the other hand, however, there is a peculiar problem presented: Under normal circumstances, even teachers who are born, raised, and educated locally experience some amount of induction (or initial) difficulties as they begin their teaching profession (Cocoran, 1981). It is therefore reasonable to surmise that international teachers would experience some amount of induction upheavals.

Owing to their peculiar circumstances, international teachers should expect to have a second tier of pedagogical problems beyond the normal order of induction difficulties. This naturally connotes that it would require extra effort for them to become effective educators in U.S. high schools. For this reason, one could therefore expect that their attrition rates would be even higher than the already disturbing current rate (which is 30% departure within five years of entry into teaching, and higher for disadvantaged school districts that offer few new-teacher supports [Darling-Hammond, 1999]).

1.4 Socio-Logistical (Support System) Issues to Know Before Leaving Home

Before coming to America, one could caption Mary, a white, middle-aged British woman as an international traveler: She had previously lived and worked in England, and two other European countries. Joe, a middle-aged white British man, had lived in Hungary, Africa, Germany, and England before coming to America. Kofi, a middle-aged black African man, had lived in Nigeria and Ghana before moving to America. Despite all their travels, they variously mentioned that moving to the United States was quite different for several logistical reasons. They also indicated that the factors involved in their move were relatively unpredictable for them. These included culture shock, emotional needs, and physical needs that were unexpected. This means that knowing what to expect on arrival is very important. A section of this book is devoted to the practical socio-logistical issues faced by real International Transitional Teachers (ITTs). It is hoped that this section will help other international teachers in this regard.

1.5 Know Why You Are Coming to America

It is conceivable that there are two kinds of people coming to teach in America. The first group may be taking advantage of the economic advantage of living in America. For this group of people (those generally moving from relatively less industrialized or relatively poor countries), it is very likely that their expectations will be rewarded with better living standards. With hard work and good work ethics, America is a place where foreigners may easily have better life, as compared to their own countries; it is indeed a place where, given the right circumstances and opportunities, people can pursue and make their dreams a reality.

For the second group of people (those moving from relatively more industrialized, wealthier nations) there is the need to be especially careful about what they are seeking as they think about such a big move. There are two main reasons for this consideration. First, caution is necessary because this group of people are already used to higher standards of living, and may possibly need to spend additional amounts (beyond their American salaries) in order to match their living standards back home, since teachers' salaries are generally viewed as unattractive by Americans. (This issue will be further discussed later in the book.) Second, the overall standard of living in America has steadily declined since the 1970s (Celente, 1997). International teachers moving in with their families should know that financial need has driven American mothers to work in order to support the family, and "the one-income nuclear family could no longer function as the standard working model" (ibid., p. 212). Financial planning is therefore vital before undertaking such a significant move.

Joe was very cognizant of some basic, philosophical issues involved in international transitions. For him, one has to count the cost before such a move. When asked what advice he would offer the prospective international teacher, he said that the teacher should

> …be very careful about the reasons why he is coming, what he hopes to achieve, what his plans are because that's going to govern various things on what he does and how he does it. So, for example, it's very easy to come from a place like England and not understand how the health system works or the problems getting teacher certification, for example, and various visa issues and when you leave a place like England or anywhere, are you just coming over for a year or two years, or are you intending to come over here for a while because that's going to mess up pension rights in England, it can mean selling a house with all the costs that's going to be and moving back again. There's a lot of additional costs so the teacher needs to be fairly clear on why they're coming, whether it's a clean break or not. If it is a clean break, then I think they need to try and make a real start at making this their home from the word "go." If you're in this half-half -- I might stay, I might go back, you're likely to end up not enjoying being here, not enjoying going back. Make a full commitment or just accept it for "Oh, I'll do this for two years, I'll see some of America, I'll survive living out of a box, and then I'll go richer for the experience," and move on [with life]. So those are the sort of big things I would suggest they need to cover.

Most international teachers one encounters are likely to be happy with their choice to move to America. After all, it is their decision to make such a move—and stay on—and there are indeed great opportunities in America. However, it is still a good idea to reflect on the issues involved in such a move.

1.6 Moving Expenses

Even within the U.S. borders, it is quite expensive to move from one location to the other. According to Homefair.com (in January 2005), moving a family of four from a three bedroom-house from Atlanta, Georgia to

Charlotte North Carolina could easily cost between $3987 and $4822 (see www.homefair.com). This is a distance of just about 350 miles.

Moving the same family across international borders would cost much more. Naturally, only essential belongings would be carried across international borders, owing to the high expenses. A single person would find it much easier to do such a move. On the other hand, people in family situations would find that the initial costs of moving the whole family could be overwhelming. It is therefore very important to do a good calculation to estimate your moving costs. Knowing that this may be a difficult proposition, it may be advisable to first have one person in the family (the one with the teaching position) move first and get a sense of the situation, before others in the family move in. There are several other reasons for using this strategy, as may be seen from the issues below.

1.7   Cost of Living

The living expenses for families in America are very difficult to estimate for several reasons. One obvious reason is the lifestyle of the family in question. An interesting article in a recent edition of the newspaper *Charlotte Observer* was captioned: "Many teachers find they need 2nd jobs to make ends meet." (The Charlotte Observer, October 13, 2003, p. 4B)

In this article, a teacher with seven years' teaching experience and a master's degree noted that she could not make ends meet on just her teacher's salary. She therefore cleaned homes and offices in order to make ends meet. She "vacuumed, dusted, cleaned the bathroom [including toilets], changed the bedding, did the laundry." (p. 4B)

This may not be a fair assessment of all teachers' living situations in America. A critical reading of this article, however, reveals that she drove a relatively more expensive kind of car, implying that she possibly had a relatively financially-demanding life-style. Her salary should be at least $33,400 (the initial salary for a certified teacher with a master's degree in North Carolina) through about $42,118 (the average teacher's pay in North Carolina) per 10-month period, in 2001-02 academic year. (Teachers also have the possibilities of summer work for extra income, although some go back to graduate schools in order to get a higher degree, thereby increasing their base salaries.) With just a bachelor's degree, one would make $25,250 for the same period of time, and possibly have a worse financial situation.

With the above noted, once again, one must ask oneself the question: Why am I leaving my current living situation to go to America? Again, depending on whether one's current living situation is at par, better, or worse, the responses would be different. For those moving just to see and enjoy another place in the world, some may realize that they may need to supplement their incomes with previous savings in order to maintain their previous standard of living. Those from poorer countries who are looking to better their economic situation and are comfortable with a thrifty life-style will find this opportunity one not to miss. In fact, many people from poorer countries will find America a true land of opportunity. Even though the first generation migrants (especially those with families) may pay a relatively dearer price for leaving their countries (mostly due to socio-cultural related issues), many migrants are known to make such sacrifices in order to seek better futures for their children.

Another significant consideration is the location in which one lives. In most American cities, a teacher's initial salary would not provide a very comfortable lifestyle. As noted earlier, teachers' salaries are not competitive with salaries in other professions in America. Granted that teachers' salaries are partly determined by the years on the job and degree attainment, it is vital that international teachers negotiate a reasonable salary, and be comfortable with the expected lifestyle they can have at the new teaching location. This can be dome by taking a cue from the local cost of living index and ensuring that their teaching experiences are taken into consideration. Again, a great website to visit is www.homefair.com.

Overall however, teachers in America may not be much worse off than any other professional groups in America. Indeed, it is very common to find several people who, after having worked in different professions, still opt to make a mid-life career change to become teachers. This may be reflected in the numbers in the alternative programs for teacher preparation in the U.S., especially during periods of high unemployment. As a former Acting Coordinator of an alternative teacher preparation program for science teachers in a large urban university, and a current instructor and advisor for many such prospective teachers, the author has learned that many new entrants into teaching find it relatively more stable as a profession, especially in a work climate where employer loyalty to employees has plummeted.

1.8   Miscellaneous Differences

1.8.1 Insurance and pension issues

In moving to the U.S., one has to know the implications of their departure in their native countries. Mary mentioned one issue as pension rights, and what one potentially loses on departure, depending on their country's policies. In this situation, it is vital that people know and plan how long to stay and work in the U.S. before certain benefits rights expire.

One significant issue that may be a shock to many (especially those from countries where health insurance is cheap) is the monthly premiums for health insurance. In the U.S., it is not unusual to have health insurance for family of four costing from a few to several hundred dollars per month, depending on the school system. Although most schools offer highly subsidized premiums, the final amounts for health insurance for teachers end up being very different. For example, for plan year 2003, teachers in the state of Georgia could opt for a plan (Blue Choice HMO) that charges $132.54 per month for the family plan. The cost for the same period for North Carolina teachers was 427.48 per month. Costs are very minimal in most cases for employees only. However, the costs increase significantly for family insurance coverage. Learning about such unforeseen costs of living is another good reason for only the employee to first move to America to scout out the best living situations for the entire family.

1.8.2 Power supply difference

Mary, for example noted that, besides the actual costs of moving, the appliances she brought over did not work because of the difference in power supply:

> There's also the expense of moving to live here, which takes a bit of recovery because everything that I bought in Europe didn't work because of the power. It was a more than expensive move. When I moved in Europe I just put everything in the car and drove wherever I wanted to go, caught the ferry over, but here is a different issue [in America].

Mary therefore asserted that if any items were of any importance to her, she had to purchase new ones.

International teachers may be pleased to know that there are several types of transformers which can either step power supplies up or down. There are also several types of adapters (for fitting appliances into various outlets) available in electronic stores that may help with this problem.

1.8.3 Stationery

Although insignificant, there are rather petty things which are still different in America, and could cause minor inconveniences. Mary noted the issue of stationery:

> Even stupid things, [such as] the size of the paper is different from the paper in Europe, so all the binders, folders, plastic envelopes that I brought with me with my notes, this paper doesn't fit. It's wider [and shorter] than the European paper.

The main irritation in this regard is when photocopies are being made. Teachers may need to adapt by copying their original documents onto longer, legal-sized papers that approximate A4.

1.8.4 Personal credentials

Personal credentials, as used here, refer to social security number (and card), credit cards, and driver's license.

It is almost impossible to live in the American city without the benefit of a credit card and a driver's license. The problem is that, credit cards are granted on the merit of trust—which takes some time and knowledge of an individual to establish. A requirement for obtaining a credit card and a driver's license is the social security number, which takes some time to get. The social security number is the *de facto* national identification system used in America for several purposes. For this reason, it is important for the international teacher to be prepared for the rigors (and some inconveniences) of waiting before the card arrives. The driver's license is easier to get, with the acquisition of the social security number.

Mary related the difficulty of acquiring a credit card on her arrival in the United States, and the consequences:

> The other major thing I found was that I was trying to get credit cards. A year ago, I got my first credit card, and I have a pathetically low limit because people don't accept the fact that I have a credit history in Europe. They just won't accept it. So I was born the minute I got off the plane. So I had to pay down payments on my electricity, telephone--I had to put deposits down because I was just a complete newborn. It has taken me four or five years to build up a credit history and that was a major hassle.

Banking and financial issues; they wouldn't give me a bank card. I found it very difficult to manage that to start with. Eurochecks were difficult to deal with when you first arrive. It took me two or three years to get credit card and I've had a credit card for twenty, twenty-five years in Europe, and car insurance.

Joe also talked about similar issues on his initial arrival in the U.S.:

I was still fightinggreen card [a permit for alien residents in the U.S.] and social security cards [and] driver's license. I mean, I had to get police records from Africa, Germany, England—all those things, and just settling down into a new country.

There are several consequences of not having a credit card. One of them is that one has to have cash immediately available or use checks for purchases. These transactions must be done in person—as opposed to credit card purchases, which could be conveniently executed in person, on the phone, or on-line (on the Internet). The other issue is that one pays more for certain services, as Mary succinctly indicates:

I paid a phenomenal amount of money for car insurance because I didn't have any history. I couldn't hire [rent] a car. Nobody would let me hire a car because they didn't know me, I couldn't rent any furniture. Anything I wanted to have, I had to buy. But that's just the way it works.

The issue with credit cards may be averted by opening a credit card account in the native country before leaving. If possible, an account should be opened with a major international bank in the native country and kept open when in America. Although credit cards are generally issued by specific banks, the establishment of credit—normally with Visa, MasterCard, or other companies (all of which are international companies)—may help to jump start one's credit rating in America.

It is necessary to know how to keep a good credit rating. This may include the frequent use of the card in order to establish a good activity history, and being consistent with payments for purchases, and not be late with payments.

1.8.5 Educational credentials

A potential candidate should be careful to have a proper evaluation of his or her educational credentials into the American system. This is very important for two reasons. First, teachers' salaries in America depend on one's current degree attainment and years of teaching experience. Second, not all the educational attainments and courses may directly translate into the American degree hierarchies. For example, Americans have the Specialist Degree (a degree between master's and doctoral classifications) which has no equivalent in many international educational systems. Although employing agencies will do this translation for potential candidates, individuals coming to the U.S. to teach on their own may do well to consult with a transcript translating agency for help. There are several agencies in the U.S. that will provide this service for a fee of between 80 and 120 dollars.

Mary's experience was a good example of the situation above. She noted her inability to transfer her educational credentials from the British system to that of the United States as follows:

> The lack of credibility of my qualifications is another personal issue, where they won't give me my master's qualifications even though I clearly have the equivalent of a master's. That's a big issue with me and that's that.

She alluded to the idea that the differences in the educational systems posed as a problem in the transfer of her credentials. For that reason, she was compensated at a lower level, and thereby suffered a financial penalty.

1.8.6 Visas

Owing to the teacher shortages in the U.S., the United States Immigration and Naturalization Service (INS), has created special accommodations for providing H-1B visas for foreign teachers. One needs to make sure that the United States Department of Labor and state licensing requirements are met. (This should be done in concert with the employing agencies.) A good website to visit is the official website of the INS section on H-1B visas, available at http://uscis.gov/graphics/howdoi/h1b.htm.

1.9 Culture Shock

A German professor on a 2004 visit to Charlotte, North Carolina, made the following remarks about the steps leading to a building: "These steps are different from what we have in Germany." He found himself being extra careful as he negotiated the steps, lest he fell. When asked how different the steps were, he noted that both the size of the steps and also the angle of the whole stairway were different.

Although this may not be the expected introduction to the idea of cultural differences, it may help to point out that culture is just the accepted way a group of people live and operate—and even build. Podolefsky and Brown

(1997) are of the notion that term "culture" includes the social organization, belief systems, and even the patterns of economy that are learned and shared by members of a social group. The issue of culture shock will therefore naturally be on the minds of every cross-cultural traveler.

"Culture shock" is used to describe the experience of disorientation and loss of identity that may result when a people leave their home culture, people, and circumstances (Kansas State University Counseling Services, n.d.). At the individual level, He (2002) expressed the notion of culture shock as a situation whereby the international traveler may initially negotiate new experiences, become influenced by the new culture, and would ultimately assume a new cross-cultural identity. The symptoms of culture shock may include irritability, anger over minor inconveniences, extreme homesickness, withdrawal from people who are different from oneself, boredom, headaches, upset stomach, loss of ability to work effectively, depression, difficulty concentrating, trauma, and the list goes on (Kansas State University Counseling Services, n.d.; Hutchison, 2005).

To the symptoms above, Sandra Hutchison of Global Trauma Consultants and Kansas State University Counseling Services suggest several ideas, noting that a cure is not guaranteed. They however encourage people to keep active, make American friends, read literature about border-crossings, exercise (also a good antidote to depression), join groups and clubs of (personal or professional) interest, introduce yourself to interesting people, and be patient. (A more exhaustive discussion is available at www.k-state.edu/counseling/culture.html.)

Certainly, international teachers need to be mentally prepared to deal with nostalgic feelings. In several places in the world, people may have firm family roots, and may be able to go back and point to their family or ancestral homes. Family relations are different in America. Nuclear families are mostly the rule, although extended the family is celebrated during special festive occasions, such as independence and Christmas holidays. The average American family may move several times per generation in pursuit of, or following their jobs. When leaving their old towns, they simply sell their homes, and would purchase another one in the new location.

Celente (1997) notes that:

By the 1950s, the [American] family had fragmented into a modern standard of nuclear units. Modern moms and dads no longer lived where they had grown up. They separated themselves from grandparents, uncles, aunts, and cousins, thereby trading off the support structure of the traditional extended family for a newfound freedom from family supervision and intervention. (p. 211)

For this reason, one's neighbors should not be expected to become emotionally close too soon. This means that it is much easier to be lonely, especially if living apart from one's family. It therefore comes as no surprise that Mary bemoaned:

I missed my family. The eight-and-a-half flight back to the U.K. is a bit of a pain. I would go more often if it wasn't such a horrible flight--and I find traveling internally in the states is more expensive than I thought it would be. Though I don't intend to fly around the States, it cost me more money to fly to Los Angeles than it did to fly to Rome, I mean in Italy. [Mary mentioned this because there are some American towns called Rome.] It was cheaper for me to go to Rome than it was to go to Los Angeles. So I find traveling internally on an aircraft to be expensive and that was a surprise.

Joe also found international translocation to be an issue of concern. He was concerned about issues of settling down in the first place, which significantly mitigated his effectiveness as a teacher. He therefore expressed similar concerns:

I think the moment you move internationally, you come to another place-you've got no friends, you're in a new house, new apartment. You've got all of that additional hassle. You just haven't got your support systems lined up. You've got to settle down and so I'm not denying my first year teaching here was by far my least effective year.

Granted that family support systems are not as easy to come by, it is still possible to find some amounts of emotional support through religious or other social institutions.

For some, the shock may be more or less, depending on how much international travel they have previously done. Another determinant of the degree of one's culture shock may be the difference between one's current culture and that of America's. For example, those moving from Western-oriented countries can expect to see similar sights and sounds. Those moving from Eastern-oriented countries, in general, should expect a greater amount of initial culture shock.

Another factor of interest regarding culture is the level of technology use to which one is accustomed. Dependence on cars, (involving driving in a different society with possibly different traffic rules), expected knowledge in the use of computers, the use of ATM machines, and the like are commonplace in America. Fortunately, these are things one may quickly get used to, depending on one's level of exposure to them, and commitment to learn. Notwithstanding the margin of differences in cultures, international teachers should expect to face some amount of culture shock. It must be emphasized at this point that international teachers should make a clear distinction between culture shock and pedagogical shock. The latter is related to educational issues; the main subject of this book.

Mary and Joe, both British, had come to the United States to teach in high schools after having traveled and lived globally. Although they knew a lot about America, they indicated that one could not learn about America by watching the movies; one had to be here to learn things first hand. Mary described the illusion provided to foreigners about America, in American movies as follows:

> Oh, here in America of course, if you don't live here, you think you know it because you've seen it in the movies. So you think you know how everything works. It looks familiar because you've seen it on the TV and in movies. When you get here, you realize that it isn't quite the same, and there's that layer of familiarity is very thin and so it seems like traffic laws, how the police work, when people say "come around" or "we must go out" or "keep in touch," they don't necessarily mean it and it's sort of odd things like that.

Inga, a German international teacher, to her advantage, came to teach as a result of her husband being transferred to America. She is a good example of how cultural preparation and awareness may help to minimize culture shock. When interviewed by the author, she shared some curious insights.

Significantly absent in her description of the issues were the basic logistical issues like visa, driver's license, credit card acquisition, and such matters that other international teachers faced. This was because her husband, who was being transferred to America, worked with a German-based, multi-national company. This company offered a good cultural orientation to its transferees and their families. During the orientation, they provided culturally-specific material as a guide to ease the transitional process into the new cultures. This is what Inga used, both for herself and any of her acquaintances traveling to the United States. They would generally talk about the differences between American and German cultures, using the hand-out as a conversation-guide:

> What I usually do is give them the hand out I got from [The Company] for the intercultural training, which tells you a little bit about different cultures; the idea about cultural truths versus scientific truths, or

something like this. Looking at those issues, looking at the idea of why people think that Americans are [what they are]. There are a few things that are typically [different] between Americans and Germans... just telling them that you have to learn about them. We usually have discussions when somebody comes. You sit down, go somewhere for dinner, talk about all those weird things that you learn [when you come to America].

Before he became a teacher, Kofi had also lived in the United States for several years. He therefore indicated that although he did experience culture shock, he had become acculturated to America before he began teaching.

In summary, some amount of familiarity or psychological preparation for the new culture will be useful for all international teachers.

1.10 Culture Shock and Race Issues

There is a good reason why many people move to America: It is a place where people with certain aspirations may find it easier to reach their goals: It is indeed the land of opportunity. There are also many Americans of all races who are willing to socially accommodate and help foreigners to feel at home and live fairly comfortably.

For the typical ambitious international teacher, success should be within reach. This is because, once a rigorous process for employment in America has been successfully executed, certain fundamental qualifications for survival in American education could be assumed to be in place. On a practical note however, a note of caution should be sounded concerning a possible roadblock to success in navigating America.

Lucius Outlaw, an American professor of philosophy once noted that the legacy of slavery in America negatively affected both the slavers and the enslaved (November 2003 Lecture). The result is that one cannot escape the issues of race and racism in America, and for that matter, in the American educational system. For the author, this was a significant culture shock to negotiate. A personal story may help buttress the point.

I, the author (an African) came to America directly from Hungary, under the auspices of Georgetown University, which is widely known and respected in America. I was coming to work as a biotechnology researcher, and was carrying H-1 visa classification; a classification granted to only specialized workers. In Budapest, Hungary, although there was a very long queue for visas to America, I was ushered into the office to directly to get my visa: I was given special treatment.

I arrived at the Dulles International Airport the afternoon of September 29, 1989. I remember being a bit apprehensive about my destination, since I was not sure if I was being taken to Dallas, another city, in Texas, USA. The flight was from Paris, France. All passengers began the disembarking procedures. As it got to my turn, a woman pulled me aside for more scrutiny, much to my surprise. My passport was taken and rechecked; baggage, fingerprints and all. I became befuddled. There was no problem—with me—except that they were suspicious of me. As I later found out from people more enlightened about the legacy of slavery in America, the immigration authorities did not believe that a dark-skinned African like me could be coming to do what I had claimed, especially in such a prestigious university.

I showed them my letter of appointment and other correspondence from Georgetown University, all to no avail. They were ready to deport me back to Africa (or Hungary); I did not know where. I collected myself, gathered some thoughts, and informed them that I was coming to work directly with a professor of biology, and that I had his telephone number on me. They called his office; he was teaching until later that day. We were not sure if he would return to his office after class. We decided to try that chance. We waited until his class was over and called his office. Thank goodness, he responded. He confirmed my story, and I was released! What if he decided not to go to his office after class that day? What if he got sick that day and did not show up at the office?

Race and economics perceptively heavily influence the American social fabric and consciousness. Unwelcome racial experiences typically occur as a result of stereotyping. As stated by Gollnick and Chinn (2004), stereotypes are the automatic associations that are made about groups of people, without justification. These stereotypes focus on characteristics, behaviors, and roles that those people supposedly exhibit. Gollnick and Chinn add that in America, these stereotypes are often perpetuated in the mass media. Despite their significant contributions to the American society, the frequent negative images and stereotypes of blacks in the American media have naturally vilified darker-skinned people within the psyche of many Americans. Granted the gains of the Civil Rights Movement since the 1960s, this problem still largely persists.

People from relatively poorer nations may also have less social regard in America. Arguably, this can be partly explained by the fact that there are patterns of existence for the wealthy and for the poor (Payne, 2001). Such patterns are believed to be exhibited though mannerisms, language, contents of conversations, and general behavior. American residents would readily agree that many Americans are inclined to value material wealth fairly highly. For this reason, the wealthy (including the middle-class) are deemed successful in life. (This is not meant as an indictment of America, but to state a fact which is mirrored in several other societies around the world.) The wealthy also possess cultural capital (since their values are the standard for schooling [deMarrais & LeCompte, 1995; Bowles & Gintis, 1976]), psychological superiority, and its concomitant powers. Perhaps, such powers are also subconsciously conferred upon people from wealthier countries, since such people may be deemed financially comfortable and therefore successful in life. The opposite is true for those from poorer countries. International teachers should therefore be willing to navigate this issue as a part of their American psychological landscape.

For the reasons above, where international teachers come from and their race will be a factor in how they are both accepted and treated by the general society, and also within their schools. A person from a "developed country" may have more social regard than one from a "developing" country. While teaching in a high school for nine years, it was rather interesting for the author to still hear people (well-intentioned faculty and students alike) categorize countries into "civilized" and "uncivilized." Such people would need to be helped by the international teachers they meet. A simple retort such as, "Oh, you mean less industrialized or developing country?" may politely, but effectively correct such people.

Based on anecdotal evidences, it appears that on occasion, the tacit assumption is that people from "uncivilized" countries do not know much about the finer things and facts of life—although they are qualified enough to have been granted employment as teachers and colleagues. Some school administrators, teaching colleagues, and students may sometimes make what may be perceived as condescending statements. International teachers should however understand that this is not a common experience, and such people may not be ill-willed, but are probably just uniformed on the relevant topics. Using such issues as points of conversation may then help to inform such people and also learn from them. Indeed, the more common experience is that Americans are generally curious about international people and cultures, and are willing to engage them in a hearty conversation.

The additional burden on people from developing countries may therefore be a need to prove themselves in various capacities. Students may challenge them more frequently, and see them as lesser than others from countries comparable to America in economic status. Even people from industrialized countries should expect certain issues from time to time, although the nature of such issues may be milder and more tolerable. (Inga from Germany made a note of this issue in her interviews.) The rule of thumb for international teachers may be that, the more similar their race and native country's culture is to the dominant American culture, the easier it is to become successful.

In conclusion, international teachers (especially those from developing countries) should be willing to pay their psychological rent for living and working in America.

Overall, however, Americans are curious and generous people. Many are interested and willing to learn about new cultures, and are willing to open up their homes to foreigners from all parts of the world. For this reason, international teachers from any part of the world should find it manageable to navigate their professional lives in America.

1.11 Recreational Needs for the Newcomer

Coming to America is a great adventure, since it opens up a whole world of opportunities—especially for people who come here from the developing world. It is a place where they could significantly better their lives, and even help their family members back home. No matter what one's background is, it is still very easy to become overworked. In fact, Mary was surprised by the fact that Americans are extremely hard-working people, and that work never seems to end, making it necessary for her and other colleagues to spend some weekends working in their schools:

> ... the work ethos in the states is very different than the work ethos in Europe. Americans work too hard from the start; they never take breaks. They seem to work longer days... There is no cut off; it seems to spread. You know, people don't say well it's five, I'm going home to be with my family, do some shopping...people don't tend to do that. It just seems to spread [so] Americans are certainly very hard-working compared to most Europeans.

One therefore needs to find means of recreation, or some other outlets for maintaining mental sanity. Although the television is ever-present with several hundred channels (on paid cable), others may find that just watching TV is not enough. For such people, physical activities may be the answer. Although local state agencies may have such recreational centers available, the problem is that it may take some time to find out where the better facilities are located.

Joe, being a new-comer to America, observed that it took him some time to become familiar with preferred recreational facilities, in order to relieve his stress. So he continued,

I think we all need to have ways that we can calm down, cool down, relieve the stress, but I had no way then. I hadn't found a soccer team to play on. I hadn't found a nice river or place to go fishing, or go walking, running--green land--concrete doesn't do me any favors—all those things took a while to sort out...

Going from the frying pan to the fire; a man without a means of recreation, he had to work even harder, and longer, just to be on par with work:

...and every time I'd have a holiday, it seems that I was just trying to catch up with stuff like that. You find that when you need to go shopping, buy things, etc. etc. There's a lot of problems when you move internationally.

When asked about how he used his holidays, Joe noted that his holidays were the times he could catch up with this work. The nature and volume of work in American teaching is very demanding, at least for the new teacher. He therefore commented that holidays were:

...were just catch-up days; gotta go buy a sofa, gotta go do various things. That was really what it was all about. And though I arrived well before school started (in August), it was not possible to get those things done. I was still working on them well into November.

It is therefore a good idea to ask employers or neighbors for information concerning where to find recreational centers or activities. There are general tourist centers in larger towns with packages for new arrivers. These are useful resources for a start.

1.12 America: The Consumer Reigns

In America, capitalism reigns, and money is the basic index for almost everything. Money can buy most things conceivable to the human imagination—and many things conceivable may be available to buy. For this reason, people generally work hard to earn money in order to buy things. This works in the interest of the international teacher, since the consumer reigns in America. As a potential consumer, all one needs is money, and most basic conveniences can be obtained, and quickly! Mary mentioned that she found some pleasant surprises, which made an otherwise difficult transition more bearable:

> It's easy to get things you want, easy to buy. It's much freer for movement than I think in Europe. Renting an apartment in [any] of the three cities I know: Munich, Lisbon, and London, is much more difficult than here. It's almost impossible to find [an apartment] in Germany, so there's a lot more freedom, much more consumer [oriented]. I'm a consumer, so people go out of their way to try and sell me things. It's easier. It is an easy place to live and many things are much cheaper mainly because gas is cheap. People who come from Europe are amazed--eating out--all the nice things in life are accessible and so I didn't have any major transitional things.

International teachers should find America a pleasant place to live, and the people helpful. Although the job requirements may be demanding, after one has had time to sort out the initial living hassles, one should be able to maintain a good life. In fact, Mary sang the praises of Americans, noting that, "Americans are very helpful, interested people, so I didn't find any problems here."

1.13 Summary

Teacher shortage in the U.S. has become critical, and this trend is expected to continue for several reasons. Several states have therefore modified their long-standing hiring policies and have been inviting international teachers to help minimize the problem. For international teachers, the shortage of teachers in the U.S. can be seen as an open door to work in America, the land of opportunity. On the other hand, it presents some potential issues to work through. Some of the issues are likely to include socio-logistical (support systems) and pedagogical or classroom-related difficulties.

There are certain important issues to consider or know before leaving home. International teachers should ask themselves why they are coming to America. Although this is a rather philosophical question, it may determine how life in America may be later viewed. Such a move may also affect one's insurance and pension benefits back home. Other important considerations are moving expenses, and cost of living in America. Once teachers have moved to America, some miscellaneous issues such as educational credentials and personal credentials (security number and card, credit card, and driver's license) need to be quickly resolved or obtained. Culture shock resulting from leaving one's home culture, people, and circumstances should also be expected and resolved. Recreational needs should also be considered.

In America, money can buy many conveniences. For this reason, new international teachers should be able to manage their transitions relatively well.

Chapter #2

EDUCATION IN AMERICA
A Brief Glance at Points of Relevance

America's strong proclivity for democracy and its concomitant phenomena may be definable along the axes of freedom of thought, and freedom of action within the law. Such freedoms may have contributed to the rapid innovations within the nation. As was noted earlier, the typical middle class American is likely to move several times in his or her lifetime. People may be born in one place, work in several places, and then retire and die in a completely different location. This phenomenon of psychological independence from one's birthplace may have borne several social, technological, and emotional implications.

Independent-thinking such as Ford's contributed to the invention of such technologies as the mass production of personal motor cars. The rise of a modest-size middle-class with enough purchasing power to buy emerging technologies must have fueled the process of urbanization by permitting nuclear families to move far from their original families. While the motorized vehicles took members of the family away from home, the invention of the telephone and other forms of communication made it possible for family members to keep in touch with those back home. Most of these people ended up in the cities, where job opportunities were available. Cities were also the natural educational centers. (For more ideas on how individual Americans operated within the greater American society, read Bellah and others' Habits of the Heart.)

Although education in America may have begun with an emphasis on religion (Christianity), it did not take long before educational critics and leaders began reforms in aim to make schooling more practical and responsive to the needs of society. By 1918, 48 states of The Union (the then emerging United States of America) had passed compulsory school attendance laws (Urban & Wagoner, 1996). Through the years, more reforms were put in place as needed by the emerging society. These reforms were generally accompanied by curriculum revisions. (See DeBoer's A History of Ideas in Science Education for more on this.)

After the Second World War, new issues emerged in American

education. The pursuit of equality in the society was prominent, crowned with the Civil Rights Movement of the 1960s. By this time, America could name several large metropolitan cities such as New York, Washington, D.C., and Chicago. Such locations had witnessed large immigrations of poor working-class populations who did not have enough economic means for comfortable family sustenance. These populations segregated into specific, "more affordable," or more functionally put, "poor neighborhoods." These are where they still remain today. With the government's policy of education for all children, there was to arise an urban educational issue, partly because of the way schools are organized in America.

2.1   The Philosophy of American Public Schools

The popular axiom, "All men are created equal" is an approximate summation of the American educational philosophy. In the ideal situation, Americans believe that:

- Every American child has the right to an education, and that the pursuit of basic education should be independent of parental financial situation. For this reason, schools are set up within easy distance of children's homes, at public expense.
- Every child is educable: American schools try to educate every child (even those with some disabilities) to the full extent of their intellectual capabilities.
- One of the main purposes of education is to provide citizens with enough knowledge, and to assist them in defending the individual freedom.
- Although some amount of group conformity and general respect for law and order is important, the needs of the individual child should be considered first.
- Schools should be decentralized in control and administration: Although all states recognize the value of a universal education, each state accepts the responsibility of educating its citizens. (Adapted from Hillway, 1964, pp. 3-4.)

2.2   The Structure of Schools in America

Because the American Constitution does not mention education at all, the responsibility of education falls under the domain of the states. This is based on sections that imply that anything not specifically designated as federal is "reserved" for the states. (For example, Article IV, Section 4 of the

Constitution states that "The United States shall guarantee to every State in this Union a Republican Form of Government," and Amendment X of the Constitution states that, "The powers not delegated to the United States by the Constitution, nor prohibited by it to the States, are reserved to the States respectively, or to the people.") The State Constitutions do indeed pick up from this point. For example, the Constitution of the State of North Carolina states that,

> The General Assembly shall provide by taxation and otherwise for a general and uniform system of free public schools, which shall be maintained at least nine months in every year, and wherein equal opportunities shall be provided for all students. [Art. IX, sec. 2 (1)]

According to the U.S. Department of Education,

> Education is primarily a State and local responsibility in the United States. It is States and communities, as well as public and private organizations of all kinds, that establish schools and colleges, develop curricula, and determine requirements for enrollment and graduation. The structure of education finance in America reflects this predominant State and local role. Of an estimated $852 billion being spent nationwide on education at all levels for school year 2003-2004, about 90 percent comes from State, local, and private sources. (On-line)

In the past, the federal government restricted its influence mainly to "categorical" areas where certain groups are protected under federal law. An example of this is the 1975 Public Law 94-142 (Education for All Handicapped Children Act, later [1990] reconstituted as Individuals with Disabilities Education Act).

Recently, the federal government has been involved in providing block funding; that is, giving blocks of money to states to spend as they see fit. "Federal block grants are used to pay for a variety of projects in Oklahoma [and other states]. Transportation, job creation, health care for women and children, programs to assist the handicapped and elderly, anti-poverty, and education programs are all recipients of these grants." However, "[s]tate agencies also are required to report on how they spend federal funds," according to the Oklahoma state Joint Committee on Federal Funds (On-line).

More recently, federal money has been tied to each state's compliance with high stakes testing. Although there are no national tests the current government is now pushing for annual testing in order to measure how American children are faring in academic achievement. This requires huge amounts of money that many local schools cannot fund. Federal funding may therefore be partly used to pay for such tests. The U.S. Department of Education indicates that:

Under *No Child Left Behind Act*, states and school districts have unprecedented flexibility in how they use federal education funds. For example, it is possible for most school districts to transfer up to 50 percent of the federal formula grant funds they receive under the Improving Teacher Quality State Grants, Educational Technology, Innovative Programs, and Safe and Drug-Free Schools programs to any one of these programs, or to their Title I program, without separate approval. This allows districts to use funds for their particular needs, such as hiring new teachers, increasing teacher pay, and improving teacher training and professional development. (On-line)

American schools are ultimately controlled by the state. Although there is a general "myth of the local control" in American schools, Grieder, Pierce, and Jordan (1969, p. 4) emphasize that "local school districts have always had only such powers as the states have granted them, and those 'necessarily implied' to enable them carry out assigned functions" (ibid.). Although the U.S. created the Department of Education in 1867 to oversee the general issues of education in the U.S., the department was not intended to have any administrative responsibility for the schools.

In most states, schools are headed by a state board of education. The most important of the state functions (which are not exercised by every state department of education, nor considered of equal importance in different states) are as follows: distribution of state funds or of federal funds coming to the state; enforcement of state laws regarding education; determination of curricula and courses of study; adoption or recommendation of approved list of textbooks; certification of teachers; approving or consulting on school-building standards; provision of library services; and the operation of teachers' colleges (Cramer, & Browne, 1956, p. 44).

The U.S. Department of Education (in December 2004) reported that,

Today, ED [Education Department] operates programs that touch on every area and level of education. The Department's elementary and secondary programs annually serve approximately 14,000 school districts and nearly 54 million students attending more than 93,000 public schools and 27,000 private schools. Department programs also provide grant, loan, and work-study assistance to over 9.5 million postsecondary students. (On-line)

With the exception of Hawaii, all states within U.S. use their local school districts as agencies for carrying out their educational functions. One hears about the counties, which are regional administrative jurisdictions within the states. In many states, these counties may serve as the local school districts (Grieder, Pirece, & Jordan, 1969). It is common, however, to have large urban cities such as Atlanta and Chicago Public Schools serve as functional school districts, partly owing to their high population densities. On the other hand, equivalent land masses in the rural farming or colder areas may have as few as several thousand people. Each school district has a superintendent who oversees its functions in concert with a local school board.

2.3 Local Responsibility for Education

Owing to local variations, it is virtually impossible to define the American local school system. Instead, one could better talk about the nature of a specific, local school district, which may have its own peculiar, definable characteristics. In part, local school districts are definable by their historical, cultural, and current contexts, and thus these are prone to change, especially in more politically-sensitive school districts.

Although they follow the curricula and other legislations set by the state, local school districts make the more immediate decisions which affect the schools. They reserve the powers to "employ and discharge school employees, purchase sites, build and equip buildings, purchase supplies and services, determine the curriculum, exercise control over students in the schools, and levy taxes to pay for carrying out these duties." (Cramer & Browne, 1956, p. 46)

As mentioned above, the local school districts are agencies created to carry out the state educational mandates. In general, the strongest administrative voices are heard at the county level. It is also the level at which the voices of the people are most active, thus capturing the notion of "local" within the organizational title. It is here that concerned parents and other organizations with educational interest operate, since schools are financed with property taxes, raised within the school districts. It is also because of this that a poor school district may collect much less money than a rich district. Recently, however, states have embarked on initiatives aimed at redistributing some of the tax funds in order to even out the money available per student. Even with this effort, some school districts still can have much more money per child than other districts.

It must however be noted that, the federal educational legislations are now being increasingly felt more at the state level. Such legislations are then passed on to the local level. An example is the current *No Child Left Behind Act*, which legislates some educational expectations, and partially funds them at the local level. Although the federal government may not be constitutionally capable of imposing mandates onto states, any state that wants federal funding for federal initiatives must thereby comply, or lose the money.

2.4   The Urban Issue

For decades in the United States, the urban areas of the larger cities have experienced a phenomenon called "white flight." This is a situation whereby, as the poorer, mostly minority populations immigrate into a neighborhood, the relatively wealthier white populations moved out. This resulted in the problem of "urban decay," whereby the neighborhood lost their economic luster, creating social problems.

Since school districts operate, in part, with the funds raised from local taxes, the resulting problem was that, such schools began having financial problems. Since it is normally the relatively wealthy who can afford higher education and the life-style that goes with it, this also meant that the nature of urban students also changed—both in socio-economic and demographic terms.

In recent years, the U.S. government has been making attempts to reverse the financial problems of urban schools by providing special grants and financial allocations to help such schools. In several cities, such as Boston (Massachusetts), Atlanta (Georgia), Charlotte, (North Carolina), and Illinois (Chicago), there have been attempts in creating "urban renewal" programs. Such cities have seen a partial return of the wealthy back to the downtown or inner-city areas. Meanwhile, American suburbs have become highly developed, with several attractive schools. This has opened up various options for teachers to compete for positions in the schools of their choice. The result is that urban schools and schools in smaller, rural towns are out-competed of teachers. This makes it more likely that international teachers may end up in such schools. (For more on urban education issues, please see chapter three.)

2.5   Progression in School

The progression of students in the schools is determined by age. Most American states require a minimum of ten years of compulsory education, usually from ages 6 to 17 or 18, depending on the state. Schools are organized into elementary (from pre-kindergarten through fifth grades), middle or junior high (sixth through eighth grades), and high schools (ninth through twelfth grades). Many schools may have a birthday cut-off date for enrolment into the school. For many schools, it is August 31. If available, pre-kindergarten applicants must be fully four years old before August 31. Kindergarten students must be fully five; and grade one applicants must be six years old; grade two seven years old; and so on.

Since it is the states that issue teacher certifications and licenses, they may certify their teachers in order to optimize the use of available teachers. However, most teachers are licensed to be elementary, middle, or high school teachers, although some amount of grade-overlaps may occur. In practice, however, it is not likely to have a teacher teaching at two or more different levels (for example in both middle and high schools), since schools are normally physically separated by school levels for a combination of reasons, including safety, logistics and convenience.

The British Council-U.S.A provides a good guide for the modified summary of the American educational system found below. It must be noted that the groupings may differ according to state or local school district jurisdictions. Most large school districts follow the general grouping system for easier transferability of students, while smaller districts with fewer students, teachers, and other resources are more innovative with their grouping systems. It is possible to find such rare grouping as Pre-Kindergarten-6th grade, 7th -12th grades, and other variations in some small school districts. In the scheme below, the most common classifications are presented, with some variations in parentheses:

2.5.1   Elementary School (Ages 4- 11/12: Grades Pre-Kindergarten - 5 or Pre-Kindergarten - 6)

Although some schools may include pre-kindergarten experiences, elementary schools cover the first five years of school, following a broad curriculum outlined by each state; there is no national curriculum. Subjects covered include reading, writing, math, social studies, science, health, music, art and physical education. Emphases are variously placed on certain subjects, as the local school system may see fit.

2.5.2 Middle School (Ages 12/13- 14/15: Grades 6- 8 or 7- 9)

Middle School follows elementary schools with the same style of curriculum. The seventh and eighth grades are sometimes referred to as "junior high," as these are the two years before high school.

There is a difference in philosophy between the middle school and junior high school concepts. The middle school environment is a virtual continuation of the elementary school. The students are taught by a core of (four) teachers specialized in their disciplines. As in the elementary school, emphases are variously placed on certain subjects, as the local school system may see fit.

The junior high school concept, on the other hand is fashioned after the high schools system. Students change teachers with each class period, with the potential of meeting as many as seven teachers each day. The schools may also have larger enrollments, and students are more likely to be tracked according to ability level (Rice & Dolgin, 2002).

2.5.3 High School (Ages 14/15- 18: Grades 9- 12 or 10- 12)

High school covers the last four years of compulsory education. High school students are usually required to study English, mathematics, social studies, science, health and physical education. They can also choose from a list of elective subjects, depending on their future plans and the state system. Foreign languages are obligatory in some states, but are considered elective courses in others. Many schools also offer honors and advanced placement courses for the students who want to be academically challenged. Advanced placements (AP) courses are usually recognized by the colleges by granting college credits, and students may elect to be exempted from those courses in their early college programs. Most high school curricula are designed to meet college entrance requirements.

2.6   Levels of Tertiary Institutions and Faculty Responsibilities in the United States

Tertiary institutions in the United States may be categorized into two main levels. In general, the term "college" is functionally employed to describe an institution which grants undergraduate degrees, and the term "university" is used to describe an institution which grants both graduate (master's and doctoral) and undergraduate (bachelor's) degrees. It is important to note that within American universities, the term "college" is used synonymously with "faculty" to describe the various larger divisions within them. For example, the College of Education is equivalent to Faculty of Education in other countries. On the other hand, the term "faculty" is used to designate "staff" within the institutions.

Universities are categorized according to the number of doctoral programs they offer, the level (or volume) of research they undertake, and the related amounts of external research funding (or grants) they are able to procure. The Carnegie Foundation (2000) classifies tertiary institutions based on their degree-granting activities from 1995-96 through 1997-98 academic years. Accordingly, there are Research I (One or Research Extensive) Institutions at the highest level of the research category. According to The Carnegie Foundation, these institutions awarded 50 or more doctoral degrees per year across at least 15 disciplines from 1995-96 through 1997-98. In these institutions, faculty are expected to spend roughly half of their work time conducting research, disseminating their research findings through publications and presentations, and finding grants to support their work. The rest of their time is shared between teaching and service to the community. (These amounts of time may vary, depending on the philosophy of the given institution.)

Research II (Two) A (also called Research Intensive) institutions attract less research funding, and have relatively fewer doctoral programs, and Research IIB institutions, with even fewer external funding and doctoral programs. During the period studied, The Carnegie Foundation reports that such institutions awarded at least ten doctoral degrees per year across three or more disciplines, or at least 20 doctoral degrees per year overall. The fewer the doctoral programs and external funding (and consequently less research and publication expectations, the more time faculty are expected to devote to teaching and service. For this reason, it is common to find Research I faculty teaching only 1-2 classes per semester; Research IIA faculty teaching 2-3 classes a semester; and Research IIB faculty teaching 3-4 classes per semester. The research publications expectations decrease in inverse proportion to the teaching load.

Comprehensive Institutions award baccalaureate and master's degrees, do not offer doctoral programs, and consequently do not focus on research. The Carnegie report recognizes two levels of these institutions: I and II, depending on how many degrees they award per year.

Baccalaureate Colleges are primarily undergraduate institutions which focus on bachelor's degrees. Associate's Colleges are institutions that may not have equivalents in other countries. They offer associate's degree and certificate programs (which take about two-years) and generally do not award bachelor's degrees.

Finally, The Carnegie Foundation recognizes Specialized Institutions which offer degrees ranging from bachelor's to doctorate, and typically award a majority of degrees in a single field. These institutions may include theological seminaries and other faith-related institutions; medical and health-related schools; schools of engineering and technology; schools of business and management; schools of art, music, and design; schools of law; teachers colleges; and other specialized institutions.

2.7   The American School Year

Most American schools begin their new year in mid-August (for many schools in the southern part of U.S.—although some states are currently considering revisions)—or early September (for many schools in the northern part of U.S.). They respectively end during early or late June. With some breaks, most schools aim for 180 days for the school year. Schools normally have five or more days built into the school year for teacher workdays and other professional development activities. Most schools observe all the national holidays.

The basic year is divided into two semesters; Fall and Spring, with some students going back to school for remedial work in the Summer.

The first semester, Fall, begins the school year from about mid-August. Thanksgiving break is nationally observed on the fourth Thursday in November and the following Friday, making for a long, four day weekend. Most schools close for Christmas holidays which mostly begin a few days before Christmas, and return to school during the first week of January; about two weeks total.

The Spring semester begins in early January, and has a "Spring break," which about one week during March or April. There are also a few one-day holidays (which normally match the national holidays) scattered throughout the school year. Many of the holidays are "movable," and are strategically placed on Mondays, which therefore provide three-day weekends.

Some school systems have a voluntary Summer school. During this time, students may elect to go to school in order to take some advanced courses. On the other hand, Summer school is compulsory for students who have not completed, or failed the requirements to move up to the next grade. Summer schools may last about four weeks, and selected teachers are given the opportunity to teach for a flat, handsome payment of several thousand dollars, depending on the school system.

A five-day week is the norm, with a school day of approximately six hours for elementary schools, and seven hours for middle and high schools, including a short lunch break.

2.8   The Profession of Teaching in America

Through the years, the profession of teaching in America has had its struggles for recognition as a legitimate profession. According to deMarrais and LeCompte (1995), this struggle is partly is due to the generally-held notion that anyone can teach. Not until recent years in America, teaching was one of the highest attainable occupations for minority groups and women (Lortie, 1969). Traditionally speaking, classroom teaching is not the profession of choice for white males in America (ibid.): those who are in positions of power to make, or significantly influence public policy. Since the profession of teaching in America has lacked powerful political allies, it has not managed to attract competitive compensation.

According to Teachers' Advantage (n.d.), teachers' pay continues to lag behind that of other college-educated professionals by an average of $8,000 a year, at the start of their careers. By the time they reach 50, their pay is lagging by almost $24,000 a year. When the economy of the Untied States is near full-employment and knowledge workers are in great demand, more teachers leave their teaching jobs and take jobs that offer higher pay. Another interesting point noted by Teachers' Advantage is that, average salaries for master's degree recipients outside teaching increased $17,505 form 1994 to 1998. Teachers, however, got less than $200 increase in salary within the same time period. Since women and minority groups do not have the power within the American society to alter the status of the teaching profession, teaching continues to struggle for a fuller recognition as a legitimate profession. (See DeMarrais & LeCompte's The Way Schools Work for more on this topic).

2.9 Professional Organizations and the School Curriculum

There are numerous professional organizations which help to organize and articulate teachers' voices. Some wield significant political powers, and aim to promote the general welfare of educators, the teaching profession, and education in general. An example of this is National Educators Association. Other professional organizations are more content-oriented, and serve to promote standards, research, and the instruction of specific content areas. Examples are National Science Teachers Association, and National Council of Teachers of Mathematics. These are national organizations with local chapters all over the United States. These professional organizations are a means through which American teachers exert their influence, and try to influence educational policy.

Although there is no national curriculum in American schools, the national content-oriented organizations have a strong influence on the curriculum in the local schools. For example, in the local Gwinnett school system in Georgia, the overall school system's curriculum was called Academic Knowledge and Skills (AKS). The science curriculum requirement, for example, is in alignment with the state of Georgia's Quality Core Curriculum Standards (QCC) science component, which in turn, is in alignment with the National Science Education Standards (NSES).

Professionally-savvy teachers are therefore expected to become members, and participate in some of these organizations' activities.

2.10 Accreditation of Educational Institutions

In concert with the efforts to make teaching a more standardized profession, all accredited teacher-education institutions in America are expected to follow certain professional standards in the training of their students. There are several accreditation bodies which provide legitimacy to the education provided in these institutions. An example, the Commission on Colleges of the Southern Association of Colleges and Schools (SACS) notes that,

> The Accreditation of an institution by the Commission in Colleges signifies the institution has a purpose appropriate to higher education and has resources, programs and services sufficient to accomplish that purpose on a continuing basis. Accreditation evaluates whether an institution maintains clearly specified educational objectives that are consistent with its mission and appropriate to the degrees it offers and whether it is successful in achieving its stated objectives. (SACS, on-line)

The U.S. Department of Education recognizes National Council for the Accreditation of Teacher Education (NCATE) as the professional accreditation body for colleges and universities that prepare teachers and other professional personnel for work in elementary and secondary schools. NCATE is a coalition of several specialty professional associations of teachers, teacher educators (college education professors), content (subject) specialists, and local and state policy makers. Its two missions include accountability and improvement in teacher preparation. According to NCATE, their accreditation process establishes rigorous standards for teacher education programs and holds accredited institutions accountable for meeting these standards. They also encourage unaccredited schools to demonstrate the quality of their programs by working toward professional accreditation. In this regard, NCATE provides periodic reviews of teacher education institutes. In summary,

> NCATE is the profession's mechanism to help establish high quality teacher preparation. Through the process of professional accreditation of schools, colleges and departments of education, NCATE works to make a difference in the quality of teaching and teacher preparation today, tomorrow, and for the next century. NCATE's performance-based system of accreditation fosters competent classroom teachers and other educators who work to improve the education of all P–12 students. NCATE believes every student deserves a caring, competent, and highly qualified

teacher. (NCATE, on-line)

Although NCATE regulates the functioning of educational institutions on the organizational level, it is the Interstate New Teacher Assessment and Support Consortium (INTASC) which provides the framework for professional teacher expectations. (More on this below)

2.11 The General Responsibilities of the American Teacher

The primary job responsibilities of American teachers may be quite different from those in many other countries. Unlike in many other countries where teachers could just teach their classes and be done with their school duties (except perhaps grading students' homework), American teachers are normally expected to do much more. Several teachers have significant after-school responsibilities. These may include coaching a sport (popular ones being baseball, football, basketball, cheer-leading, soccer, etc.), coaching a social or academic club, or attending a school program of some kind.

A lot will be said later about the nature of teaching in American schools in subsequent chapters. However, in brief, teachers are expected to show up at school at a set time, and plan to stay in school until school is over—at minimum. In many schools, depending, classes may begin as early as 7:30 a.m.-8:30 a.m., and end at about 2:00 p.m.-3 pm. Teachers are normally expected to arrive at least 15 minutes before classes begin, and stay about 15-20 minutes after school is over.

In general, teachers may report directly to their classrooms (where they hold all their classes). Each class period may last 50-120 minutes, depending on the type of schedule and programs being run in the school. (The longer periods are generally found in some high schools.) Sometime during each work day, teachers are given a planning period when they may plan their lessons, activities, and make photocopies, etc. In the middle schools, planning periods are normally times when teachers from the core subject areas (mathematics, science, social studies, and language arts) meet in groups called "teams," to plan their teaching activities.

There are several kinds of duties and responsibilities available in the schools, depending on innovations within the school. These are normally spelt out in faculty handbooks that are provided to new teachers, and updated at the beginning of each academic year. The handbook explains what new teachers need to know about school procedures and policies in-depth.

In many schools, a part of the first staff meeting is devoted to the discussion of new inclusions in the faculty handbook, and the parent-student handbook. Many schools ask all teaching staff to read both handbooks within the first week or so, and to indicate that they have read them. This is critical, since school policies and responsibilities are of legal interest in the United States, and it is in the best interest of all teachers to both know and follow policies in order to avoid possible lawsuits. In point of fact, students' grades are considered a secondary legal document. This means that they could possibly be summoned in court, should it become necessary. In addition, students' grades are a private matter, and are not supposed to be openly exhibited to others. This may be the opposite of what is true in many countries, where grades may even be openly posted on bulletin boards. Therefore, knowing the policies, and following them is vital for new teachers' success.

There are general staff meetings which may be held periodically; once a week, two weeks, or one month, depending on the school. These may be scheduled for early mornings or afternoons. These are meetings for discussing any issues of school interest, and in most schools the meeting format is a model of the democratic process. The meeting may be facilitated by the school principal, or another administrator. Teachers may be expected to speak out about various issues of concern, depending on the agenda set for that meeting.

There are bus or driveway duties, whereby teachers stand in the school, driveway, or a designated area to monitor the students as they get in or out of school buses or cars. This is done twice a day; before and after school. There are also hall duties, whereby teachers stand in their hallways to monitor the students as they change classes (and therefore classrooms).

Lunch may begin as early as 10:30 a.m. or as late as 1:30 p.m., depending on how large the student body is, and therefore how many sessions the cafeteria or dining hall can accommodate in order that all the students may eat. Teachers are expected to be on duty during lunch times, according to a schedule. Lunch times are generally 20-30 minutes for students. Supervising teachers may not have time to eat during the students' lunch break, and may need to plan to eat during their planning periods.

There may be other duties and responsibilities within the school, as deemed necessary. If so, they are spelt out in the faculty handbook, or are communicated to faculty in other ways.

2.12 Teacher Responsibilities, INTASC Standards, and Licensure

The responsibilities of the teacher are inherently outlined in the expectations of INTASC. INTASC is a consortium of state education agencies and national educational organizations dedicated to the reform of the preparation, licensing, and on-going professional development of teachers. Created in

1987, the primary constituencies of INTASC are state education agencies responsible for teacher licensing, program approval, and professional development. Its work is guided by one basic premise: An effective teacher must be able to integrate content knowledge with the specific strengths and needs of students in order to ensure that *all* students learn and perform at high levels.

INTASC encourages that state education policy and teacher licensing standards under their jurisdiction align with professional standards. States' licensing policy establish what teachers need to know and be able to do in order to effectively help all their students. New teachers are therefore expected to fulfill certain requirements in order to be licensed. For example, in the state of North Carolina, the Department of Public Instruction requires that all professional education candidates pass certain standardized tests (Praxis I and II examinations), and satisfy Advanced Technology Passport requirements. This formula of requirements for licensure is generally followed by most states.

Praxis I test comprises reading, writing, and mathematics. This test is normally taken by students before their junior (third year) in college, as a requirement for entering a teacher education major. Praxis II is a test measuring teacher candidates' mastery of content knowledge in their specialty areas, and is required before being granted a state teaching license. (You may read more about Praxis Tests from the website of Educational Testing Service: http://www.ets.org/praxis/index.html.) Where required, the technology requirement measures the extent to which teacher candidates have mastered advanced computer competencies. States with technology requirements may be expected to provide professional development courses or college courses which provide such required competencies as a part of their education degree programs.

INTASC has ten principles (or standards) which serve as the overarching goals and objectives of courses in professional education courses. The ten standards are:

Standard 1: Content Pedagogy. The teacher understands the central concepts, tools of and structures of the discipline(s) he or she teaches and can create learning experiences that make these aspects of subject matter meaningful for students.

Standard 2: Student Development. The teacher understands how students learn and develop, and can provide learning opportunities that support their intellectual, social and personal development.

Standard 3: Diverse Learners. The teacher understands how students differ in their approaches to learning and creates instructional opportunities that are adapted to diverse learners.

Standard 4: Critical Thinking. The teacher understands and uses a variety of instructional strategies to encourage students' development of critical thinking, problem solving, and performance skills.

Standard 5: Motivation and Management. The teacher uses an understanding of individual and group motivation and behavior to create a learning environment that encourages positive social interaction, active engagement in learning, and self-motivation.

Standard 6: Communication and Technology. The teacher uses knowledge of effective verbal, nonverbal, and media communication techniques to foster active inquiry, collaboration, and supportive interaction in the classroom.

Standard 7: Planning. The teacher plans instruction based upon knowledge of subject matter, students, the community, and curriculum goals.

Standard 8: Assessment. The teacher understands and uses formal and informal assessment strategies to evaluate and ensure the continuous intellectual, social, and physical development of the learner.

Standard 9: Professional Development. The teacher is a reflective practitioner who continually evaluates the effects of his/her choices and actions on others (students, parents, and other professionals in the learning community) and who actively seeks out opportunities to grow professionally.

Standard 10: School and Community Involvement. The teacher fosters relationships with school colleagues, parents, and agencies in the larger community to support students' learning and well being.

(The above INTASC standards are available at http://www.ccsso.org/content/pdfs/corestrd.pdf. At this website, the ten standards are greatly expanded.)

Each of the ten standards is further elaborated into three areas; knowledge, dispositions, and performances.

Knowledge describes what teachers are expected to know about both their content areas, and also about the art of teaching (pedagogy), in order to effectively help their students. This may include the teacher's "understanding of major concepts, assumptions, debates, processes of inquiry, and ways of knowing that are central to the discipline(s) s/he teaches." (INTASC, on-line)

Dispositions are the general attitudes of teachers, and therefore what they are likely to do owing to their beliefs. For example, "the teacher realizes that subject matter knowledge is not a fixed body of facts but is complex and ever-evolving. S/he seeks to keep abreast of new ideas and understandings in the field." (INTASC, on-line) Terms such as "appreciation," "commitment," and "enthusiasm" are used to capture the attitudes expected of teachers. Such attitudes are expected to help bolster student learning outcomes.

Lastly, *performances*, in response to knowledge (above), describe situation-specific applications of both pedagogical and content knowledge in order to help student learning. For example, "The teacher effectively uses multiple representations and explanations of disciplinary concepts that capture key ideas and link them to students' prior understandings." (INTASC, on-line) Some key ideas included here are the use of teachers' content knowledge for the evaluation of student knowledge, the use of resources and curriculum materials, engagement of students, and the creation of learning experiences.

International teachers coming to America are generally employed by recruiting agencies. These agencies may normally be expected to provide all the required information needed to satisfy the United States Immigration and Naturalization Service (INS), United States Department of Labor, and state licensing requirements. State licensing agencies may then be expected to issue a provisional (temporary) license, which is normally good for one academic year. (A good website to visit is the official website of the U.S. INS section on H-1B visas, available at http://uscis.gov/graphics/howdoi/h1b.htm.)

Once in the U.S., international teachers may decide to work towards full licensure, if they plan to stay longer in the U.S. One recruiting agency, Visiting International Faculty (VIF) and some school districts do have arrangements with local universities to provide professional development courses to bring the teachers in line with the local licensing standards, or even earn a master's degree in the process.

2.13 Summary

America's love for democracy and the resulting freedom of thought spill into the schools. The philosophy of American public schools may therefore be summarized in the popular axiom: "All men are created equal." Although education in America began with an emphasis on religion (Christianity), a series of educational reforms were undertaken with a view to making schooling more practical and responsive to the needs of society. After the Second World War, several new issues emerged in American education. The pursuit of equality in the society was prominent, and that was crowned with the Civil Rights Movement of the 1960s. This became reflected in the schools.

American public schools were initially conceived to be ultimately controlled at the local (state) level. Through the years, however, several educational reforms have increased the role of the federal government, especially as a funding source. The school curriculum, however, is still created at the state level, although federal educational policies may influence both the curriculum content and delivery. Schools are directed by a board of education at the state level. The next administrative layer is the county or local board of education, which administers the local school districts.

Most states require a minimum of ten years of compulsory education, usually from ages 6 to 17 or 18, depending on the state. Schools are organized into elementary (from pre-kindergarten through fifth grades), middle or junior high (sixth through eighth grades), and high schools (ninth through twelfth grades).

Most American schools begin their new year in mid-August (for many schools in the southern part of U.S.) or early September (for many schools in the northern part of U.S.), and respectively end during early or late June. Excluding breaks, most schools aim for 180 days for the school year.

There are numerous professional organizations which help to organize and articulate teachers' voices in order to influence educational policy. Some are more content-oriented, and are instrumental in creating the curricula in their disciplines.

The responsibilities of teachers are implicitly outlined in the expectations of INTASC. INTASC is a standards-oriented national organization which encourages uniformity in teacher preparation across the U.S. The licensing policies within the states establish what teachers need to know and be able to do in order to effectively help all their students. New teachers are therefore expected to fulfill those requirements in order to be licensed.

Chapter #3

RESEARCH AND ISSUES OF INTEREST FOR INTERNATIONAL TEACHERS

Education in the United States is guided by various theories. Such theories are used to shape classroom practices in order to achieve the best possible teaching and learning. In the past, guiding theories were mostly generated in colleges and universities. Recently, however, teachers' voices are being heard more in the educational literature, through action research. In action research, teachers actively participate in the observation of phenomena of educational interest, and document them in order to help address classroom issues. In this chapter, selected theoretical frameworks of interest to cross-cultural teachers are discussed. The theories in this chapter form the matrix of this book.

3.1   The Influence of Culture in Schools

Atwater and Riley (1993) relate a story that illustrates how cultural competence can make a difference in instruction.

Setting: Panay, an Island in the Visayas: One of a Group of Islands that Comprise the Middle of the Philippines' Archipelago:

A sun-bleached, crushed-shell walkway cuts through the tropical vegetation and leads to the open door of a woven grass and bamboo structure. Inside are grey, hand-hewed, double-seater desks, weathered but sturdy. About 40 children sit quietly at the desks, bare feet on the floor, their plastic sandals arranged in orderly rows outside the door. The translucent shell clutters are pushed back as far as they will go. The room is dark and cool. Batteries, bulbs and wires lie on the desks untouched by the hands of the covering each face.

The teacher, a foreigner... had read about and seen this disturbing student behavior before. It is termed "nahuya," and while it has no direct translation in English it captures what we might describe as a mixture of shyness and respect. Nahuya is expected and rewarded in this culture.

With an accent guaranteed to bring out smiles behind the hands, he starts the lesson. "Maayong aga sa tanan tanan." With encouragement, the hands slowly creep down and hesitantly reach for the batteries and bulbs.

Setting: An Inner-City School Bordering Washington, D.C.:

A concrete wall and chain-link fence surround the large brick turn-of-the-century building, separating it from the urban sprawl of three-decker houses, iron-barred shop windows, and abandoned stores. Inside about 35 children... noisily talk at their desks. The desks are wooden surfaces with cast iron sides placed in rows and bolted to the floor. The students have just returned from recess. The teacher is preparing to teach the same lesson on batteries and bulbs. The class behavior is nervous and anxious. Something is in the air. It seems everyone--but the teacher--can feel the tension. The students are avoiding Princeton, moving away from him. All eyes are on Beatrice, who reigns from the back of the class and whose domain extends throughout the school and beyond the fence. Chaos explodes as the first battery crashes into the wall. Students scramble for cover as Beatrice and Princeton circle the classroom hurling batteries at each other, reloading at each desk. In time, order is restored. The science lesson resumes. The batteries, bulbs, and wires, confiscated and hidden away, are replaced with safe ditto sheets. (Atwater & Riley, 1993, p. 661-662)

In their discussion, Atwater and Riley note that in the first episode, this American teacher had the advantage of cultural preparation as a part of his pre-service teaching program. For this reason, he was familiar with that culture's heroes and heroines, thereby making it easy for him to believe that "from these 40 barefoot children could come doctors, teachers, farmers, and nurses. All things were possible for these children." (p. 662) In contrast however, the same American teacher, in the second episode, "did not speak the language" of the children he was teaching. (Ibid.) Although he was in his home country, the United States of America, he was not familiar with the children's culture, nor their heroes and heroines. Atwater and Riley suggest that this teacher was more effective in the first episode because he considered it a cross-cultural experience. His experience in the second episode, however, was less effective: Although in reality, he was teaching in a cross-cultural situation, he failed to recognize that, because he may have felt that he was still teaching in the United States. He therefore did not prepare adequately for it. Cultural preparation, therefore, is one of the keys to success in a new teaching environment.

3.1.1 Culture and Reality

It may be an understatement to suggest that human beings are quite perfunctory in their day-to-day activities. Hobson (1993) posits that the natural environment where a person is raised is not a passive, but social construct in two senses: a) We act upon and change the natural environment and thereby construct and reconstruct it through our collective social actions, and b) We perceive the natural environment in a way that is dependent on the prevailing socio-cultural framework. Should these assertions hold merit, then it is prudent to suggest that humans are, concurrently, the creators and the products of their own actions, and that this is a subconscious human functionality.

In a philosophical vein, Bronowski (1972) would agree with the suggestion above, noting that, "There is no evidence for the existence of things" since, for example, "seeing the left profile of a person, and later the right profile of the same person is no warrant to assume that we are seeing the same person." (p. 31) To Bronowski,

> By the canons of logic there are no grounds: no one can deduce the man. We infer him from his profiles as we infer that the evening star and the morning star are both the planet Venus; because it makes two experiences cohere, and experience proves it to be consistent (ibid.).

This is something that humans do not question, but assume to be a part of reality, whereby two different experiences are conjoined into an integral whole.

Implicitly, therefore, if there is a sense of consistency in our everyday experiences, "reality" could be assumed. Perhaps, this is comforting, since humans would not like to exist in a surrealistic helplessness. Consistency provides a framework within which we operate, with a tacit assumption of reality. It is therefore necessary for humans to be conformists (even in the absence of logic), in order to exist in that "certainty" of reality.

The concept of culture provides the medium in which human beings can exist in a "conformist reality," without laborious, tedious questioning. Perhaps, this is why culture is a natural outgrowth of human civilizations (Podolefsky & Brown, 1997), and cultural practices influence our thinking and understanding (Fleer, 1997) and therefore education at large.

The concept of culture is difficult to capture, unless it is contextualized. Bodley (1997, p. 9) recognizes the following as admissible domain-specific definitions of culture:

- Topical: Culture consists of everything on a list of topics, or categories, such as social organization, religion, or economy.

- Historical: Culture is a social heritage or tradition that is passed on to future generations.

- Behavioral: Culture is shared, learned behavior; a way of life.

- Normative: Culture is ideals, values, or rules for living.

- Functional: Culture is the way humans solve problems of adapting to the environment, or living together.

- Mental: Culture is a complex of ideas, or learned habits, that inhibit impulses and distinguish humans from animals.

- Structural: Culture consists of patterned and interrelated ideas, symbols, or behaviors.

- Symbolic: Culture is based on arbitrarily assigned meanings that are shared by a society.

In synthesis, Bodley (1997) demonstrates that, "culture involves at least three components: what people think, what they do, and the material products they produce" (p. 10). He continues that, "It is shared, learned, symbolic, transmitted cross-generationally adaptive, and integrated." (ibid) Should this be the case, then he is in agreement with Kuhn (1962), who argued that even scientists who profess empiricism, are influenced by paradigms (or boundaries of logic and common sense), although they may be oblivious to it.

Kuhn believes that there is a "strong network of commitments--conceptual, theoretical, instrumental, and methodological" which serve to confer the metaphor of "puzzle-solving" on normal science (p. 42). Scientists therefore work from models which have been "acquired through education and through exposure to the literature without quite knowing or needing to know what characteristics have given these models the status of community paradigms." (p. 46) Hence, the manner in which knowledge-creation is conducted may be influenced by this silent, extrinsic factor: cultural traditions or paradigms. Spector and Lederman (1990, p. 23) suggest that some of the parameters specified by a socio-cultural framework or paradigm may include the following:

1. How the world works
2. What questions should, or can be asked
3. Procedures for answering questions (i.e. research method)
4. What constitutes acceptable hypotheses, and
5. What constitutes acceptable answers

There are several ways Spector and Lederman's assertions may be manifested. An Amish farmer in America, for example, may plow hundreds of acres with just a team of horses instead of modern machinery. This practice may violate the more widespread cultural value of efficiency. However, from the Amish point of view, hard work may serve to generate discipline, which is crucial to Amish religious life (Macionis, 1997). The Amish culture, and the normative thoughts of the Amish may not necessarily question why that horse-mediated plowing is the normal practice; it is just a cultural practice.

Rakow and Bermudez (1993) are of the conviction that cultural perspectives may even influence the way we see people. They refer to studies which suggest that European-Americans teachers, for example, were inclined to see boys as silent, steady, open, factual, rational, and independent, among others. Mexican teachers, on the other hand, rated boys as morose, dependent, talkative, shy, protective, emotional, sweet, and imaginative, among others things. For this reason, Rakow and Bermudez believe that teachers may possibly carry a variety of cultural stereotypic images with them, based on their own cultural heritage. These stereotypic images, in turn, influence how they view their own students.

Cultural images may serve other roles, including that of metaphors. Tobin and Tippins (1996) maintain that even the metaphors used by a teacher to make sense of a particular teaching experience may be saturated with the semantic networks associated with the culture of that educator. In their studies, a Navajo (Native American) science teacher used the metaphor of the "teacher as a gardener" to relate her role in the learning of her students. She used such phrases as the gardener having to prepare "Mother Earth" to receive the seeds, as a metaphor for planting. The harvest; the products of education are "given back to the people to use in ceremonies," in the tradition of this particular Native American's tribe (p. 719). Tobin and Tippins therefore raised some questions, including the following: How would a teacher's approach to teaching and learning likely to be received by students from different backgrounds? This question should be addressed by the international teacher, as he or she encounters a new culture.

In summary, the literature suggests that teaching and learning activities are heavily influenced by cultural factors. The international teacher would therefore be better prepared if he or she is conversant with the cultural variables in the new culture, or at least conscious that culture is a critical issue in his or her new educational encounter.

3.1.2 Culture versus Worldview Theory

If culture were a human body, world view theory would be his or her eyes.

Different countries naturally have different cultural practices (Bodley, 1997), and so it is reasonable to expect that international teachers will experience some cultural barriers as they come to teach in United States high schools. Such cultural differences and barriers may be expected to have an impact on their classrooms. This is implicit in Mahan and Stachowski's (1994) work whereby, on reversing the situations of teachers in this book, American student teachers needed to reorient themselves in an international teaching environment.

Kearney (1984) asserts that people's "world views" influence how they receive and generates knowledge. World view theory suggests that one's background influences the way one views the world, and consequently, learns (Cobern, 1993; Shumba, 1999). If well understood, the idea of world view theory could enhance cross-cultural pedagogy. This is because it has the potential of eliminating cognitive impediments to the flow of knowledge, and therefore construction of knowledge (learning).

Roth (1993) argues that learning could be viewed as a "process of cognitive apprenticeship" (p. 147). More importantly, learning is simultaneously a "process of enculturation similar to growing up in a particular society and learning its sign systems such as language, behaviors, and other culturally determined patterns of communication" (ibid). Driver, Asoko, Leach, Mortimer, and Scott (1994) confirm this point by reiterating that learning science, for example, involves "being initiated into scientific ways of knowing" (p. 6). Factors such as language, behaviors, and sign systems are all learned, integral composites of one's culture (Bodley, 1997) and can influence one's world view.

Kearney (1984) employed the notion of logico-structuralism to explain world view. He used seven tenets, namely: self, non-self, relationship, classification, causality, time, and space. These tenets are the basic frameworks by which individuals in a society make sense of the world around them. For example, one could see causality as the attributions given by local individuals to explain phenomena such as rainfall; perhaps, the gods making the rains, as opposed to the conventional scientific explanations of the causality of rains—as explained by water cycle.

Ultimately, people "know" things using their filters of world view. Such filters could be also comparable to Kuhn's (1962) "paradigm" noted earlier under cultural considerations. In this sense, paradigm speaks simultaneously to both world view theory and the phenomenon of culture. It could be thought of as the yardstick by which new knowledge is created, and new information measured.

For example, Kuhn noted that the scientific community operates using as their guide or their world view, "universally recognized scientific achievements that for a time provide model problems and solutions to a community of practitioners" (p. x). Ultimately therefore, when even scientific textbooks are written, they are indeed written in the vein of history, or better put, scientific culture. In other words, new knowledge is somewhat influenced by currently-accepted knowledge (which itself resides in cultural norms or paradigms). "It therefore makes sense to refer to our scientific community as a community of 'practitioners,' since we are in a constant practice of a set of community norms." (Ibid.) Perhaps, it is for this reason that Bronowski (1972) suggests that "the scientist does not merely record the facts; but he must conform to the facts" (p. 28). He or she is under a kind of "social injunction" (p. 58) not only to exhibit the "power of virtue," but to "uphold the standards of the community" (p. 58, 59). Effectively, this is the world view of the educational community: This is where people's cultures meet their world views.

Cobern (1991) believes that understandings of nature arising from one's world view may be either epistemological or mystical in origin. The epistemological flows along the axis of reason and thinking, leading to comprehension, while the mystical pathway flows along the axis of intellect and knowledge, leading to apprehension. Both pathways can be useful in making sense of one's world. Indeed, religious people around the world who are trained within the empirical traditions arguably employ both avenues of knowledge certification in order to understand different aspects of their world. Ultimately, the objective of either pathway is to make sense of one's world.

In the light of the preceding argument, knowledge, whether it derives from the mystical or the epistemological route, is still a social creation. It is influenced by the world view of its creators and consumers. Consequently, different societies have different views of schooling, teachers, students, and the essence of education. Gao (1998) notes that in the People's Republic of China for example, the teacher is viewed as a model of good conduct and learning, since Chinese teachers model themselves after Confucius, whom they consider a great teacher. To the Chinese, good teaching should therefore incorporate the modeling of both high academic and moral conducts, both inside and outside the classroom. Hence, in the classroom, Gao notes that the teacher dominates, since the view of the class time is for the teacher to provide students with good examples of learning. It is also noteworthy that this is a society where respect is paid to elders, those in higher positions, and those with more education.

International teachers coming to America will find that Americans make the fine distinction between one's personal life and professional life. Although the notion of the virtuous teacher is tacitly expected of teachers, the sheer inertia of Americans' value for personal freedom and independence subordinates any issues of communal values to a secondary consideration. This is understandable, if one considers that America is a very diverse society. Theory and principle backed by the law reign supreme in the United States, and that is what should be expected in American schools.

3.1.3 World View Theory and Multiple Realities

In his research-based book, <u>The Geography of Thought: How Asians and Westerners think differently and Why</u>, Nisbett (2003) maintains that Asians and Westerners do think and see the world differently because of differing ecologies, social structures, philosophies, and educational systems. He notes that Asians are more inclined to see the world holistically, and to look for relations among objects. Therefore, they may excel in one subject area, but not necessarily in others. On the other hand, Westerners have the proclivity to focus on salient objects or people, and to use their perceived characteristics to assign them to categories. They also are likely to apply rules of formal logic to understand behavior, and are therefore more likely to perform better in subject areas which demand such logical skills.

So what happens when people from different backgrounds are trying to make meaning of the same material? Ogawa (1989) would agree with Nisbett (2003) that it is possible to have multiple realities, since humans have different ways of knowing the same thing. In his work in Japan, he indicated that students in the elementary school performed well in science. However, when the same students reached the high school level, they performed relatively poorly. The problem, he believed, was that the curriculum in Japanese elementary schools was designed after the Oriental world view, whereas that of the high schools was more Western. His explanation was that at the high school level, the everyday worldviews of the students did not harmonize with the high school curriculum. Therefore, they performed relatively poorly.

Dzama and Osborne (1999) concur with Ogawa's argument. They maintain that although Japan has had a long scholarly tradition, there occurred a "conflict between science and established traditional cultural values..." (p. 395). This happened because the traditional Japanese believed in living in harmony with nature and studying about nature in the natural environment. This idea, however, was in conflict with the Baconian interventionist culture of Western science, whereby nature may be killed, and then brought to the laboratory for study. This cultural conflict may have translated into a practical problem of doing Western science imported into Japan. Dzama and Osborne think that the same argument could be made for the problems of doing Western science in India and Africa.

By extrapolation of the above discussions, therefore, Hobson, (1993) cautions that when teachers (especially in America) talk of assisting children to a greater understanding of the world, they need to be clear what they mean by the term "world." To them, the "world" could variously refer to the immediate world of the child, the world of the teacher, or the conventional Western world view of science.

The message above also rings true for international teachers coming to teach in America. International teachers should be expected to come into the U.S. high school bearing their own personal world views. These are worldviews they must have developed in their countries of origin. Once they enter the U.S. classroom, there may be clashes of their world views with those held in their new environments, where they are conflicting. The consequence would be that the flow of instructional information (which naturally flows along the axis of worldviews) may be hindered. An understanding of issues regarding worldviews could therefore be helpful in minimizing such impediments to information flow.

3.2   The International Teacher and Cross-Cultural Issues

The idea that language and thought are closely related is firmly buttressed in the Sapir-Whorf theory (in anthropology). This theory makes the claim that one's view of the world is partly influenced by one's language. For this reason, it is possible for speakers of different languages to live in different perceptual worlds (Bodley, 1997). For example, it is not possible to think of, or imagine the shape of a cocoyam, if this plant is not found in a particular culture or location (assuming that photos are not available). The term "cocoyam," as a mental or linguistic symbol, has a name and shape only because of its existence in a given location, and therefore culture. The location (via its climate, etc.) determined whether or not such a plant could grow in the first place. Since this plant is found in the given location, it is therefore known by name (and uses), and is a part of the local culture's parlance and thought.

Another illustration is to think of a phenomenon which is peculiar to a culture only through historical incident or accident. Such a phenomenon may have a name (or term) and meaning only within the context of that given culture and incident. Since language is inextricably intertwined with culture, the concept of literacy also entails the concept of world view.

Phelan, Davidson, and Cao (1991) make the argument that people's success in managing transitions in new cultures is "smooth" when the cultures of the family and science are congruent or similar. Transitions are "manageable" when the cultures of family and science are somewhat different. However, transitions are "hazardous" when the cultures are very different; and "virtually impassable" when the differences are highly discordant. For this reason, they believe that a science student's success, for example, will depend on factors including the following:

> a) the degree of cultural difference that students perceive between their life-world and their classroom
> b) how effectively students move between their life-world culture and the culture of science or school science, and
> c) the assistance students receive in making those transitions easier.

Traweek (1992) agrees with them by noting that cross-cultural issues are inherent in the educational setting. Even within a professional physicists' community, he observed that there existed belittling humor, sarcasm, and other cultural reprisals, all of which were attempts to encourage conformity within the academic community. He therefore not only affirms the existence of cross-cultural issues in the academic community, but also suggests that hazardous border crossings should be negotiated with great care and subtlety, by using humor, selected conformity, power, and politics.

For the international teacher, care and subtlety are certainly appropriate and instructional, since their transitions into American educational system are forms of border-crossing.

3.3   Urban and Rural Schools and the International Teacher

As noted earlier in chapter one, there is a shortage of teachers in the U.S. for several reasons. One factor playing a significant role in the shortage of teachers is the migration of teachers from mostly urban schools to those in the suburbs (Herriott & St. John, 1966). As old as this phenomenon is, the problem still remains. The main reason for this migration is that teachers' salaries are based primarily on years of experience, academic degree, and type of school district. Regardless of quality, teachers are given wholesale, equal increments based solely on experience and degree. For this reason, teachers naturally migrate to the areas where they will have the best combination of pay and working conditions (ibid.). Unfortunately, this also means that, even if pay is higher in an inner city school district, the combination of pay and working conditions often means that more qualified teachers will migrate to middle class or higher school districts with good pay and students (Grissmer & Kirby, 1997).

If the claim above is tenable, then one may safely expect that teacher shortages will be more critical in the urban and rural schools than those in the suburbs. For the same reason, it is more likely that migrant teachers will find more employment opportunities in urban and rural schools. Urban and rural education issues are therefore a part of the international teacher migration phenomenon.

3.3.1 The United States urban school and the international teacher

Herriott and St. John (1966) participated in an extensive study of urban schools that was begun in 1958. Their findings were that within the central city, there were population shifts with respect to social class: As neighborhoods grew old and decayed, second generation ethnic clusters broke up. White families left, as members of minority populations arrived. Since minority populations in general did (and still do) not have strong financial resources, such demographic shifts produced communities with a weak financial base. Schools in the community therefore reflected this financial weakness, and their students paid the socio-educational price. Of particular interest were their descriptions of the schools attended by the children of the very poor:

> Usually located in the oldest sections of the city, where building costs are high and play space at a premium, faced with rising enrollments of the children of multi-problem, migrant families, these schools report the difficulties that might be expected. They suffer generally low achievement, high rates of transiency, antisocial behavior, dropouts, overcrowded classrooms, and teacher shortages. (p. 4)

One could question some of their assertions such as "low achievement" and "antisocial behavior" since such variables may defy a strict definition (Liston & Zeichner, 1996), and reflect the cultural stereotypes of the students held by the observers. The issue of teacher shortages in urban schools, however, may be difficult to dispute (Grissmer & Kirby, 1997).

Herriott and St. John (1966) further noted that this issue of teacher departure, as early as in the 1950s, was common enough to have been named the "horizontal mobility hypothesis" (p. 9), whereby teachers left one school for more preferred ones. "Inequality hypothesis" (p. 9) also became an issue of social interest, dealing with the issue of resource allocation. It maintains that school systems do not distribute their resources equitably, but favor middle class schools in the assignment of staff, provision of maintenance, teaching materials, and special resources.

By some accounts, the very schools which need help are the ones which go without it. Russo and Cooper (1999) remark that such inequities in educational spending in the cities, compared to the wealthy suburbs, are virtually scandalous. They note that in 1998, for example, the average expenditures per pupil in the city of New York was $8,200, as compared to $14,000 per pupil in a wealthier suburb like Great Neck or Manhasset, and rising up to $19,000 in the highest districts in the state. They therefore conclude that equity remains a serious issue in urban schools, and that social class and family are possibly the best predictors of the quality of education.

International teachers who come from schools with good resources could therefore be disappointed to find such situations, especially those with a romantic image of the U.S. as a nation with rich resources, and therefore ample provisions for all her young citizens. This lack of provisions in some schools may result in frustration for some teachers, and could potentially affect the effectiveness of their instruction.

Another area mentioned in the Herriott and St. John's (1966) study is the issue of discipline. It was noted that although there were discipline issues in the suburban schools, it was more pronounced in the urban schools. Several other variables were studied and found to be significantly different between the urban and the suburban schools. These included achievement, parental reinforcement, and home background—all of which were found to be more favorable in the suburban schools. Russo and Cooper (1999) agree with this assertion.

These issues have implications for international teachers and their pedagogical experiences in American schools. For example, Stenlund (1995) observed that students have a lot of impact on teacher enthusiasm. In a cross-cultural study, he noted that secondary school teachers from United States, England, Germany, Japan, Singapore, Canada, and Poland were all either encouraged (gained enthusiasm) or discouraged, in direct response to student motivation. International teachers moving into schools with student motivation problems need to be alerted to the potential issues and be appropriately prepared to have them resolved.

3.3.2 The United States rural school and the international teacher

Urban schools share some issues with rural schools: They both have a relatively weaker financial base, since local taxes are partly used to finance local schools. Sometimes, owing to their smaller populations, they may not have influential political stakeholders to fight their cause. They therefore share the problem of financial inequities, as opposed to suburban schools. For this reason, they are likely to share the problem of inadequate educational resources, the most important of which are good, veteran teachers.

Rural schools, on the other hand, are more likely to be composed of a single ethnic group, as compared to the more diverse urban schools. The socio-cultural dynamics should therefore be expected to be different and relatively more predictable. Their world view may be expected to be directed more by the local issues than world affairs, since they are socially more insulated. Conversely, the urban student world view may be more likely to be influenced by extenuating, and possibly global factors—especially in schools where migrant populations abound. The nature of rural students will be different from rural schools, and so will be the parents and the citizens with whom the international teacher will relate.

Whether teaching in a rural or urban school, international teachers will find new worlds to explore, and new minds to influence.

3.4 Behaviorism, Constructivism, and the International Teacher

3.4.1 Behaviorism and the international teacher

It is likely that most international teachers are familiar with, or have operated in a school environment where behaviorism is the rule. Major contributors of this theory include John Locke, A. H. Thorndike, and B. F. Skinner. In essence, this educational theory makes the assumption that the mind of a learner is passive, but has potential. It assumes that because the mind is neurally-wired with certain reflexes connected with human needs, it is therefore trainable. This training is effected in three steps: 1) a stimulus occurs in the environment, 2) a response is made in the presence of that stimulus, and, 3) that response is reinforced, punished, or extinguished (Dacey & Travers, 1996).

Based on the notion of the reflexive, input-output, action-reaction pattern, behaviorism supposes that given adequate amounts of practice (via reinforcement, drills, and repetition, etc.) and the appropriate reinforcements, students may reach higher behavioral-cognitive potentials. For this reason, the task of the teacher is to employ systematic instructional activities which will elicit the desired student responses.

The discussion above has very significant education implications for teaching, classroom management, and learning. In many parts of the world, such as Africa and Asia, the teacher is viewed as the sage: an embodiment of knowledge. Students and the society at large behave as such toward teachers. The implication for teaching and learning is rather extensive and profound. If teachers are indeed sages, then they are the authorities in their subject matter, and final arbiters of knowledge in general. They teach with authority, and student voice in the classroom is subordinated. The questions and inputs of students are likely to be more solicitous of the facts and clarification, as opposed to being contributions to the developing knowledge. The teaching style tends to be the direct delivery approach, since the teacher is actively "pouring" knowledge, as it were, into the passive minds of the students.

Another implication is that, since the students are mental and psychological subordinates to the teacher, their behaviors would tend to be relatively contained. This is in harmony with the operative terminologies likely to be found in the behavioral environment. For example, even teacher education colleges may be called "training" colleges, as has been indicated elsewhere in this book. The term "teacher training" has a stricter, more behavioral connotation as compared to "teacher education."

Depending on where they are coming from, international teachers will find the world of behaviorism as discussed above to be similar or different from the classroom environment they may expect in American schools. In countries where the selective function of schooling is high (which may include the tracking of students for relatively fewer higher educational and economic opportunities), behaviorism may be expected to be stronger. Conversely, in more egalitarian countries (where individual freedom and equal rights is stronger), it is more conceivable for constructivism to take stronger roots.

Other factors such as educational reforms may interfere with such patterns. For example, Ghana, a listening (relatively hierarchical and traditionalist) society, undertook an educational reform which embraced constructivism in order to foster student comprehension. Constructivism, however, is inherently at odds with the behaviorism germane to a traditionalist environment. On the other hand, a caveat is order for the American teaching environment: Although American colleges of education espouse the constructivist, hands-on, minds-on approach to teaching as the ideal philosophy, many practicing teachers employ different degrees of the behavioral approach in order to keep abreast with rigorous curriculum pacing guides.

3.4.2 Constructivism and the International Teacher

World view theory was suggested as a paradigm or basic framework within which people operate and make sense of the world. Through their cultural activities, people both change, and are changed by their environment (Hobson, 1993). This is where the concept of world view meets constructivism.

In consonance with social transmission theories, whereby cultural values may be passed on from one generation to the next, education has historically had its own share of cultural transmission. Roth (1993) observes that this may be done primarily by bringing a newcomer into the "community of knowers" (p. 164) in order to share in the authentic practices and discourse patterns of the culture. He adds that it is through this shared participation that we learn our mother tongue, traditional apprenticeship training, law practice, and so on. It is for the same reason that in the scientific community, there are such practices as medical apprenticeship (and internships) as well as post-doctoral programs to introduce novice scientists to their work. This is the bridge between the shared, cultural values of the scientific community (world view), and the learning of actual practice–or the dynamics of constructing new knowledge (constructivism).

If education is about teaching and learning, then it is very difficult to circumvent the idea of process as an issue. Constructivism is concerned with the process and philosophy of teaching: It is a double-edged sword. Tobin and Tippins (1993) suggest that constructivism could be simultaneously viewed as a referent and a strategy for teaching and learning, both of which are processes.

Duit (1992) notes that several empirical research studies have shown that students essentially do not learn the "scientific view." He believes that two main reasons appear to explain this. In the first place, students' current views guide and determine their understanding of the new information being taught. They therefore try to integrate aspects of the "science views" into their own native views. "This results in 'interesting mixtures' of intuitive and science views." (p. 7) Secondly, there is a strong resistance to change native ideas in order to adopt new ones. This happens because the old, native ideas have been successful, and therefore students have no need for any new ones. Duit therefore concludes that constructivism helps to establish that:

i.   Pre-existing conceptions guide understanding
ii.   Knowledge construction is only possible on the basis of already existing conceptions
iii. Old ideas are not easily given up without severe resistance; to give up an old idea is to consent that one held a wrong idea for a long time (p. 7).

Cobern (1993) believes that if constructivism were an epistemological model of learning, then constructivist teaching would be mediation, and that the teacher's role is that of an "interface between the curriculum and the student, in order to bring the two together in a way that is meaningful for the learner" (p. 51). There is an emphasis placed on the term "context" since constructivism (the process), as in the construction of new knowledge "takes place at a construction site consisting of structures standing on a foundation" (p. 51).

Driver et al. (1994) support this view by observing that knowledge is something that is constructed and agreed on within the community. It then becomes a part of the "taken-for-granted" way of seeing things within the community (p. 6). They conclude that "public knowledge is constructed and communicated through the culture and social institutions of science." (p. 6)

Coming from culturally different backgrounds, international teachers will need to find novel ways to help their students in the new culture to "construct" new knowledge. They will need to bring to a convergence the dual processes of enculturation and knowledge construction. This done, they can more successfully adapt their native curriculum and instruction to that the local context.

3.5   The International Teacher and Teacher Induction

The earlier sections of this chapter indicate that international teachers can be expected to go through significant cultural and pedagogical changes. Since they would have new pedagogical and cultural experiences, it is reasonable to suggest that they will also experience some kind of "induction" into the new teaching environment. The ultimate goal of such an induction would be to develop better quality in teaching. The Center for Educational Research and Innovation (1994, pp. 14, 15) defines teacher quality using the following five dimensions:

1) knowledge of substantive curriculum areas and content;
2) pedagogic skill, including the acquisition and ability to use a repertoire of teaching strategies;
3) reflection and the ability to be self-critical, the hallmark of teacher professionalism;
4) empathy and the commitment to the acknowledgement of the dignity of another; and
5) managerial competence, as teachers assume a range of managerial responsibilities within and outside the classroom.

Out of the above, Odell (1989) believes that the two most frequently identified needs of new teachers may be pedagogic skills ("support in the instructional process" [p. 49]) and managerial competence ("managing children," specifically, discipline concerns, [ibid.]). A lot is expected of the teacher, new or veteran. It is therefore not surprising as Reinhartz (1989) points out that it is not only unrealistic, but also unfair to expect new teachers to function as proficiently and successfully as veterans. Reinhartz is a proponent of teacher mentoring programs for new teachers, together with several others (for example The National Commission on Teaching and America's Future and NCTAF State Partners (2002); Huling-Austin, (1989); Henry (1989), who are of the conviction that many potentially good teachers would leave the profession without the benefit of such help.

Mager (1992) believes that "[t]eacher competence is transportable," and that an individual teacher may "bring competence from prior experience and study to the work of teaching in any classroom and school: she will take her competence along when she comes to the next setting" (p. 17). Notwithstanding the possible portability of competence, Weiss and Weiss (2000) suggest that new teacher induction is not an easy venture. This, they claim, explains the inordinate rate of attrition among them. Bullough and Baughman (1997) are also of this conviction. They point out that teaching is a stressful job, particularly as teachers' roles become less and less defined. International teachers may benefit from these observations.

3.6   Pedagogical Content Knowledge

Pedagogical content knowledge (PCK) is a re-synthesized knowledge; a form of teacher's knowledge. It incorporates basic pedagogical knowledge and content knowledge of a given discipline (van Driel et al., 1998). In other words, effective, trained teachers are conversant with the basic art of teaching. Beyond that, they also have a mastery of a subject area or discipline of interest. The problem is that, in a real classroom, raw, factual knowledge needs to be converted into a more digestible form for the students. Once this feat has been accomplished, the converted knowledge has then become a new kind of knowledge: the pedagogical content knowledge for that material (Shulman, 1986). This is the knowledge base a practicing teacher eventually creates from experience, and is environmentally-influenced (Cochran, DeRuiter & King 1993).

Although earlier researchers have written a lot about PCK and developed the concept (Shulman 1986; Tamir, 1988; and Grossman, 1990), Magnusson, Krajcik, and Borko (1999) explain PCK in the recapitulation of the typical teacher's soliloquy:

> What shall I do with my students to help them understand this concept? What materials are there to help me? What are my students likely to know and what will be difficult for them? How best shall I evaluate what my students have learned? These questions are common for every teacher, and central to describing knowledge that distinguishes a teacher from a subject matter specialist. (p. 95)

They have re-synthesized several previous research, and re-conceptualized PCK as consisting of five components namely,

1) orientations toward teaching
2) knowledge and beliefs about the curriculum
3) knowledge and beliefs about students' understanding of specific topics

4) knowledge and beliefs about assessment, and
5) knowledge and beliefs about instructional strategies for teaching (p. 97).

It is particularly interesting that "knowledge and beliefs" appear several times in the list above. It may be granted that educators are in the knowledge construction business, and so have to necessarily possess specific knowledge base for their professions. However, the term "belief" is very personal, non-standardized, and value-laden, and that could raise concerns in the minds of public education stakeholders. Gudmundsdottir (1999) suggests that "values are embedded in teacher education curricula, just as they are hidden in school curricula. These need to be 'lifted out' and examined." (pp. 50, 51) To him, most people who go through teacher education have had to develop an orientation "not by choice, but by default" (p. 51). Therefore, he believes that all teacher education students need to make informed choices that would guide the development of their PCKs.

To illustrate the points above, international teachers should note that in American schools, personal values are expected to be separated from one's teaching practice. For example, an American teacher with a Jewish religion background may not impose his or her personal, religious values on a Moslem student. However, this teacher's personal values and background may determine his or her personal heroes, and conceivably therefore, influence his or her examples during classroom instruction. A further example involves ethnic or cultural values. African Americans, for instance, show much more interest in black history than other United States cultural groups; are more knowledgeable in black historical facts than other cultural groups in America; and are more likely to cite black historical figures as examples in their lessons. As natural as such inclinations may be, they indeed do influence the products of learning in the classroom.

In several trials while teaching pre-service teachers at a large, urban university, my colleagues and I administered two sets of questions to our racially diverse students. One set of questions contained conventional American historical figures, and the other set contained questions on black (African American-related) history. Although all the students naturally knew the conventional American white historical figures, most of the white students did not recognize significant black personages in American history—but the black students overwhelmingly did.

The above example is illustrative of two points: First, that black (and probably all other ethnic) students value their own cultural heroes more than others; Second, that different historical facts are not placed at an equal value in the American school curriculum. This is indeed a global phenomenon, and it is a part of the hidden curriculum in schooling, whereby different ideologies and information are differentially emphasized; some more than others, depending on the dominant cultural norms. This curriculum issue is addressed in the book, History Lessons: How Textbooks from Around the World Portray U.S. History, and recaptures the African proverb, "No one points to his or her father's village with his or her left hand." In other words, "Dirty linen is best washed out of public view."

International teachers should be interested in PCK issues, since local examples and analogies may serve a better purpose than foreign, unfamiliar ones (S. Magnusson, J. Krajcik, & H. Borko, 1999). This is in agreement with Cochran, DeRuiter, and King (1993), who recaptioned PCK into "pedagogical content knowing," in order to acknowledge the dynamic, on-going nature of knowledge (PCK) development.

3.7 Diversity Issues in American Education

America is a nation of both voluntary and involuntary immigrants. The voluntary immigrants, mostly Europeans, relocated to the United States for various reasons. Initially, religious freedom was of paramount importance for the European immigrants who were primarily from England. Later on, voluntary immigrants came to America mostly for economic opportunities. In order to fuel the economic infrastructure (which was then mostly agricultural), African slaves were brought in to provide labor on the plantations. During this period, the slaves did not have the luxury of education, and in many cases, those who attempted to read were prohibited to do so by their masters.

After slavery was abolished, freed slaves were left with very limited economic opportunities to live decent lives. Even though the value of education was well recognized in the larger American society, the freed slaves had few educational opportunities open to them. People such as Booker Washington (1856-1915), a freed slave, and Mary McLeod Bethune (1875-1955), a daughter of former slaves, began to open schools to formally educate their fellow slaves.

Notwithstanding the harsh racism, Booker Washington, Mary Bethune, and several other freed slaves became very powerful people in America. They were also advocates of education for all Americans, including the slaves, and this movement towards true liberation for all by means of education was widespread among black Americans. Many black Americans viewed education as the means to their freedom. Not surprisingly therefore, some of the most notable black American historical figures lived during this period of time, including George Washington Carver (1864-1943), W.E.B. DuBois (1868-1963), Marcus Garvey (1887-1940), and the two mentioned above.

History testifies that the struggle for racial equality in America was rather long and difficult. During World War II, numerous Americans from minority extractions were sent to war. Having had the opportunity to experience racial equality at the warfront, but still being relegated to second-class citizenship on their return to the United States, African Americans increased their clamor for educational and economic equities. Although there was initially a lot of resistance by the majority population, African Americans were able to organize enough support from more and more influential white sympathizers and other minority populations. With the help of several organizers such as Malcom X, and Martin Luther King, the Civil Rights Movement of the 1960s was born.

The Civil Rights Movement was a clamor for equality of all people, no matter their race, gender, religion, or national origin. The most popular hero of American Civil Rights Movement, Dr. Martin Luther King is popularly known to have said that, "Injustice anywhere is a threat to justice everywhere." Minority groups such as Native Americans, Latinos, Asians– and indeed all other minority groups in the U.S. stood to gain from this Movement's activities. Women also derived significant benefits. Such gains included relatively better economic and educational opportunities for all Americans. The educational gains included better schools for minority neighborhoods, and later, the struggle to include the contributions of women and all minorities into American history books, and in certain cases, to correct certain historical facts.

Since schools are a reflection of the larger society, in time, the then current societal issues became the educational issues, with two contending philosophies: "Assimilationism" and "Cultural Pluralism." The "Assimilationists," as the term may imply, believe that schools should teach immigrants to seamlessly become a part of the American fabric. In part, they believe that this could be achieved by learning to speak English, and to value and take part in the cultural heritage of America. For them, new immigrants are expected to become a part of the American "melting pot." They believe that, as the American axiom goes: *E pluribus, unum*, meaning, "Out of the many, one," both the immigrants and the American society stand to gain, as all Americans stand as one people, with a common destiny. (Proponents include such names as Diane Ravitch and Dinesh DeSouza.)

The Cultural Pluralists, on the other hand, believe that there is no such thing as the melting pot. To them, America has had past racial and cultural discriminations, leading to the intervention of the Civil Rights Movement. They contend that a person does not have to lose his or her cultural heritage in order to develop loyalty and allegiance to the United States. Many minority groups sharing this opinion believe that they need to fight for their historical contributions and cultural peculiarities to be recognized by the

American society at large. For these reasons, they have fought for schools to respond by making certain changes in their curricula. This brought about the phenomenon of "multiculturalism," or "diversity issues" in American schools. (Proponents include Molefi Kete-Asante, James Banks, and Asa Hilliard III.)

At its roots, multiculturalism (or the notion of embracing diversity) is a concerted effort by teachers to respect all cultures represented by individual students in their classrooms. Students are viewed as human beings with cultural pride. Cultural pride is believed to influence self-esteem. Teachers are therefore expected to plan their lessons in such a way as to intellectually and emotionally connect with, and respect all their students from all backgrounds.

Campbell, (2004) asserts that the American school system is designed after the values and culture of the American middle-class. Middle-class families provide most of the teachers and administrators in American schools. With the massive influx of immigrants into the U.S. (who are generally poorer, and have different cultures), there have arisen significant educational crises.

Poverty, by its very nature, creates its own culture; a culture which may be disregarded and misunderstood by the middle-class. (For more on this, see Payne's book: A Framework for Understanding Poverty). Secondly, the cultural values of the poor are sometimes assessed negatively in the school system, thereby excluding poor students from achieving success through education (Bowles & Gintis, 1976). Campbell (2004) therefore argues that middle-class educators need to learn about the poor, and also how to work with the poor to achieve success. He states that,

> Multicultural education assumes that teachers want all their students to succeed and that they are looking for positive and effective democratic responses to the economic and demographic changes taking place in U.S. schools today. We need teachers who are willing to search out the potential of all children. A significant percentage of the U.S. labor force for the next decade will pass through our urban schools. These citizens must be prepared to work, investigate, explore, and decide on public policy that will benefit the entire community. If schools fail, even if only the urban schools continue to fail, then the U.S. economy will fail. (pp. 38, 39)

The education of all Americans is a serious national issue. In fact, the current education reform (the *No Child Left Behind Act* of 2002) is the government's attempt to ensure that all American children receive the best possible education. (A good resource on multicultural education is Handbook of Research on Multicultural Education, Banks & McGhee Banks [Editors])

3.8   Teaching Diverse Learners

As multiculturalism or the notion of diversity gained roots in American classrooms, another issue emerged. This was the need to recognize the finer differences among individuals, even within the majority white populations. With the discovery of cognitive sciences in the 1960s, and later brain-based learning, the nature of teaching and learning in American schools changed. Teachers are now expected to find out more about individual students and discover how to effectively teach them.

A popular approach to teaching in diverse classrooms is the recognition of "multiple intelligences," which employs the "learning styles" of students. Howard Gardner for example, recognizes eight "frames of mind," outlining eight different "intelligences." These include linguistic, logical-mathematical, spatial, musical, body-kinesthetic, interpersonal, intrapersonal, and naturalistic intelligences. To him, it is unfair for society to assess students' intelligence based on only a few of them; especially linguistic and logical-mathematical abilities, as exemplified in the lecture, or "chalk and talk" instructional method, or IQ, and other standardized testing. (For more on this, please refer to Gardner's book: <u>Frames of Mind: The Theory of Multiple Intelligences.</u>)

So, how does one teacher teach a diverse class of 25-40 students with different intelligences and still be able to reach all of them?   There are several techniques in current use. One popular response is differentiated instruction. In brief, this is a lesson planning process whereby the teacher plans with different learning styles and cognitive needs in mind. (See a sample lesson plan in the appendix.) The result is that the teacher teaches the same concept using different instructional approaches. Cooperative strategies are at the root of this. This partly means that the role of the teacher changes from that of the "sage on stage," (whereby he or she may predominantly use the lecture method to "deliver wisdom" from the podium), to that of a "facilitator" who moves around the cooperative groups to help students "construct" their own knowledge. The term "facilitator" is commonly used in conjunction with the notion that students bring in some form of native knowledge to the classroom to be remolded. (This is the concept of constructivism). (For more on this, please see Chapters 3 and 6.)

3.9   Summary

International teachers are necessarily crossing cultural and pedagogical barriers. For this reason, they need to create their old worlds anew. This may include the embracing of the culture and world views of the new society. One's world view is the most salient (even if silent) determinant of the foundations of that person's knowledge. World view theory attempts to explain the factors which influence knowledge, knowledge construction, and knowledge re-construction. Pedagogical content knowledge is concerned with teachers' knowledge reconstruction, in the interest of their students.

U.S. public schools are fashioned after the values of the middle class. Urban and rural schools, however, have peculiar social, cultural, political, and economic factors that are important to understand in order to meet the needs of the students.

Unites States is a multi-ethnic society. Therefore, there are discussions concerning how to include, and represent the interests and contributions of all ethnic groups. Multiculturalism (or the notion of embracing diversity) in the classroom, is a concerted effort by teachers to respect all the cultures represented by individual students in their classrooms. Teachers are expected to plan their lessons in such a way as to intellectually and emotionally connect with, and respect all their students from all backgrounds.

The issue of diversity also features the management of diverse students' learning needs, especially in urban settings. An understanding of these issues is necessary in order to ease the transitional process for international teachers.

Chapter #4

INTRODUCING THE PLAYERS
Modified Backgrounds and Contexts of Five International
Teachers

In this chapter, some information about the author and each of the participants of this study, nick-named Mary, Joe, Inga, and Kofi are provided. Excerpts from interviews with them have been used in order to provide useful, close-to-real-life accounts for the reader. The information included will hopefully help to shed some light on the lives of the participants, as they make their teaching transitions into American schools. This section is also included in order to help buttress, and provide contexts for the later chapters.

It must be mentioned that caution has been exercised so as to protect the true identities of the participants in this study. Just enough information is provided in order to help the reader understand each participant's international transitional issues. Any limitations in their background information, where missing, are thus explained.

This chapter begins with the author's personal experiences as an international transitional teacher. As mentioned earlier, the study that resulted in this book was borne out of the author's personal experiences as he began teaching in United States middle and high schools.

4.1   The Author's Pedagogical Biography

World view theory harmonizes with the adage that, "No man is an island." It asserts that people's backgrounds invariably influence their worldview. Written in the first person, this pedagogical biography is meant to relate my past experiences which have, and still do influence my teaching life, both in Ghana and in America.

4.1.1 My early perceptions of teachers and teaching

In Ghana, being a high school teacher is considered respectable. I therefore respected the teaching profession, although I initially did not plan to become a teacher. I did fantasize about becoming an engineer (and of course sometimes, a medical doctor). However, I could not get the required score to gain admission into the very few, coveted spots in the related universities. Luckily, I did qualify to enter the pedagogical university, and I was very grateful for the opportunity. I therefore became a teacher purely on the basis of tracking.

4.1.2 My socio-cultural influences

After the colonization and independence of African countries, a new society has emerged. Although there is a strong socio-cultural intercourse between the traditional African and European systems, African traditions still reign supreme. Syncretism (a hybridization of two or more, especially religious practices) is prominent. Although modern, Western education has become the new avenue for social mobility, traditional respect, and even reverence for the elders is still evident in the educational system. For this reason, students hardly ask questions in classes, as compared to American students. The teacher is seen as the elder, a wise person, and a custodian of knowledge; one who knows it all, or at least should. Questioning (especially with the wrong attitude) could therefore be seen as an affront to the teacher's dignity.

Most high school teachers, especially in the sciences, are males. The traditional family role for males is that of a breadwinner; unlike mothers, fathers are generally not perceived as caring, gentle, and loving figures. One can therefore easily understand why reluctance to ask too many questions of teachers in class could almost be a second nature to the Ghanaian student.

Several of my teachers were apt to speak to us in parables, or in proverbs. African value systems (some of which we learned from "Brer Rabbit" and "Ananse" stories and the like) added color to the teaching and learning experience. Certainly, personal stories added flesh to the pedagogical experience, and the best teachers always had the best stories to match the lesson. Proverbs and stories therefore were cherished, and honored by society.

African traditional religions and Christianity are also inherent in our educational system. The marriage between African and European traditions has given birth to several issues loosely called the "African dilemma." This dilemma has been given a voice in several African literature, captioned the "African Writers' Series." This series is a large body of literature mostly relating everyday examples of life in post-colonial Africa. Such everyday life examples have become fictionalized, global best sellers.

In consonance with the themes carried in African Writers' Series, African education is at the crossroads of African and European cultures. Ghana has not been an exception to this phenomenon. In fact, one could argue that the commonwealth of the independent nations of the world share this same dilemma. I too, personally share in this larger experience.

4.1.3 The educational system in Ghana and its influences.

The educational system in Ghana is centrally-controlled from the capital, with sub-controls in regional offices. One however, cannot discount the influence of the local headmaster or headmistress in the hiring of teachers and acquisition of facilities. At the high school level especially, the role of the alumni is significant.

When I was in school, children began schooling at about five years, entering into "class one." Students remained in elementary school for six years, through "class six," after which they went on to middle school. This was for four years (forms one to four). In the middle school, the real educational competition began: All students who wanted to go on to secondary (high) schools needed to prepare themselves and sit for the Common Entrance examinations. One could begin as early as the first year of middle school, all the way to the fourth year, to attempt passing this examination. Depending on one's marks (scores), one would get their first, second, or third choice of school. This exam was very competitive, because all the students in the nation were competing for very limited spaces in the high schools. Those who did not make the score to leave middle school for the secondary track would then finish off middle schooling by sitting for the Middle School Leaving Certificate. Such people generally became artisans such as carpenters, mechanics, apprentices, blacksmith, etc.

Those who entered high school would then have to make it through the first tier; the General Certificate of Education (GCE) Ordinary Level Examinations, affectionately captioned the "Os." Depending on one's scores, one would either move on to the technical (or trade) schools, or find a job. If one made good enough grades to gain admission into the "sixth form," one would spend two more years in the high school in preparation for GCE "Advanced Level" Examinations (the "As"), and subsequently, a college career, if one made the cut in the competition.

Owing to the high level of competition for high school education, there existed a general spirit of competition among classmates. At the end of the semester, in many schools, all the grades one earned were averaged and ranked against all the students at that grade level. This was then openly posted for public view. The idea was that this would urge on the weaker students to fare better. There were also inter-school competitions, not only in athletics, but also in comparing GCE scores. Schools therefore asserted a kind of "superiority" by the index of their GCE scores. It may therefore come as no surprise that the last year to the O-level or A-level Examinations were mostly geared toward teaching in preparation for these tests.

4.1.4 Tracking in schools

Although students may have had personal aspirations, such aspirations were generally contingent on making good enough scores as to make it to the right academic track. I mention this because only the first three years of our high school education was generic. At the end of the third year, those good in math and science were selected to opt for the science track. All other students were barred from the science track. It was therefore a source of student pride, especially the fresh, form four students to carry their "Abbott" around as a symbol of academic superiority. (A. F. Abbott was the author of a rather voluminous, blue physics book).

On a side note, it may be interesting to mention that in the boarding school where many in my generation went to high school, "Abbott" was also a weapon. The relatively junior students who did not accord respect to their "seniors" (i.e. those in higher grades) would be made to carry an "Abbott" with an outstretched hand for a significant amount of time, as their punishment.

Forms four and five (roughly, junior and senior years) were a preparation period for the Ordinary level examinations in a selected or tracked area of discipline. The examinations would further limit those on a given track to continue in sixth form. If one made it to the sixth form, those on the science track had two package options: one selected physics, chemistry, biology, and general studies (for general paper examinations—a form of aptitude test), or physics, chemistry, mathematics, and general studies. In college, one would then directly begin to work in their major area, in my case, zoology, botany, and chemistry, in addition to my education courses. What may be interesting here is that in Ghana, the coursework and course loads are essentially set in stone all the way from primary school through college (depending on one's major).

4.1.5 My high school environment

Growing up in a Ghanaian city during the 1960s and 1970s, high school education had become the secondary rite of passage into puberty. This was a time when children left home (normally at about 13-15 years old) and braved "the world out there." It was also a critical period of life, because it was the place to "make or break" one's future aspirations via academic work: This was a time for students to define their future social placement. Even if one came from a poor family, one could still succeed in life, with academic performance. On the other hand, even if one came from a wealthy family, one could still end up in worse social situation if one's grades were not good enough. The educational process was indeed no respecter of people's economic background.

I passed the Common Entrance Examinations at about fourteen years old. Since I was bound for a boarding school (which was the norm), I said my last farewell to my parents, siblings and other relatives on the 18th day of September, 1974. From that time on, they would see me only a few months a year when on holidays, or when we visited each other.

My high school was located on twin hills, on the outskirts of Cape Coast. There was a student population of about 900, with about 500 boys and 400 girls. The girls lived in three dormitories, and the boys four. In order to mitigate and control potential adolescent problems, the girls' dormitories were located on the hill to one side of the road, while the boys lived on the other. The main campus, comprising the administrative, classroom buildings, and the dining hall, were on the boys' side. The campus was generally maintained by the students, who each went to "do their duties" before attending classes. We also had a large contingent of teachers living in bungalows on campus.

4.1.6 Academic life in high school

Each morning, about 7:15, the girls would cross the street (and later a bridge) to the main campus for the first two classes. Breakfast would then be eaten in the dining hall, and classes would resume until about 1:30 p.m. During classes (each of which lasted about 50 minutes), the students, unlike in the U.S., kept in their classrooms with permanent seats. The teachers moved around the classes. Generally in the lower levels (forms one to three), the science teachers taught general science in the classrooms. We had several double periods a week, which helped us to do hands-on, laboratory work. Group work was encouraged (in part, because of inadequate apparatus for all students).

At the lower academic levels, emphasis was placed on simple experiments and demonstrations. Although most of the work in science was theoretical, simple, common-sense reasoning skills were held in high esteem. Memorization was also rewarded. The textbooks used were thinner; consisting of no more than 100 pages; very readable; and placed a lot of emphasis on practical work.

At the higher levels (form four and higher), however, the students held classes in the science laboratories. General science would then give way to the individual sub-disciplines; physics, chemistry, and biology, since students were at this level working in their major academic areas.

Since it was too expensive to purchase certain chemical supplies and glassware for practicals (laboratory work), several of our chemistry laboratory work were done as demonstrations by the teachers, if the supplies were available. However, it was possible to do most of the physics and biology practicals. The reason was that, physics apparatus were normally hardy, and could be repeatedly used for several years, and were well maintained.

Being a tropical country, biological specimens could easily be collected right in the natural environment. One could therefore have a dissection of frogs anytime by just going to collect frogs from the local pond, or cockroaches among discarded boxes, or collect some plants or flowers for dissection right in the school backyard. Here again, group work was emphasized. The syllabi were daunting, but we had approximately two years to cover the same volume of typical books used in the United States in physics, chemistry, and biology. This is about twice the amount of time that one typically has available in the U.S. for covering the same amount of material. It was therefore possible for some of us to work out every single problem in the textbooks with classmates outside of classes, in preparation for tests. Some even had the time to create their own question banks, and challenge each other to tough line of questions expected in teachers' tests.

Perhaps the rigor of high school work could be maintained for a few simple reasons: In the first place, students lived on the school campus, and had no jobs. All the serious-minded students therefore had enough time to concentrate on schoolwork. Secondly, there was no opportunity of leaving the school campus for about three months at a time, except about three Saturdays in that period. Any student therefore who had any personal aspirations and internal drive to excel had the opportunity to do so. Besides, most of the teachers lived in bungalows on the school campus, and so it was possible to reach those who were on hand for help. In fact, it was a common experience to have many senior level classes meeting for extra lessons either in the afternoons or at night in order to finish a practical work, or a topic. The classrooms were also available to the students officially till bedtime, although several students stole away to keep studying into the night--a phenomenon among Ghanaian students which we called "mining" at the time. During mining, students would chew caffeine-laden cola nuts, known for its potency to keep one vigil.

4.1.7 Assessments and grades in Ghana

Most of the term's final grades came from tests during the course of the semester. The nature of our tests were generally unknown, since the onus rested on the student to know the material well enough to "attack" any question on any topic. The teachers' attitude was that of surprising the students with an obscure question, while that of the students was to surprise the teacher with a good mastery of the material as to "butcher" the test--and put that teacher to a "secret humility." It was a kind of cat-and-mouse game. The comparative grading scales in my high school and university are shown in table 4-1 below:

A COMPARISON OF APPROXIMATE GRADING SCALES IN U.S. AND GHANAIAN SCHOOLS

Designation	*Assigned Grade*	*U.S.*	*Ghana*
Excellent	A+	98-100	70+
Very Good	A	90-97	65-69
Good	B	80-89	60-64
Satisfactory	C	71-79	55-59
Pass	D	70	50-54
Failure	F	0-69	45-49

Table 4-1

Although it was possible for a few good students to obtain the "excellent" designation in high school, the general, tacit acknowledgement was that in the universities, for example, no one could expect to obtain an "A." This grade expectation was generally reflected in the final degree in the universities: There was the acquiescent absence of "first class" designated graduates, and a minority "second class upper" graduates. The general grade was "second class lower," and there was the detestable, but frequent "pass" designation.

It was generally difficult to know exactly the "marking scheme" by which one was given a grade. This was so, because, for the same reasons assigned earlier, we normally did not question the elders, or authorities. It may therefore be asserted that throughout the educational system in Ghana, a student's grade almost literally lay at the mercy of the teacher.

4.1.8 Recollections of my teacher education

At the University of Cape Coast, Ghana's primary pedagogical institution, the instructional mode was very traditional. The instructors mostly lectured in classes. (In fact, we generally call the college teachers "lecturers"—perhaps, for a good reason). There was a tacit assumption that there would not be discipline problems in the classrooms. Therefore, most of the curriculum centered on content acquisition and a separate degree program for pedagogy.

As a part of the curriculum, I had two "teaching practice" (internship) experiences in two different schools. Apparently, I did such a fine job of teaching that my education professors made a video recording of my teaching for instructional purposes. This is interesting to note in the light of my later teaching struggles within the American school system.

4.1.9 My teaching life in Ghana

Having graduated in 1986, I began teaching in an all-girls' high school of about 600 students. Apart from having female students, the life and the teaching traditions were similar to what I did experience in my own high school. I lived in a flat (apartment) on the school campus, and did not have to be in the classrooms unless I had a class. I taught general science in the lower grades, and biology to the sixth formers (6th and 7th year high school students).

I do remember that it was a pleasure to go to the classroom: at the lower classes, there was near-reverence for the teachers. The students were always in class, in their assigned seats, when the teacher arrived. They were very eager to learn. Occasionally, one would come across a deviant student, but the general atmosphere was replete with discipline. Added to the regime of discipline in the school was the fact that the campus was the residence of a Catholic convent, with which the school was affiliated. There was therefore a strict religious presence on campus.

In general, a student would not have discipline problems. If they did, depending on the gravity of the problem, they would be met with extra duties (such as cleaning the dining hall, weeding in the school farm, cleaning the chicken coops, or suspension (whereby the student would be sent home from boarding school). If suspension were the case, the student would be met with added severity from the parents (since it is a shame on the parents for neighbors to know that their children have been undisciplined in school). It is therefore obvious that students would do their best to avoid any such situations.

My sixth form students had similar discipline situations, although they were normally given more freedom than their younger counterparts. In general, students were hard-working, and it was a normal occurrence to see even freshmen students (14-year olds) going to "mine" (study in a rather obscure location through the night, into the wee hours of the morning, by a flashlight or candles). The teachers on night duty would sometimes drop by, on a surprise visit about midnight, only to find young miners in the lower grades. However, it was normal a expectation to see several upper level students burning the midnight oil in studies.

4.1.10 Teacher's responsibilities

The main job of the teacher was to show up during his or her periods, and teach. After that, he or she could depart the campus to do anything until the next teaching period. Staff meetings were rare, and when the teachers did gather, meetings were held in the afternoons, with full refreshments and lunch served. Teaching loads were generally not more than about 22 hours per week, and the younger teachers living on campus had assigned dining hall supervision duties, for which they were given free meals. Most teachers also had evening classroom supervision duties.

Students were not required to stay in their normal classrooms during evening studies. It was therefore common to find the senior students teaching the junior ones in the subjects of their specialty. This was a source of personal pride for them to "strut" their academic stuff. Perhaps, more so, these teaching experiences were necessary to help them refresh their own memories of the material over which they would be tested during the Ordinary, or Advanced Level Examinations mentioned earlier. Teachers normally felt responsible for the performance of their students in their subjects in the examinations. It was partly for this reason that it was common to find teachers instructing their senior level classes in the afternoons, and sometimes well into the night. Homework was not a norm for all subjects, although section review materials were generally assigned in most classes for practice and later testing.

If students had any psychological issues, it was not easy for anyone in the educational system to know, since that was not a part of the tacit educational responsibilities of the teacher. If any student experienced a physical or psychological breakdown, there were ample hierarchical structures for the student to get the necessary help. There was first the class prefect (or leader), the elected dormitory prefect and his assistant (senior-most level students), the house master and his assistant (in charge of the dormitories), a senior house master (with an oversight of all the house masters), the assistant headmaster, and finally, the headmaster.

4.1.11 Transitioning into my American school

By the time I left Ghana in October 1988, I had not only attended school all the way through college education, but had also had teaching experiences in a co-educational school, an all-boys school, and an all-girls school. I also had very close acquaintances who went to school all over the country, with whom I exchanged stories about school, friends' adventures, and, of course teachers. I had therefore a well-developed sense of the Ghanaian educational system.

I began teaching in a U.S. high school in August 1993. I clearly remember the first day of school: I arrived bright and early, since I had just moved into town the previous week, from the state of Oklahoma, and lived in an apartment about five minutes from school. The first day was mainly spent filling out paperwork for new teachers. The veteran teachers arrived the next day. We received our supplies and further information about the normal operations of the school: This included such activities as the class rotation schedule in the school, how to handle class schedule changes, and also parent-student handbook (and changes therein).

Apparently, we were also informed (to my oblivion) about the fact that grades were sent to parents whose children were not doing any better than a C- grade: We had to send them a deficiency report, using a specific format. There were also the sixth week grades, which were sent home three times per semester. There was separate paperwork for students with special needs, such as special teacher "contract" etc. with them. This I later discovered was the individualized educational plans (IEPs): something that cross-cultural teachers will hear a lot about in American schools.

I kept notes, but there was just too much with which to keep up. Some of the veteran teachers would occasionally give encouragement to the new teachers by saying that we would survive the week; the grading period (of six weeks); and so on, and that it got easier the second year, and even better the third year, and so forth.

We also had a session in which some veteran teachers shared their teaching experiences with the all the teaching staff. I heard some expressions about student management such as, "Do not smile until Christmas," and "Just be consistent with your discipline plan." On hearing some of these expressions, I began to wonder, and tried to imagine what kind of students I was going to deal with. I also listened to a series of tapes (for my personal homework).

I had my first "baptism of duties" when I was called on to help with student registration. It was nice opportunity, because it did help me to have an inkling of the kind of students I was going to meet, come first day of school. By the time the week was over, I was both physically and mentally exhausted.

4.1.12 Classroom experiences: Real life begins!

The students reported to school on Monday. By the time classes began, I was naturally anxious about beginning my life as an educator in America. I arrived at school very early in order to ensure that I had physically and mentally prepared myself. I stood by my classroom door at 8:10 a.m. in order to welcome the students as they entered the classroom. I tried to reconcile some of the conflicting axioms I had been taught about how to handle students, and I found myself yielding to my true self: I smiled all the way through my first day. The students smiled back. This was a good sign, I believed; I had established a good, human connection with my students.

Perhaps, I had a good first week for several reasons. First of all, there was a sense of newness to both the students and myself. Two of my classes were physical science. The students were in eighth grade, and did consider it a privilege to be in the high school building, I surmised. My other three classes were biology, which was taken by ninth grade students. This is a very transitional grade for two reasons; most school transfers occur into this grade, and all the students are now entering the high school for the first time. These factors may have contributed to my having a "tamed" class—at least, for a while.

The second reason I attributed to my having a good, early start was that I had an accent. This provided novelty in the classroom; several students mentioned that they liked my accent, and I was often asked to repeat expressions strictly for the students' enjoyment. I also heard several jokes, whereby the students were trying to imitate me. I believe that they possibly did enjoy the nuances of the accent until that factor faded off, as matters of content material grew more imposing, and the grading period approached.

Before long (about the third week or so), some of the students began to break the class rules. I still do recall the faces of some of students who just could not keep quiet. I became concerned, for several reasons. In the first place, this was the first time I was experiencing such kind of student misbehavior. I instinctively tried several warnings, none of which did work. Every so often, I would send a student out of class to the assistant principal in charge of student discipline. For several of these students, none of these measures did work. Eventually, unbeknownst to me, I had actually abandoned my discipline plan. I probably became "reactive" to the "perennially-troublesome" students. These students (who were albeit the minority of the class population) were enough to disrupt a significant portion of the planned lessons.

I remember some of the novel discipline problems I was encountering in class to include passing notes around the room. To this I decided to rework my discipline plan, so as to deal with it; I would read out aloud, some of these notes. In reaction, some of the students would intentionally write funny notes in hopes of having them read to entertain the class.

Besides planning to teach a good lesson, it was now a problem to deal with certain students, especially in a couple of my biology classes. Having sent these students to the office several times, I felt that it was my responsibility to personally deal with them, and not burden any administrator with my classroom management problems. Therefore, I kept the problems to myself. I was always very happy to make it to Fridays, because I needed the weekend in order to catch up with my grading and lesson plan preparations. More so, I needed the weekend in order to maintain my own mental health.

4.1.13   My meeting with the school principal

Towards the end of my first year, I was called to the office to meet with my principal. Although he was very cordial, and had personally hired me, he informed me that he had been notified about the serious discipline problems in my classes. Besides that, he had also heard from some parents that I had an accent, and that was having an "impact" on some of the students. I was therefore given the option of going to a program called "Emory at Night," in order to reduce my accent. I seized the opportunity to do that. I was also given a written note to officially document our meeting, with the provision that my contract would only be renewed if I made significant progress in my classroom management skills.

In the accent-reduction program, the instructor (who herself spoke like a British) noted that I had a good command of the English language and a "good accent." I however, stayed in the program to the end. Indeed, I did not have any misgivings about this, since the school administration was generally very cordial and fair. I took cue from my tribal axiom that says "No one person can fully embrace a baobab tree." This means that no one person is the sole custodian of all knowledge, and also implies that one had to be open to learn new things. I was therefore willing to learn anything in order to become more effective as a teacher in a new land and culture. This I realize, in hindsight, was a necessary, survivor's attitude.

4.1.14 Teaching issues

In the course of time, I noted several differences in the nature of my American high school in several categories. This included, for example, having to meet parents for meetings. In Ghana, I never had official meetings with parents in high school. My American students came in for help sessions, which were officially scheduled to be offered. The students asked a lot of questions in class, and some of them very much off-topic, and voiced out their opinions openly and without inhibition.

I also realized that some of them had a natural curiosity about my culture, and so I spent some time on cultural issues; specifically African issues. Although several of them complemented me on my accent, several others made me repeat things for them. For some, the issue concerned my use of expressions, or words, which had different meanings in the American parlance. Others asked me to repeat things for them. Certainly, there was an issue with communication.

In time, I realized that there were so many plants and animals in the area, that were not familiar to me, and I sought out to learn them—as a science teacher. I was then able to provide local examples, and therefore was better able to contextualize our interactions.

4.1.15 The teacher as a learner

Naturally, there were several things in the area with which I was not familiar, and so it took some time for me to be able to communicate effectively, and also understand both my colleagues and students. For example, I was not familiar with the local Braves baseball team, and was rather surprised that the school declared a "Braves spirit day," and had a "cheer-leading squad"; ideas which were non-existent in Ghana. Teachers came to students' games, and even made it a whole family affair. Parents came by in droves, and were very active in school affairs. The students stopped by, and personally invited me to their games, and looked to see if I was present, and mentioned it in class. All these were different in Ghana, and I needed the time to learn and make them a part of my life-style, to some extent.

By the end of the year, notwithstanding petty classroom management issues, I realized that I had inadvertently created a following of students, whom I called "my disciples." Several of the parents would also call me at home, or come to my classroom to inform me about the influence I was having on their children. I had apparently become the regular subject of their dinner conversations. A partial reason for this was that I used a lot of personal stories in my teaching lessons. I received several endearing notes from co-teachers, parents, and most importantly, my students.

In order to mitigate any problems in my classes, I used a lot of jokes, some of which were self-deprecating, and these made my students look forward to coming to my class. For this reason, there were several parents who would try to arrange for their children to come to my classes, in later years. Some of the parents wrote notes to me, using our joking class lingo, such as this one that said: "To the government: My little rascal, Brandon, has permission to migrate out for lunch on Thursday." My classes were filled with real-life experiences and anecdotes—more like applied biology, and that helped all the students to be cognitively focused on the teaching and learning process.

There were several things that I needed to change in order to survive in my U.S. high school. This included my personal attitude toward students, and my assessment methods, both of which had to be relaxed. I spoke more slowly, learned American expressions, and resorted to other teaching methods, such as more hands-on approaches, in order to reach my students. I sat in the classes of another teacher-colleague, and learned how he dealt with his students. I learned to assign homework and grade them, and also learned to use a lot of the machines used in the schools (such as the scanning grading machine, photocopiers, laser disk players, and computers), most of which were absent in Ghana when I was teaching. I learned about what materials were available in the school environment and were useful in my lessons, and also learned what the students knew, in order for me to make my lessons relevant to them.

In the end, by my fourth year in the school, I was chosen to become a mentor to other teachers, in our mentoring program, and was called on to talk to the whole faculty about cultural issues facing certain students in the school. I had survived!

4.2   Mary's Pedagogical Biography

Mary was a middle-aged British woman teaching in a private high school in a large metropolitan area. She was a serious person, and very professional about her job. Having taught biology for over a decade, she could boast of being a "master-teacher." She was also the head of the science department of her school, and had been living the in U.S. and teaching there for five full years at the time of this study. Her school (which was the same school in which Joe and Inga were teaching) had a climate that placed more emphasis on academic achievement than Kofi's.

Mary went into teaching because she wanted a career change. She made her decision during a time when there was a shortage of teachers in England and was convinced by a friend to try teaching. For this reason, she initially got in the classroom without the benefit of formal teacher training. The following are Mary's account, rearranged with minimal inclusions (in brackets), in order to provide an approximation of her teaching life:

4.2.1 Mary's early perceptions of teachers and teaching

I just wanted a career change: The salary didn't seem so important. I was earning a lot of money during my previous job, but I was not enjoying it. It was very stressful, and so I took a break, [and] was introduced to teaching by a friend, who just lived virtually next door. It was immensely hard work because I didn't have any teacher training or training in education. My biology qualifications were appropriate, but I didn't have any teaching [experience], so it was [difficult]. [It is like] one of the things, when you're allowed to teach here in the U.S., [and] you are outside looking into the profession, and you think it's easy; [thinking that] we all know how to teach because we were in school, so everybody can teach. [It is] one of the big lies of the world. For me, it became a huge revelation especially at [my first school in England], to realize that teachers didn't get time off during the day. It was a constant stress.

I had favorite teachers, but I don't know if they were models of teachers. They were probably like people when you're growing up, and you're a student. What attracts you to a teacher may not be their professionalism, it may be the fact that they don't give you any homework, or they'll let you be a few minutes late, or they'll let you talk in class, which is not a model of a teacher. I had no idea ever of becoming a teacher until I was in my thirties; it never ever crossed my mind.

So I think of teachers that way: They never drove me to want to be a teacher. In fact, they probably drove me away from it, if anything. I find that [to be true] with my [current] students, because I teach students who are a little older, and they're thinking about what they're going to do later on. Very, very few of them ever consider teaching as a job. It's a rare student I have in the twelfth grade who would say, "I want to be a teacher." So their choice to go into education and become a teacher, at this level, obviously comes later, and it's a different motivation. It may be different for people who want to become kindergarten teachers or junior school teachers, but the motivation to do that is very different than doing what we do. Very rarely; one in forty, one in fifty would ever say, "I want to be a teacher; I want to do what you do."

So I didn't have any role models in school; no. Later on, when I was moving to the international system, I [did] have a role model for how I try to run the department, and that was my first department head in [Europe]. I try to follow what she did because she was a brilliant head of department. I was in my early thirties when I started teaching, and I was the only female in the department; the only biologist in the department, and it was hard for me to find a role model. There wasn't anyone I really wanted to emulate, whether that indicates some kind of arrogance on my behalf, I don't know.

4.2.2 Mary's socio-cultural influences

Early home influences. My parents were very supportive of education because of the conditions they grew up in. I regard both my parents as extremely bright, intelligent people—[as] me and my siblings. Education was a driving course they wanted us to go, and they would have done anything to get us into the best schools. They weren't in position to send us to private schools, but the best schools the state had to offer. So that was one of the main drives--and [also] the opportunity that education would give you. For us it was considered a privilege that you went to more academic school. That was part of it, I suppose. My mother worked, which was unusual.

When I was a kid, it was unusual for a woman to work or to run a business. Having got the education, the thing is what you're going to do with it.

For [my parents], the main thing was stability; you want to get a good job, a good pension so that you have security and stability, so that was one of the major things. I grew up in a fairly large house within quite a poor neighborhood. It was not considered to be the best neighborhood in the town I came from, but people were very neighborly; there was a sense of community, and my sister and I didn't have many friends from the school. My sister is a few years younger than me. She followed me through school. My brother went to a different school on the other side of town. He's younger than me.

What's interesting is that my father traveled a lot during the war because he was in the air force. My mother didn't. We all lived overseas; all three of us. My sister was the first one to leave—she married and went to live in Eastern Africa [and later, several other places around the world.] My brother lived in Japan, and has traveled the world. That freedom to move—we are an unusual family. Where that came from; from our background, I have absolutely no idea. My father would encourage us to travel because he traveled and had seen the world, and he came from a larger family where they tended to be less nuclear, and it was expected that the kids would scatter. From that point of view, my father was at more ease with his traveling. My mother had more problems with that. She doesn't like [our travels]: at one time all three of her kids would have been scattered all over the world. I was closest. We were a close family [and] the guilt about leaving home is huge, and you never overplay that. From that point of view, we all appreciate the support our mom and dad gave us.

School influences. [In] the school I was as a student, you took an exam when you were 11 [years old] in England, Great Britain, and according to how you did, you were put in different academic levels. My sister and I went to the top level, which is called grammar school, and so there was that kind of streaming on academic basis. That tended to isolate people culturally as well. The middle level would be some sort of technical school or bilateral school, [and] that was also streamed when you got there. The third level would be the kind of school I ended up teaching in, so the school I went to as a student wasn't particularly racially or culturally [diverse]. Academically, we were all basically the same--but financially it wasn't particularly mixed. I think that's something my parents taught me—[that] people are different; [and] you are not perfect. That was [an] unsaid issue--that you to accept people for what they are, and not classify them according to some silly criteria. I think that's what made it easier for all three of us to move around and live in different cultures and make a success of what we are doing.

4.2.3 Mary's recollections of her teacher education

I didn't get any teacher training. At the time that I started teaching, there was a great drive by the government to get people in industry and business into schools, because they felt that would help drive forth the kids into working in business and industry. In fact, the school I was in, the headmaster was very interested in it. We had people coming straight out of common factory industry straight into schools to teach, so I didn't get any [teacher training].

I had two interviews before I started the school, both of which were testing my science knowledge, which was adequate. I had one visit from an inspector the first year [and] I had very little evaluations. My only teacher training was on the job and I got the support teacher to come and help me when I had too many classes. I just couldn't teach the classes: I had too many; and he came and took one class, to give me some free time. So my teacher training was on the job, and for me it worked. For others, I think they would have crumbled.

My first six weeks in school, I got two free periods a week, [and] there was nothing [to guide me]. Actually, I still have at home, framed, [a note] from a chemistry teacher when I started working in October, and she says "Don't smile 'til Easter." The other one was a piece of paper somebody gave me that said, "Try this, it might work," and on it was a lesson plan and it said "Title," underlined, "Date," "Object," "Blackboard Work," and that was underlined, and "Homework." It said, "Why don't you try writing these for each class?" And that was my teacher training. Luckily, I had supportive friends who helped me through it, and would buy me [drinks] when I started to cry.

[Another] training I got was the year I went back to university to do a degree in education, but that was not [in] teacher training [but management]. I was very fortunate; I fell on my feet, and I found something I could do and enjoy doing, but I don't know if that would suit everybody. I think some people might need more support.

4.2.4 Mary on her first day of school

School starts in September in England. I started just one Monday morning, and I got a lot of work. My main fear when I started teaching was that kids were going to ask me questions that I didn't know the answer, and I was told to start with a skeleton. I arrived at school 7:00 that morning. I could hardly stand up. My hands were shaking, my legs; everything was shaking--and I dressed up nicely. Previously I had been in business and I had nice business suits, high-heeled shoes, you know. That lasted about two weeks.

[The] kids came in, and I just looked at them, and I knew in ten seconds that the issue was not going to be that the kids were going to ask questions, but the issue was going to be getting them to sit down. I think those ten seconds were very informative. I just looked at them and I thought, "I know what's happening here. I recognize these, and I know what the challenges are going to be." Very luckily, I picked it up quite easily because of my training in business and because I was older; I mean, I wasn't twenty-one like many new teachers, and I'd been in a fairly mixed school myself, and I could change my priorities. You can't teach them anything if you can't get them to sit down. So what are you going to do to get them to sit down and listen to you? For some reason it worked for me; with my temperament and background.

What happened worked because I'm here doing what I'm doing, but I think a lot of people would have been shocked by that lack of support. I asked for a different kind of support from people—[to] tell me if I [was] doing a good job or bad job. The thing that I could've had, but didn't get was more time to prepare and I didn't get that. After that Christmas break, somebody realized I was being hit by all of these troublesome substitutes [issues], so I did eventually get the five or six free periods I was entitled to, but that was a struggle.

I was treated as a full-blown qualified teacher from the minute I walked into the school. So that's mainly one thing I would've liked to change: more time to prepare for classes, and to recover from the classes I'd just done, and to get to know the kids a bit better. A little more academic guidance [such as] what appropriate kinds of practical lab work to do for the students, because I was floundering; I didn't really know what to do.

[On moving outside the United Kingdom], I brought my industrial and business experience, and seemed to work it out. I worked immensely hard, and I almost burned out after the first year, and managed to get through it-- and the rewards come later. I think [in] the first year, wherever you go is a nightmare. It can be particularly bad if you moved countries and you moved schools. It can be very difficult on a personal level to move to a country where you may not know anyone, might not speak the language very well--I mean the infrastructure is different. The first year was a nightmare, I think.

4.2.5 Mary on teaching life in native England

General teaching experiences. I taught biology in South London, [in a] very large inner city comprehensive [school], which I did for more than five years. After that time I decided to move on and took a position in a school in [another large, European metropolitan city], [in a] private international school, where I taught biology and International General Certificate of

Education (IGCE); it's an exam they take in the U.K. at sixteen. After four years in [this place], I went back to England to do my degree in education. I majored in educational management.

From there, I took a year off and went to [Asia] and various places like that. Then I went to a German international school, where I taught International Baccalaureate (IB), and some A-levels too at the same time. I taught in the upper school, so all my classes were exam classes. I was there for five years. Then I came here [to the United States]. This is my fifth year, starting my sixth. Because of the way the timetable is constructed here, I just teach eleventh to twelfth graders. When I first came I taught eighth grade science.

Teaching in England. I taught in one school in England and that was large; over 1000 high school students: that would be from grade 9 to12. [It was] inner city, poor [school with a] lack of parental interest in the students' academic progress. If parents were involved, it was not always in a positive or supportive way. They would get involved if you wanted to keep a child back for disciplinary reasons. They would come and get them out of school and say, "No they can't, they have to look after their sister." So discipline was undermined by the lack of parental support from that point of view.

This wasn't general. There was a small minority of students I still remember who had immensely supportive parents. They were sometimes like the lifeboat that you cling to when every thing else is going down. These students were great; they come and they work and try to do their best. The best may not have been academically successful, but all you can ask from anybody is that they do their best and these students would do that. But they were, on the whole, a minority.

This was a state school; a public school and [there] was mainly lack of finances, lack of lab equipment, large classes, [and], I suppose lack of respect for the material and equipment and resources they had. Some students would regularly break things; throw things around--lack of respect for personal property.

On the other hand, one of the biggest [disciplinary measures] that you could impose on some of our students was banning them from school. The biggest thing that you could do was stopping them from coming to school, because school was the one good place they went to. They had structure, their friends were there, they knew what they were supposed to be doing, [and] there was somebody to look after them--even if they didn't feel that they needed to be looked after. And that's a big thing; what kind of restrictions or come-backs you have against students when you try to impose discipline, but basically it was all to do with money and finances.

4.2.6 Mary's school environment in native England

[The school] was urban [with] no green trees [or] very little. The streets around it had old, turn-of-the-century buildings in London. The main road that the school was from, was suffering to some extent from modern decay. Originally, it was a wealthy area of small-shops people, but the shops [were] gradually closing down and moving away, and they were taking the wealth and the work ethic. And the drive to succeed was leaving with the people who used to run the shops. Toward the back of the school, there was a large skyscraper-type of large housing blocks; [a kind of] construction with no ideas of how the people had to live in them. [They had] windy walkways, concrete jungle kind of things. There was one of the main sites of drug dealing in South London within this big housing estate in the back of the school.

On the other hand, in that part of London, there has always been a very strong community spirit: what we call "cockneys." It's a word to describe native Londoners; people who grew up and lived in London. But, that's the family infrastructure that was starting to fragment, as people moved out to more pleasant suburban areas. It was quite mixed community. We had quite a lot of Turkish, Soviets and Greeks, [but] not a large black community. Because there was some choice in the school, the schools tended to become polarized, so our school was predominantly white, with very few black people--and a lot of the black families selected to take their children to another school.

There was polarization that [took] place largely through choice; it was that time in London when there was a lot of unpleasantness going on with racism, and we tried our very best to deal with it. It was difficult at times, and our school had a lot of white racists there. It was particularly unpleasant to deal with [it], but I think it filtered itself out to some extent when the schools were almost integrated or mixed up, so there was less choice. Faculty were great: very supportive of each other.

I worked [or taught] in the lab of course; I kept the materials that were out in the lab to a minimum. I wouldn't dream of leaving anything out on the benches because we didn't have enough of them, so they had to be locked up and looked after, and sometimes the kids would deliberately damage the equipment. I did have things like an aquarium, a fish tank, and some kids put washing soap liquid in it, or put bar of soap in it. Some of the kids would open the windows and pour biological specimens out the window. It was a very tough school: quite violent, and we did have a problem with racism as well. We had some tough times.

4.2.7 Mary's classroom issues in native England

[Teaching methods were] varied. The biggest issue I felt was [that] the classes were all [of] mixed ability, so in the same class, you [c]ould have football hooligans. (I had a class of boys who used to go to football matches on Saturday and get locked up, then come to class.) [There were also] nice kids who would try to learn and do their very best, and also some recently-migrated families from overseas: Asian families.

The most difficult thing to try [to do was] control the kids who clearly didn't want to learn; who didn't feel that school had anything to offer them. If I had classes [composed of] either one or the other, it would have been much easier, but part of the issue [was] mixing them up and trying to be fair; trying to deal with these other students so they didn't interfere with the learning of those who wanted to learn. That was, I think, the biggest cause of stress.

I did as many labs I could, but I had to be very structured and organized, and I couldn't let them have anything sharp because they would throw it. It was a very tough school. I'm amazed there wasn't a major accident. It was quite a violent community. Boxing [was] a big sport that students go to. Trying to get them ready for exams was tough; tough for everybody. Kids lose faith in the system; they lose faith if they cannot get a job. Only reason they went to school was to be with their pals and create mischief, which is what a lot of the kids did. Some of the more motivated desperately wanted to move on and go on to A-levels, and preferably go to college, and that was the main cause of stress.

The number of students would vary on the class, but it would average out to over 20, 24, [or] 25. The couple of A-level classes I did would be one, two, or three; very small numbers, because academic achievement wasn't considered to be particularly important. And they were special kids. We tried our very best to help them. [I had] about 25 in the classes I taught [in] lower school; sixth to eighth grade could go up to over 30 in science classes, but I didn't teach those classes.

The faculty [was] very supportive of each other. It's almost like a war-time banding together. Sometimes kids give you a bad time and somebody would help you out and try to deal with things, but everybody else is under the same stress. It's like being in a different world, really, [as compared] to what I experienced in my international school.

4.2.8 School organization in England

[In the schools] we would have a headmaster, a deputy head, [and] there might be head of section; [it] depends on size of school. In our school, we had what's called heads of year, so you would have one principal teacher who was in charge of all these sixth graders or seventh graders. That teacher would move up with the kids as they went through [the grades]. They were in charge of the whole year, but when you had 240 students in one grade level, you need somebody like that.

And then you would have form teachers. You would have their group of maybe 30 students. So, for every grade level, you would have maybe a core team of eight teachers who had a group of students. [These teachers] would meet regularly for the year with grade leader, who would respond to the section [leader]. [The section leader, in turn] would report to the high school principal, who would then be responsible to the deputy head, who would then be responsible to the headmaster.

It was a clear cut hierarchy and the responsibilities were clear cut. We also had counselors. Counselors in the U.K. were counselors who [dealt with] educational or social problems. It's not the same kind of counselor that you have here, [in the U.S.], which is for university or college entrance: totally different job. And [that] caused me a lot of confusion when I first started to teach in American style schools; [as regards] what the counselor actually did. I assumed the counselors were almost like social workers, but of course they're not. Coming from a school of country [where] getting into a college or university was [tough], there was quite a lot of support, but the support was mainly what we would call pastoral support: looking after the kids' well-being, safety, and security.

The teachers, themselves, were responsible for looking after their academics. There were no academic deans at this particular school or it was something everybody [helped with]. The heads of department maybe took more [responsibility for it].

The curriculum was quite rigorous because, certainly in the minds of tenth graders, students were working towards their GCSUs or O-levels. That's an externally-applied syllabus. Some students didn't want to do the exams, but we still make them follow the same broad curriculum in order to get them into class, basically. Down in the middle school, we have a school-based curriculum with very clear set of objectives. I was particularly involved in that. The curricula for the ninth to twelfth grades we didn't use by choice: you just did what the exam boards expected you to do.

We [had] to keep [the students] at school and we wanted to give them an education. If I remember, it seems a long time ago, [but] there weren't any extra special courses for any of the students. They would basically do the same things, even if they didn't do the exams at the end of the course. And for the sixth form (eleventh and twelfth grades), there was a constant struggle to teach students in there, and to get students to stay on at school. We used to offer courses that were still quite [motivational], but we were not able to get them to stay on. But, because we wanted the kids to come back to school, we would offer them basically anything we thought they could do in order to keep them in education, and basically get them off the street.

4.2.9 Mary's daily routine in England

[I would] wake up in the morning, go to school in my car, [and do a] medium drive. I used to drive along the back streets. I'm not good in the mornings, so I would tend to stay at school later and then just come in and start working, rather than get to school unprepared. But my first year, I used to get to school 7:00 in the morning. School would start about 9:15 [to] 9:30 [a.m.], and start straightaway with classes. In this school, we had no assemblies. [You took] 15 minutes to register with your home group; equivalent of a homeroom, unfold any problems, read any messages, try to get the kids organized for the day.

Classes would average 40 minutes long. Occasionally we'd have double classes. [We took a] short break in the morning (about 20 minutes); we would go down to the staff room for cup of coffee or tea and a biscuit, and then some people would do duty: You would have to patrol the school and make sure no one is wrecking around; keep [the kids] outside. [There was also] playground duty. [Some staff would] walk through until lunchtime. Some would have lunch duty. We used to have to walk the kids to the lunchroom, line them up and walk them through the streets. This was high school. We didn't have anything on site. Lunchtime would be maybe 40 [to] 50 minutes, maybe; certainly not an hour. It would start in afternoon and go to about 4:00 p.m.

One of the big differences was the amount of non-contact time we had. We had a forty period week. Out of this, we were scheduled to have six free periods. I averaged two or three a week, so I would work two or three full days without break. The rest of the time was filled up substituting for teachers who were sick--and we had a lot of people out who were sick [from] the stress. There were no outside substitute teachers. That was really a difficult issue. It's all down to finances, because there was no money to pay substitute teachers, so they used people in the school, and on top of that you had meetings.

4.2.10 Mary's student-teacher relations

[Student-teacher relations] would depend on the student, but generally it wasn't brilliant or anything. It depends on what you're judging it against. Compared to International School, it wasn't in the same league. My teaching style tended to be determined by the need to keep some sort of discipline in the classroom, so it tended to be highly structured. I always had plenty of work for the kids to do, [although] I made breaks. Everything was tightly controlled for me: It was the only way I could maintain security. It was different working in a lab. You had to be careful of the kids playing with the gas tops, turning the tops on, playing with the equipment.

Books were short. Sometimes three kids would have to share one book. I'm fairly good with discipline and control, so I didn't have a problem. I could also control kids with my demeanor and my voice. They felt intimidated: I needed to do that. I think I was successful as a teacher. I got good references, [and] I became head of biology after a year. Whatever I was doing seemed to work.

When I switched to International School, that heavy-handed type of control that I had was not appropriate. It took me quite a long time to realize that I could relax: I could actually smile: I could [converse] with the students, and it wasn't going to undermine my teaching, or my discipline or anything. That was one of the hardest things for me: [to learn] about being in International School when I started. Now it's easy to go the other way. It's easy to go from what I do now to tightening up, but it took quite some time for me to realize that, "It's OK, you can smile at the kids; they're not going to do anything unpleasant to you."

4.2.11 Mary's comparison of native British and American schools

This is a topic that Mary discussed at length, in a different context. For more about this topic, please read more about it in the next chapter.

4.3   Joe's Pedagogical Biography

Joe was a British man in his late forties. He had taught chemistry for several years in his school, and sounded very confident in his content matter. He had previously taught physics as well in the same private, cosmopolitan high school as Mary and Inga. He was open to the students, and tried to get to know them better through coaching soccer. He will speak for himself in this section.

4.3.1 Joe's early perceptions of teachers and teaching

General influences. I really wanted to work in research. I'm a microbiologist by trade, so I actually started off doing research, and then going from one research job to another. If I stayed in England it was probably fine, but I didn't. I moved out to [Eastern Europe], and when I came back, I planned to do just a year's teaching before going back into research, then I found [that] once you've left research, it's very difficult to get back into it. I actually started enjoying teaching, so I stayed there.

I worked in a town school [which] had some problems (not severe by anybody's standards), but there were some technical problems and I actually felt I was starting to make a difference: it was to keep the kids out of trouble from the police; try to keep them in school. It was similar problems you get in inner city schools (not to the same degree), but I was having some successes.

Early perception of teachers. [While growing up in school,] I got [teachers] who would've put me off to [taking teaching as a profession]. There were certainly a few of those. I wasn't impressed with the way I was taught. There were certainly one or two teachers I respected. There were quite a few whom I did not respect; whom I swore I would never ever teach like they. The ones [I liked] challenged me appropriately, and I was challenged in a comfortable environment, which allowed me to have a go at a particular problem, and if I didn't succeed, I still felt comfortable. It was a comfortable environment in which to accept a challenge, knowing that even if I blew out totally, everything was still OK.

[In the classrooms of the teachers who had a negative influence on me], I got the feeling that, "Why am I here?" Why am I at school?" "Why am I having to write this stuff down and learn it?" "If I need to know it, I'll look it up." History was a classic one. I disliked it intensely, because there was no challenge: learn a heap of facts and regurgitate them; be a tape recorder. I learned thousands of lines of Latin poetry, [but] I couldn't translate a word of Latin. I would begin a piece of Latin prose, and look for a few words that I did know and say, "Nowhere in these thousands of lines did I learn this," then go "Oops! Yes, it's verses 3, 4, and 5. Out comes verse 3, 4, 5: perfect translation!" but I couldn't translate Latin.

Obviously, one has to learn, keep some facts into memory to develop an argument. Certainly that is a useful skill, but not the way I was taught. I had that civility already. What I do find interesting was that I hated history with a passion back in school, but right now, if I'm doing some research out of my subject specialist area, very often it's historical. I do like reading history books, so I believe the material could have been interesting. I believe I could have been challenged, but I was [taught] "out of my mind." So, there [are] the things that do challenge, keep the students interested, challenge them in a relatively warm environment, and that didn't happen to me in some subjects.

Obviously I've come into contact with a lot of teachers. Some I dismiss as idiots; others are fine; and others I like, and respect. One [that] springs to mind is a person I can't stand on a personal level; a friend of mind he is not, but he is an excellent teacher, and he does those things that I just suggested. The students loved his physics. As he came to the school where I was teaching, you could see the steady increase in the number of students that took up physics, and clearly, a lot of the students had a deep respect for him.

Obviously for many students, physics is an awkward subject, but he had a way of bringing it down to a level which the students felt comfortable taking on, and they certainly enjoyed it. I've seen that particular subject taught in a way in which most students were just turned off. So in many schools I've taught at, you would see that the students, given the free choice, most would take biology, least would take physics. That school virtually managed to turn it around. Most took physics, fewest took biology, and I would say that guy was the primary factor that was responsible for that.

Joe's early school perceptions. [In the grammar schools], they were trying to maintain tradition. I can imagine the teachers maintaining a discrete distance from the students and, as you got down to the "lesser regarded," then I think you were more likely to find a teacher who lives in the community where the students are from: It's going to be far more typical. That's my perception: I can't say if it's really true. [So in general, the lower the academic level of the school, so to speak], the less rules, and the rules they have are frequently flaunted. You go into the elitist, more rules.

Look at my school [growing up]: I went to a grammar school. In the town where I eventually taught, I went to a boy's grammar school. I was not allowed to play soccer. I had to wear a school cap; I had to wear it from the moment I left my house in the morning, all the way through school, until I got home. If I was seen without my cap, my tie properly done, my jacket buttoned, I could be given detention by any teacher driving past, or any of the seniors that were so-called prefects could stop me. I could be reported by anyone who knew me as being improperly dressed anytime.

That's a whole heap of rules. We might make rules here about, "You should not do drugs even after school." OK, but I'm talking about stopping me from playing soccer. I was not allowed to go and play soccer! I remember there was a friend of mine who was not allowed to go fishing. School rule: No fishing. That was the big ["public private"] school in town. We're going back to when I was in school in the early sixties, but I still think they might have gone down a bit, but you might see photographs where they still have those very rigorous school uniforms and you can bet, you go in there and, when the teacher walked in the classroom, kids still have to stand and the teacher will say, "Now you may sit," and they would have to address you as "Sir" all the time.

4.3.2 Joe's recollections of his teacher education

I went to teacher training, not because I particularly wanted to be a teacher; I wasn't totally against it, but my friend was finishing up university and I wanted to just wait that year, and that's how I took teacher training courses. We had to do educational theory, which I regard as almost irrelevant. Learn it as much as you want, but when you're out there, you've got so many diverse cases in front of you: I believe it's by experience that you get through. What we had was teaching practice, and that was the useful thing, but again not so useful. It virtually is, "throw them in the water and see if they can swim," but in order to pass my teaching, I have to pass my teaching practice.

I think the problem with teaching [is that] you need experience; a wide range of experience to cope with a variety of situations. I don't believe there is one formula, and we were being given one formula [by] this [instructor, who] had very limited teaching experience. She didn't know what certain problems were; she didn't know what inner city kids were like. She was trying to teach us to teach a rigorous academic program, whereas many of us were going to be going to secondary modern schools, and a rigorous academic program was not what we were going to be delivering. So there was a marked difference between us, and so I do not feel I gained much out of my teacher [education in] college.

Other than that teaching experience, [I worked with] this one guy, who was my geography teacher [in college]. I had a lot of respect for him because he was a college professor, but because he wanted to keep his finger on the pulse, he'd go and teach in inner city schools; and he'd go and teach some of the rough ones. Every week, he spent time in a classroom teaching. He didn't go into [a] grammar school; he'd go into the inner city, and he told us so much what life was going to be like: You're there writing something on the board, and this missile comes whistling past your head and hits the board: bang! What do you do? We're "sitting duck"? He says, "You better find out who threw it, and you better nail him because otherwise they're going to nail you: That's what you're going to be up against!"

4.3.3 Joe's teaching life in England

[The school I taught in] was a very weird school. You have nothing like it in America. In England when I was there, we had what we call grammar schools, which were supposedly for the top 25% of students in a particular area (location). We had what we called "secondary modern," which was for the rest. Those are essentially gone now, in favor of what we would classify as almost a typical American high school, but this one school was very weird in the fact that it didn't fit into either category. I saw some quite important things educationally happen there. In this one school, we had both [academic levels]. They went on to good universities, so I've been pretty much against this segregation at age eleven from what I've seen now. I've seen too many students pull through, and I've seen many [good] students go the other way.

This vocational school was very heavily supported by industry and strongly tied to industry. So, even when the recessions were on in England in the 70's [and] 80's, this school would get most of its pupils into industry. We would go to [the industry] and say, "We do technical drawing, how could we modify our courses for what you need?" And we had a reputation for being tough with discipline. When [an] industry got a good reference about a student from us, they knew us--and our students had a distinct advantage, and so in that sense it was a great school.

I really enjoyed it, and the reason I left England was because that school was due to close. For those of that worked [in that kind of school]—there were only a handful of them around the country—it was excellent, and I was just so depressed, [and] fed up [because it was closing down].

We had a "catchment" [or feeder] area for the students, and it was the center of the town, so we did have some very poor kids in the [school], so we had some of the usual problems. [These included] social problems at home, and some of the kids, particularly because in England they could leave school at sixteen and particularly when they were twelve to fourteen, they could get a little bit unruly.

There were some teachers that were there a heck of a long time, and they got the system sorted out. You saw the change because the kids knew, "These are the rules, you got to stick with them; because if you stick with them, you're going to get the qualifications, you're going to get a job." And so, although you see them relatively unruly, as they got closer and closer to school leaving age which was 16, the problems, whereas in many cases they got worse, in our case they got better. [This was] because the flip side was, "Ok, you don't want to play by the rules, go to another school," and that was a big "No, no."

One thing I should also point out: it was a single-sexed school, all-boys' school. On the same campus, but separate, was an all-girls school. It's called a "bilateral school" in England, so I taught in the boy's school. The upper school, which was grade 11 and 12, was mixed, but grades 6 to 10 was single-sexed.

4.3.4 The physical environment

Nothing like you're going to think: I'm not talking about inner city; we're talking about a town of maybe 5,000. The school [was] on the very edge of town, so beyond it was rural, but the sector of town that we covered had some of the [government] housing projects. We had one-parent families, people on social, and we had students that had one pair of pants, and it was tough; if they ripped those, to get another pair [was difficult]. So we got quite a few people where money was really tight, and we had quite an ethnic mix in Britain. We had quite a few Indians [and] Pakistanis in that area of town. In my particular town, the number of West Indians wasn't a lot. What we had was Bangladeshi, Pakistanis, [and] Indians.

Very often there was a linguistic problem, because many of them were relatively new immigrants to the U.K. We also [had] some of the poorer British-English on that side of town. We had some wealthy [people] I would classify [as] middle class. If you had to put your average, I'd put it at lower middle class, so it was not a significantly deprived area, but it had it's problems, particularly as in the 80s, the industry was sizing down—the 70s and 80s.

[The schools were mostly] brick [and] peach [in color]. We had woodwork, metalwork, tech drawing in major sections of our school. Most of the schools in the area may have minimal, but we had lots [of resources], so we were in a sense an early technology school. [Inside the classrooms], we had, instead of these solid stone tops [as in the U.S. science lab], solid teak (hard wood), and the school was fairly old. These solid teak surfaces [were] hard stuff, and the kids got their work cut out to carve their names in it. Only a few managed. It was solid stuff: chemically resistant wood; it certainly was good quality wood. The campus was fairly pleasant. We were on the edge of town, so we had large playing fields [and lots of greenery].

4.3.5 Joe on teacher-student relations

I left in the 1980s, but I'm still in contact with some of the students I taught. One of the guys is coming out to [the United States] in two months' time. He's going to do some fishing with me, and when I go back to England in a few weeks' time, one of the girls I taught in the eleventh grade, [is] about to give birth to her first baby. I shall drop in and see her and her husband on my way around England.

The hardest part is that, I was a form teacher, which means I was in charge of social development of a few of these kids. They always gave me the bottom band, and keeping them out of juvenile court was the big thing, so I ran a fishing club, and the headmaster said, "You can't take fifty boys fishing: not these fifty," and I said "No problem!" We're talking really inner city, you see. Still, very few people ever did anything for them.

I used to write fishing articles, and for the money I used to get from that, I would subsidize them on a fishing trip. We used to run it in a very democratic way so everybody got some subsidy. We'd work out who needed it the most, and we put it up to a vote. I would tell them how much money the trip would cost, how much money I was putting in. We'd have a committee to decide how much each paid, and everybody knew if they mocked up that was it; they were kicked out. So peer-pressure…

I never had any trouble with them on these fishing trips. They were great. They knew, and the parents knew their son was safe when the fishing season runs up, he's not going to get in trouble because if he's out all night, he's not out doing drugs, not going to get in trouble burglarizing some house; he's all-night fishing, probably with me. That's a part where I started to really feel I was making a difference, and so that makes it a very nice, rewarding job in that sense. Of course, I can't claim that I succeeded with every kid, because I did not. But you can't spread yourself too thin, otherwise you'd have no effect on anybody, and so I would say there were some kids I succeeded with, but some kids I didn't.

4.3.6 Joe's daily routine in England

My teaching experience was tough at the start. I didn't have the experience to deal with all the various problems that came my way, so it was tough. I think it's tough for any new teacher starting anywhere. You can learn all you want about educational theory, but when you're in the classroom, it's there in front of you. It's a different ball game entirely; and so what we're actually doing here is comparing me now as a very experienced teacher with a lot of confidence. Go back there at the early days—inexperienced [with] not much confidence and so it was tough, but I think the difference is more my experience rather than any thing else. I would say that's the major thing.

Kids are kids; if you've got a weakness, they'll find it, and they'll exploit it. You say, "Never smile before Christmas," and it takes a while to develop a good rapport with the kids. It can't happen overnight. You come in and be all, "I'm your friend and I'm going to help you," [and] they don't trust you. It's actions, so my fishing club was one of my ways of trying to get to meet them outside the classroom. [It says to them that], "I'm actually a member of the human race"—and I also coached sports: [cross country in England, and currently soccer]. I've done that ever since I started.

[In Britain], you have to keep a certain distance, or it was expected that you did, and I think, very often, that makes the teaching less effective. As we keep a distance, we're using fear; fear of the unknown in many cases, to keep control, whereas I personally believe that once the students know what I'm doing and why I'm doing it, they realize that we're on the same side essentially. I believe that essentially we're preparing them for college and they've got to do what they've got to do because they want to do it and because then they go onto college. If I were to run a repressive regime, then OK, maybe it would be easier for me, and I would actually say yes, it is, I don't have to deal with discipline problems because, "Bam!" You say the wrong thing or breathe out of turn, "Wham!"

In England, we used to have the cane back then, but you know there's one thing I remember: One of the students saying to me: "We do so much more work in Mr. Thesis' class. In your class we don't do nearly as much, and we mess around." And I said, "Ah yeah, and how did you do in history—in the exam"? [He answered,] "Oh we did lousy." I said, "How did you do in my class?" "We did well." "Now there's a coincidence isn't it? And we do all this work. We have been hit down, hit down, we have these external exams, but done lousy in history, but have done great, in this case in biology. Yes, but you didn't realize you were working did you?" So I believe in a friendly environment, then the students can proceed toward their maximum achievement, and I don't believe that was the case in the environment.

That often was so in England; fear motivated the students to learn. Blow out the test and they'd be in detention all week. [But], blow out one of my tests, [and] I'm going to pull a kid in a corner and say, "What's going on here?" "How can we sort this out?"—a totally different atmosphere; [I was more student-friendly.] So, [I am basically not the typical teacher]; not by English standards, and certainly that's why I would say, my methods run a more dangerous route, in that, in order to get the students where I wanted them to be, I had a more laid-back approach. Now that is going to cause a few probable ruffles early on, as the kids try and push the parameters of the rules I set. It would certainly be easier to be a strict disciplinarian, but it would not get all the students to where I believe they should be.

The students that know me typically know they can come in and talk to me, mostly about chemistry, but not always about chemistry. They know if they blow out on a test, they're not going to be yelled at. We're just going to sit down and try to sort it out, get them on line, get them ready, and we'll look at the end product. In this case, typically at this [current U.S.] school, it's the IB, and there are various different ways to get different students there, but that's what we're working for. We might have a few ripples on the way [owing to the] different environment. [For] some students, I know I really need to coax [them] along.

Certainly, fitting in the English system wasn't so easy for me, particularly in that school, but I did eventually fit in, and partly that was because I didn't have to discipline the kids. It was peer-pressure working, and certainly you would not have the kids in my class sitting rigidly to attention. Sometimes we'd have two-hour classes. We'd get rather tired. [I would say,] "Come on you guys, does anybody know a joke about..." let's have a laugh for ten minutes or something.

4.3.7 Joe's comparison of British and American schools

The first thing I'd tell you about teaching [in England is that] there's greater contact time than there seems to be in the U.S. Here [in the U.S.] I teach my five classes, but there, I would teach probably 12, 15 different classes per week, [although] not meeting as often. Here [in the U.S.], very often, you have your five classes, but it's the same preps. [In England], I would go from a bottom band sixth grade class to a top band twelfth grade class, to a middle band ninth grade class, back up to an eleventh grade, back to seventh, and I could meet in one day, eight completely different classes.

It was a forty-lesson week, and typically the teacher would teach 35 of those. The number of repeats that you could do was quite minimal, so this is the most extreme I've been to teaching. I would teach in these schools geography, chemistry, biology, math. The biology was anything from six to twelfth [grades], and chemistry anything from six to twelfth [grades], and anything from low level to the equivalent of AP. So, some classes I might only see twice a week, but you get to know a heck of a lot of kids that way. It was challenging sometimes.

Sometimes the kids would say "Look Mr. Key, we are not sixth graders, we are seniors," and you'd say, "OK boys, sit down." It's typical; suddenly you're coming out of, you know, "This is the end of the test tube you put the chemicals in," and then you're going into an AP-level class, and it's a certain change. So in England, I found the workload heavy. Getting into the International System, I found the workload a lot easier.

[The British educational system] is rigorous and obviously, it's got an unfairness. You get students—and I had one go through this year who just suffers from exam nerves. Never ever has this girl done as well as she has done throughout the year. Yet, very often in the exam system, it doesn't matter how good she was in [her] grade 11 class, or grade 12; it's this one exam. It's taken over two days. She happened to be sick the week before, and so she's not going to get the grade she deserves. I'm far better able to predict what she's really worth, having taught her.

And so there is a problem with the exam system, but it is rigorous right to the end. And then of course where it really hurts is that the students don't know what they're doing until they get the results, which could be mid-June or mid-July. And so you've got students now waiting to find out if they've gotten into college, and it's going to come on a piece of paper; somebody that never met this girl is going to determine how they've done. So that's hard, but it does get them to push to the very end, which is the one big difference between there and here.

Student power is a lot more evident here [in the U.S.]. The students fill out forms on how they regard me as a teacher. Student evaluation forms--I've never come across that before. I know if students didn't like what I did, they would complain to the administration, and the administration would likely listen here than in other places. It certainly means that the students are going to question more what I do, and [are] not going to blindly accept it, which in a way is good. So, I'm not totally against it, but that is a difference.

Certainly, it has had its effect on the school; certainly a big difference. Students are going to argue, "You didn't give me a point on this." [In Britain, I would have said to the British student], "Yeah, keep your mouth shut or I'll take another point off." That would be totally inappropriate here and, obviously, being British, sarcasm is the lowest form of wit, but it's still funny. I have to be a little bit more careful about what I say. That could also be a product of the times.

I mentioned before that I want the learning environment to be friendly, and obviously with sarcasm, you can cut a student to the bone and not even know you've done it. In that sense, I have to be far more careful with what I do. Still, I want a friendly learning environment, so I'm going to make a lot of fun of myself, and if I make fun of a student, let's say, you give me 2+2=4, [and] you are a lousy mathematician. I might just quietly ask you to "check the 2+2=4." If you are a really good mathematician, then I'm going to get you for that: "Oh yeah, 2+2 is 5, you do high level math, do you?" Things like that. I had one of the best mathematicians this school had ever had. Every time [he] made a bad mistake like that, I'd make fun of it, and I knew he could take it. He knew he was a good mathematician; everybody else knew he was a good mathematician.

I noticed [that] with one of the British kids, I'm far ruder to him than I would be to a student I didn't know. You can't always see the damage that you've done, so you have to be very careful about that, and so that is a difference, and I find that, British versus American, the ruder I am to you, if you were British, probably the more I like you. There's a mutual respect. If you were a good friend of mine we'd be trading insults. If you're polite, we hate each other's guts. [The American] "Have a nice day!" took me a while to get used to, so there [are] certainly different cultural differences. Obviously, having been in many different countries, that's something one has to be aware of.

Comparing school administrations. Here [in the U.S.], I feel I could walk into the administration and say, "You really mucked up today. Come on, get real; this is stupid." I feel I could do that here. I would not feel I could do that in England. Actually it is very hierarchical [there]. Of course again, one has to be very careful. When I was in England, I was a starting teacher. So again, in that sense [of] comparison, as they say in science, we're not holding the other variables steady on this.

4.4   Inga's Pedagogical Biography

Inga was a German lady in her early thirties. She had been in the U.S. just about two years at the time of her interviews for this research. She had moved to the U.S. with her husband, and had been working on a part-time basis with the same school as Mary and Joe's for a year, before she was employed on a full-time basis. She was very easy-going, and wore a smiling face throughout the interviews. Being a new teacher in the U.S. (and having taught only a year in Germany), she was going through her initial transitional issues. Therefore, her responses were a good complement to those of her teaching colleagues in the same school.

4.4.1 Inga's early perceptions of teachers and teaching

I decided to become a teacher when I was in fourth grade, because I think it was the best I could do. I think everybody should do what they can do best. [In] tenth grade, I wanted to be a chemist, so I had an internship at a company. I figured out they sit in the labs all day long, and they all kind of [had little social life]; not the way that I wanted to be. Then I wanted to be a journalist, and I figured out I'm not good enough in writing, so I came back to the initial idea of being a math teacher.

In Germany if you want to be a teacher, you have to have at least two subjects. Where I came from, you don't have many choices you can match with math, so you can only match economics, which I hate, or P.E., which I [did not] apply to, and religious education, which I don't like either, and there was physics, so I took physics. And so that's how I started with the whole thing.

I didn't like the teachers in high school. I had a lot of teachers that didn't think girls were capable of doing physics, so I just figured out: "Leave them alone, because it's just too much of a pain to go through this." And it was [similar issues] at college. The more I did, the more I liked it, because math is nice, but it gets boring easily. [In] physics, you always have more challenges: you can build things, play with things. I did computer science as well.

Everybody connects immediately [that physicists are smart], which I think might be quite right, but you should connect it with other subjects too. Somebody who's incredibly good in English, or writing poems or art, [is also] incredibly good, and you need a different kind of intelligence for that; a different analytical intelligence to analyze a character and to implement things. It's nice that people think I'm incredibly smart because I'm a physics teacher; sometimes you can use it; it's helpful because they trust your judgment easier than other people, but it's hard, because it's hard for the students who feel they aren't good in math and physics.

4.4.2 Inga on socio-cultural influences

Gender issues. I had a math teacher in eighth grade in a girls' school who told us he's not going to give us the best grade because girls are not capable of good grades in math. We have too many people who think in that way. We still have too many people who project that on gender issues instead of seeing that girls and boys learn differently: approach things differently. Well, there might be a genetic reason, or how they're brought up, but they react differently; they act differently; they approach things differently.

I have to control myself because [of] the way that boys react, because boys are usually more forward and more expressive, not so afraid of making mistakes. So they're the first ones to raise their hands, come up with ideas; you usually you work more with them. The girls are a little bit quieter, and I have to sit down from time to time and tell myself that I have to change that pattern because it's just what suits the subject. You want to have ideas. You want them to make mistakes, to learn from their mistakes, and the girls are usually more hesitant to make mistakes in the first place: that is a hard thing. But we're working on it. I'm getting like 40% of girls next year in high level [physics] and I had no girls last year. I have one girl [currently], but I only have five in that class this year, and next year we're going to get 4 out of 10.

The high school years. My favorite teacher was my chemistry teacher in high school. Because I didn't like physics [then], I took chemistry, and he taught me how to structure my work, organize, prioritize, [and] work through things in an organized way. I even still know most of the facts he taught me ten years ago. He taught us to learn, and he had time, and he listened. He first listened, and then made a judgment or decision about something, and I think that is the most important. He gave positive feedback and would say, "Just go for it and do it." It was treating us as young adults, which we were at that time. I was seventeen. I think I take everything from everybody that I think is good and put it together. I don't want to focus on one thing, because I'm going to miss out on other things. I read a lot of things, I listen to people and I just do what I think is best.

4.4.3 Inga's recollections of her teacher education

It was not a nice time. There are some sayings that I really can't translate,

[but] they say, "As long as you are in training, you have to earn everything from the bottom to go somewhere." That is a very German thing. So in those two years (you're usually around 23 to 24 years when you go in there), you just work for two years, and "you don't know where your head is."

What you do is, you go to college, and you have to do a first year exam, which is a national state exam which is [very] subject-based; a lot of physics and math. You [also] have a little bit of psychology, and then you go into the teacher training. Most people get through—and right now it's not a big issue because we have teacher shortage everywhere—but I remember even two years back, only about 15% got a job the first year, because they only hire you by your grades. So there was a lot of pressure in that too.

They demand a lot of you and I hated that at that time. I really hated it, [but] I think I learned a lot. I think they could've changed it a little bit, but it is a power thing: You're the little student here and some of the [classroom] teachers are really happy that you're there, because then they don't have to do that much work. [During internships,] we had to teach in the morning, and we had lectures in the afternoons, and then we had to prepare on the weekends or in the nights. Then we had a big exam at the end, and you had to do demonstration lessons that they grade—three of them. They're very strict in timing things and organizing things and what you have to prepare.

What I definitely learned that helps me here right now is that I learned to prepare students for an exam. In [some] American high schools, it [may not be] necessary, but as I'm teaching the IB, the experience of dealing with a syllabus—getting it done and then preparing for an outside exam—is what I really felt I learned very well. We had a lot of planning. We sat down and made plans for half a school year or whole school year—how we organize all the work load that we have, how we structure or where we put spaces in what you definitely need—so I felt very well prepared for an exam.

And you go in there, and you have to deal with the students—and the students know that you're a teacher in training—and they really bother you. They try to play with you—and it's good because you're still not completely responsible, so if something doesn't work out that well with one class, you say, "OK, I have that experience, let me move onto something else. I might have just stepped in the wrong way," so you learn. You see many classes.

I basically changed the classes that I taught every few weeks. They give you new classes so you learn to deal with students within your situations. So you have to prepare [several] times for classes, and write all that stuff up, and I remember that my teacher told me to do that carefully, keep them carefully, because that's going to be the best prepared classes for your whole life. I thought he was kidding, but he was definitely right. I learned a lot. I didn't like the way people treated me because I was already grown up. That is one of the issues—which is cultural.

[If I could reform the teacher education system in Germany], so many things would be changed. Definitely, I would try to give teachers the opportunity to do something between going to college and going to school, because I see a lot of people who went to school, went to college, [and] went back to teaching without ever being out there in the real life. Probably even encouraging people [to go] into fields where they have to prepare their students to go to; getting more mandatory [experiences] like going to conferences, [and] giving them more opportunity to see what is out there.

The problem is always if the people want to deal with this. But, I think if you create a little bit more of this during the whole process, like if you send high school teachers into [places] like Montessori schools, and see how 40 kids can work in a classroom quietly, intensively—give them those opportunities; send them to different countries. When you have Russian immigrants [as students], send them to Russia and see what [goes] on there. It's all about looking at different things. That's why I learned so much when I came here [to America]. Just living in a different culture—you learn so much about your own culture when you see the differences, or when you're open to see the differences. Then you know how much is culture, and how much is just what you thought is really true.

4.4.4 Teaching life in native Germany

The school system in Germany. The school that I was in was a *Realschule,* [which] had from fifth to tenth grades, around 800 students. There are three different school types in Germany. They split up the kids after fifth grade, depending on their learning abilities, [and then] they go to [the] three different types. The lowest [is] where they graduate after ninth grade [and] usually go and learn [to become] something like a carpenter or electrician; they don't go into college; they go into company-based training for three years. Then we have the *Realschule,* which is the middle track, where they graduate after tenth grade, and usually go onto banks, accounting, [and] things like that, for training. Then we have track for college, where they graduate after thirteenth grade. (More on this topic is discussed under the topic, "Inga's comparison of native Germany and American schools" in section 4.4.6 below.)

4.4.5 Inga's daily routine in Germany

School starts usually at 8:00 [a.m.], and the teachers are supposed to be there [about] 20 minutes earlier. I had to drive nearly an hour in morning, because I didn't want to move. I got up like at 6:00 and got into the car at 6:45, drove my hour. You prepare, go and make your copies; whatever you need prepared, [and] go into the classroom.

You usually have four or five classes a day out of six. School is over at 1:00 [p.m.], so we go home at 1:00. You go and you prepare most of your things at home, grade your papers that you have to grade. There's not that much to say because [there's] not so much of a school life, because you come at 8:00 [and] you teach four classes out of six. They have one big teacher work room; basically where all the teachers meet during the two breaks that you have, and during their free time. They have a lot of tables and a little space somewhere, which is yours and that's where you work.

You're expected there from 8 a.m. to 1:00 p.m.: That's your time. What is different is, when there is a teacher sick, you don't get any external substitute. The teachers have to cover within themselves. So you have to be available if someone gets sick; you go in [according to a] schedule. You have certain assigned times, I think two periods a week, where you are supposed to be available. Other than that, they really just look. If there should be more people [absent], which just happens when you have flu season or something, then you have so many people that are sick, then you have to cover more, then they come and look around.

4.4.6 Inga's comparison of native Germany and American Schools

The physical environment. It's very different. You have two types of classrooms in Germany. You have one that is mainly for lectures and one more for student experiments (which usually don't have much possibilities, because the classes [were] too big). If I have 35 [students], it is nearly impossible to do a physics lab, because they're all going to need some help at some point, and one person with 35 is impossible. I would say impossible: It doesn't make sense to do it.

You have mainly public schools in Germany. The big difference in Germany [is that] you have to teach at least two subjects. You don't have your room; you have to move [around]. [For example], you teach first class in the morning. You teach math, and the second one you teach physics, and you have basically two minutes. [During] the transition, [you go] from a math classroom to a physics classroom, get all your stuff on a cart, get it in the room, get started, and then leave the room cleanly after 45 minutes— which is nearly impossible. That is something I always had a problem with, because, usually, when I started teaching, I was just into the whole thing then the bell rings, and everything is a mess.

Here [in the U.S.], I have my room, my five minutes [between classes], I can just put it on the side, I can ask the next group of students just to put it on the counter tops; it makes teaching more efficient. You tend to show more experiments, do more things because it's just more practical. I'm sort of spoiled now; I had a group this year of five in high level physics, and it's wonderful because you sit around a table and you say, "Let's [do] something," and they go out of the room and get the equipment that they want, [and they will] put something together. They get the generator and they just basically do so much on their own, because you see what they're doing, and they know each other so well, and they learned to work with each other over the years. For me, it's perfect, in that sense of class size. Definitely, we have things that can improve, but it's better than anything I ever dreamed of.

[My] school [in Germany] expanded the[ir] program, so they had some issues with rooms, [and] it was very crowded. I have seen other schools where it wasn't that crowded, but it's general because you have those classes staying in their room. It's not like here that, when I don't have a class, we have a lot of rooms that are available in between. I think it's more crowded, less space outside, but that's a general European thing because you don't have that much space [there]: It's expensive. [The kids] play, but it's just not that much space.

Comparing teaching experiences. It is very different, but the thing is, it's not only [an issue of comparing] Germany and America; it's [comparing my current International School to] public German School, where I was. Going to an American International private school, where we have kids that have everything—if I have a good reason for saying, "I need this and that equipment," then I basically can have it—[this was new to me]. It's also having children [whose] parents want their kids here. In the German public school, they have to go there. You can't kick them out of school. They have to be there, unless they do drugs or something that's illegal, where you can send them to another school. But here [in the U.S. private school], if there are problems, you can talk to the parents and counselor, and work on the issues, instead of just dealing with kids that have problems

It is just so different [for several reasons], and all the different cultures of the students and teachers. In my physics class right now I have a student who came from Pakistan last year, who keeps telling me that women are supposed to stay at home and cook and take care of the kids. I have [another] student from Taiwan who doesn't speak at all because he thinks it's impolite to speak out loudly in front of the class. Getting all of those together is fascinating and sometimes really challenging, but it makes your life so interesting, and you think so much about your teaching style, which you can't when you have to go into a classroom of 30 kids.

You just have to think, "OK, this is my classroom, and I somehow have to get that into their heads." Here [in the U.S.], I have not [only] more time, but more time for students because I have so few. And I can sit down with them, and they work on things, and the students really come and talk with the teachers. They trust the teachers; they come when they have problems. Sometimes they come too often. They tell you everything and sometimes they tell you things you don't want to hear. It's so different.

Back in a [German] public school—in a country where you obey when the teacher says something, [it is] very different. From this teaching climate], coming to a school here [in the U.S.] where a fifth grader stands in front of you and says, "I think, you know, I have my own opinion." And they all have opinions—and they are [just] 17 years old or 18 years old. We have 16-year-olds that are going to graduate today, who know who they are, who go up on the stage and give you a speech on the political issues in Israel, because they went to "model United Nations." They have prepared resolutions about this, and, Wow!

Yes, I read my [German] newspaper, yes I try to be up to date about what they're doing down there, but [U.S.] kids have way more ideas than I have, and that is the incredible thing, because I learn from my students. I have a student in twelfth grade right now who is developing software for computer companies ([and] making good money with it), who helps me with the computer when I have problems. And it's all possible here [in the U.S.]. No one says, "You don't fit in that system, so stay where you are." And that's also the way they [in this school] handle the languages they have; classes where you have eighth to tenth graders sitting in one room because they all have right now the same level of Spanish -- and they study together.

Inga on comparing the profession of teaching. You have two groups of teachers: [the] ones who just do their job because they get their money, and not really care too much, then you have those that still have some idealistic beliefs that work a lot, don't get very far, [and] get frustrated. In teacher training I had a very good teacher who was teaching German and history, and she taught us psychology and teaching techniques, and she was burned out completely. She just had to take two months off because it was too much: She wanted to change things, but there are so many walls you run into, if you want to change something.

First of all people are way more afraid of change. The German society is not a society of risk-takers, compared to Americans. First of all, people are afraid if [something] doesn't work out. Second of all, it is too much work to do changes and [one would] probably fail, and have to go back. Here [in the U.S.], we see way more teachers that are open to have discussions with other teachers; open to say, "Let's try it. Realistically let's look to see if it's possible. If it's completely outrageous, we don't do this." [They] sit down, ask other people—try to involve more people in things, sometimes accept that it's not going to work—not being afraid of failing.

Also, a lot of people are here that really care about the students, and I think we have a lot of people [in this school] that have a good background on psychology, the history of students, and also of different cultures, where we all need each other. [For example], when Musa came from Pakistan, I had to talk to our Indian teachers, because we had no one from Pakistan to figure out [what his cultural issues were]. That makes things so much easier.

***Inga on comparing school organizations*.** I always had a good relationship with everyone. I think that was very typical, [although] I have way better relations with my administration here, but you don't have such a big administration [in Germany]. You have a headmaster and an assistant headmaster, and two secretaries, and that's it. You have somebody who keeps the building, but you don't have so many different departments.

Here, [in this U.S. school], we have a development office, a business office, an instructional technology department—which was not that far developed in Germany—with the IT things. Internet is expensive, so you don't have the schools online—because you have to pay for your local phone calls, so that makes it a [money] issue. Therefore, you don't have much administration; only two or three people, and as usual, that is a personal issue too—whether you like that person or not. You [may] get along with one [and not the other].

Here [in the U.S.] it is way more complex, because you have so many people, and you first have to learn who's responsible for what, and you have certain people you have to talk to [in order to] get something from them. And that is easier in a way. In Germany, because we have basically one or two people, you have to talk to [them], but if that person doesn't like you, you don't get anything. If the person likes you, you might get more—but it's kind of unbalanced, if you have personal issues with the headmaster.

4.5 Kofi's Pedagogical Biography

Kofi was a Ghanaian (from West Africa), and had been in the U.S. for at least a ten years. He taught high school in Nigeria before coming to the U.S. to pursue two graduate degrees. In the U.S., he was teaching in a large public school of over 2000 students in a south-eastern U.S. suburb. Although this suburb was in a relatively wealthy area, the students in his school came from varied economic backgrounds, and he observed that it was easy to distinguish among them by the kinds of cars they drove, as teenagers. The school campus was very large and rather overwhelming, and one needed ample time and hand-holding, in order to find one's way around the school. Kofi was very confident in himself as a teacher, since he was very competent in all the science content areas, and was being enticed by other institutions for employment. He shared his early experiences as in international transitional teacher with a very clear memory and several anecdotes.

4.5.1 Kofi's early perceptions of teachers and teaching

I think part of my reason for becoming a teacher was the influence that certain teachers had on my life. It was not a career that I was looking at earlier, but after college, after I looked back at my life and saw how many teachers had impacted my life, I decided that's something I would like to do. I had a teacher in middle school who helped me. He was from Togo, West Africa. [At that time,] I thought I was smart, but I was just foolish, because I would not focus on my work, and I would do the work for the bigger boys in the class, so they would protect me. Many times, I didn't do my work, because, by the time I finished their work, it would be time, and I so would [make up] an excuse for not doing my work.

This teacher caught me one day, called me in front of the class, and gave me one lash in my palm, and told the whole class about what I've been doing, and it changed my life. He actually put me on the right track: I started focusing on my work more than [that of] others. I didn't care whether they would beat me or what, and that's when I started seeing progress. So, even though that's the most painful experience I've had in all my school career, I still see this teacher as somebody who made an impact on my life.

Life as a student. [Growing up in school], you talked only when a teacher asked you a specific question, and I found that was very stifling. I've been in classes where teachers asked a question, and [to] all the questions I knew the answers. The other students would be struggling with it, [but] I would sit there and watch. Sometimes I got upset with the teacher because the kid couldn't do it, and nobody could help him, and the kid got so frustrated, and the teacher got mad [American term for anger] because the kid can't give the right answer, and so part of that was building frustration also in me. I felt that I wasn't learning because, here I was, I had to watch this scenario, and it was an interesting movie.

I've had time to think through since I've been out of that setting, and I think that [it] was not normal for you to even talk while the teacher was teaching or talking—in fact we hardly asked any questions. It's only when the teacher asked a question that you raised your hand. In some classes it was impossible to have a question to ask the teacher, and so I thought learning in those environments are not really positive. Overall, a few kids may catch on, but you lose the majority of the students.

I was very shy [in school]; one of the last kids to speak, but when it came to class discussions, I had an opportunity to say something that wasn't totally out of the way. That was one way of overcoming my shyness. If you left me by myself, you could hardly hear a word I would say. I would not utter a word out of context, but in context, you could get me to say something. So for me, [the discussion format] was very positive.

I find that there are a lot of students who have the same kind of problem, and so if we can only let them be able to express themselves in our presence without being humiliated, that might encourage them to even learn more. That's why I've had that kind of attitude in the classroom, and I think that most of my students have learned a lot more chemistry than they have ever imagined in their lives. I think most teachers probably [teach] out of their own experiences—a number of them sometimes out of their own context [and so] approach the classroom differently.

You find that most teachers, if we have any real bad experiences [during] our career, sometimes we transfer that. Unless we take time and do a real serious, self-analysis and try to overcome those experiences, we sometimes inadvertently transfer that to our students.

Admired or model teacher. My model teacher is Professor Hendrikson from Oxford University, in England. He came over to Cape Coast [University in Ghana] my senior year, and taught us organic chemistry. That was a course I dreaded. Everybody dreaded it because no one had made a "B" in that course before in the department; everybody was so scared. [To] anybody who chose chemistry as a major, the first thing they would tell you is: "Watch out for organic chemistry." That was the last course I wanted to take. I delayed it to my last year, when I didn't have any other choice, and then Hendrikson came in when he was on Sabbatical leave, and he was asked to teach us that year.

He made it the most interesting, simplest course. He was regarded as [one of the] world's greatest synthetic chemists. He taught us from one side of the board to the other with his colored chalk, drew patterns, made everything make so much sense that finally, at the end of the year, everybody felt organic chemistry was the most interesting course. It carried through when I finished college and started teaching. It's not an accident that the textbook I wrote was in organic chemistry. It was he who actually inspired me: The course I feared most became my most interesting course.

There have been so many teachers who have really impacted me, from elementary school to college and grad school and all those areas, but Hendrikson stands out because I dreaded chemistry. Most students, even teachers, don't want anything to do with organic chemistry, because it's so complicated. It's difficult to understand and to teach. I think the way Hendrickson helped me through that stage of my life, he would be my "teacher of the century."

[So my favorite teacher, admired teacher, and model teacher would all be different people, depending on their impact on me]. All of them had certain qualities about them. My middle school teacher who helped me through that stage of my life; he could see something in me that I didn't know, so he focused on that and tried to bring it out of me. He could see that I could do more than I was doing because I was so distracted and totally unfocused on my own academic achievement. Prof. Hendrikson, showed me that there should be no fear in any academic course. In fact, he totally took away my fear of any course in education because he showed me that organic chemistry is something that everybody can do. He made it seem that even the dumbest kid in class could understand this stuff, and since then, it has really impacted my life: It has helped me to go higher than what I expected of myself earlier. It has helped me to see that whatever I set my mind to, I can do it. All of that has to do with him showing me how to come through this dread of organic chemistry.

4.5.2 Kofi's socio-cultural influences

I would say we [had in Ghana] the best type of education, with all its limitations—and there were several; textbooks, [low] teacher compensation, [and] classroom setting were comparatively less [favorable]; but mostly textbooks [was an issue]. But, with all those limitations, I think we got the best of education, where the emphasis was on being a total student, a total person, not just learning something that you can't use.

I think our educational system was very challenging, more challenging than I've seen elsewhere in some of the advanced nations. I think what also helped us was that education was meaningful in the sense that, for those of us who came from very small towns, the educated were well respected. It felt like, an educated person could be a community leader. The poor community would look to you for leadership, and so education was meaningful. It wasn't like you become one of the [elitist] groups or anything; there was [a greater]t expectation of you. For example, during that time, there were still communities that would contribute to send one kid to high school. It means that a whole community invested their whole future into you, so that you could come out and be somebody different than who they are, but also guide them to somewhere that they wished to go, but couldn't go.

There was that kind of relationship between the school system and the community. The community depended on the school to train those who would lead the community at every level, and so the educational system was meaningful, and therefore we also put in a lot of effort. We didn't have many students who just went to school. People went to school for a purpose, especially high school. There were still just a few whose parents could afford

[it], but majority of students who went to high school went for a purpose, so they were really achievers. We took the system serious, [and] every opportunity we had, we made the best of it.

4.5.3 Kofi's recollections of his teacher education

The most useful part [of my teacher education] was the practice teaching. That's where we had the direct interaction with students, and I think that was very important. It helped me a lot when I actually had to teach students. When these were supposed to be my students that I had to teach, now I had to look back at the interactions I had with my students during practice teaching and that helped me a lot.

The classroom content is more [a] confidence building [issue] than actually application: It helps you to know that you know a lot more than you're required to teach, and so that is very good. The academic part is good for confidence building, and so you know that you're the teacher, and you're not deficient in your area that you're teaching.

[The education courses] were very helpful. In fact, if I had a recommendation, I would recommend that they increase the amount of time spent in teaching practice [and] cut down [on] the content, because what I've found is there is no better way to learn to teach than to teach.

During teaching practice, you have a supervisor around you to observe what you're doing. It's just like we take driver's test: You don't just get in the car and start driving. Somebody has to observe you and make sure you're following the rules, and that you're on the right track, so you don't become a hazard to people on the roads, and that's what the education department does. We are molding people. This is a people business, and if we don't equip them properly, they may end up on the wrong side of town, and then become a hazard to all society, so it's a very important department—a very important work that we do, and that's good.

4.5.4 Kofi's teaching life in Nigeria

This was a day school. [The students] walked to school; no buses, no transportation. It was twenty to thirty minutes' walk. Usually, they walked in groups. The school was almost at the center of the town. It was a big school. It had a population of nearly 6,000. I used to say it was a school for models, because they had so many [beautiful] girls [with] just a few boys scattered amongst them.

It was a very interesting school because the academic level was very high as compared to the other schools in the region. They were more focused on schoolwork and activities. In fact, I would even compare that nationwide, because when I started working with the West African Examinations Council, I could tell exam results from different regions around the country, and I could see that this school had a much higher standard than the majority of the nation. Part of that has to do with the maturity level and the desire to learn. School was a lot more fun both for teachers and the students because they were all on the same page.

The instructional setting was more "interactionary." There was a lot more interaction between teachers and students. I taught math and chemistry, and even in the math class, students were very much into the subject. There was a lot of discussion. Kids challenged each other; if you gave a problem to the class, everyone wanted to be the first to finish, or the first to get it right. So there was that kind of competition which was very positive. There were a few slow learners in the class but they were not penalized. The other students gathered around them in group sessions and worked with them, and helped them through the work during class time. The setting was very conducive to learning, and that's why it showed up in their achievement tests—final exams. They were achievers.

[Classroom dynamics], I think, has to do with the teachers. My classes are mostly interactive. I prefer to let my students talk about the subject, become a part of the teaching experience. So [in] most of my classes, when the students come to class, they have that expectation. They know that I expect them to be a part of the class, not just sit quietly like they are in a movie. They come in with that expectation, so the classes are very active. I have seen that, that has been helpful to me when I was a student and teachers allowed me to express myself; to be a participant in the class. I learned a lot more than when I just sit and watch.

I find that a number of [American] students have very low concentration levels—attention span—and so [my classes] are more interactive. You can engage them to be part of the discussion—the classroom activity—for more than an hour. But, if you leave them to sit by themselves while you just lecture or give them info, you find that their attention span is no more than fifteen minutes, and so you lose them after a few minutes of the class time. Because of that, I found that getting them more involved, posing kind of a leadership: leading them to actually learn the lesson helps them better; makes them a part of it, and then [that knowledge] becomes theirs because they learned it.

This is something I learned from watching a few teachers; all the different teachers I had in my career. I learned that the ones who allowed me to really be a part of the discussion; a part of what was going on in the class, I came out of the class knowing a lot more about the lesson than the others. I thought if I could help students do the same thing, they would know a lot more chemistry than they've ever learned in their lives. So that has been part of my style.

4.5.5 The physical environment

All the buildings were brick. Some of them were theater-style buildings, where you could seat maybe 120 to 150 students in a lecture hall type. The labs were different. We had different classrooms for labs and for lectures, and so when we were doing lectures, we used the lecture halls. Most [classrooms] had individual tables. The labs were pretty well-equipped, compared to many high schools.

Most of the labs were hands-on, and the classrooms were big enough, and the students were attentive to instruction, so you could instruct them as to what they were supposed to do, and you can count on very few errors or accidents. Safety was first, especially in my class in chemistry. I made sure that they understood what safety meant, and that you can be permanently damaged. I told a few stories about some experiences, and so they understood that if you don't handle things properly, you could end up with permanent damage, so they did well.

The classrooms were much bigger [than in the U.S.]; we had about a minimum of 40 to 50 students per class. Their physical space was much bigger. There were 1,002 students in the business department [alone]. Out of that 1,002, there were only three boys. Eastern Nigeria had just come out of the Nigerian civil war, so many of the young men had died in the war, so there were more girls than boys, both in the towns and the school systems. This was a senior high school.

The setting was that these students, who had come through elementary, middle and junior high school, were a little bit more mature, pretty close to junior college level. The civil war had taught them a great lesson about life, so they had that experience. Many of their loved ones—fathers, uncles—had died in the war, and many of these kids themselves had experienced the struggles of the war, where they had been deprived of practically everything, including food, [and] shelter. Many of them had to live in the woods for several days [or] weeks, and so the impact was there—and they have come out, and now they have the opportunity to have an education in a more favorable setting, with all the facilities available.

Some of them had become the heads of the households, so that had impacted their maturity level, plus many of them were very keen on education. They thought it was their way out of the struggle, so they were very active in class: eager to learn—and they paid attention.

4.5.6 School organization and relationships

I really enjoyed working with the students, and the teachers themselves were very cordial: very good relationships going. I was the chairperson of the science department, but I was free [or cordial] with all the teachers. They all came to me with their problems. If somebody was having difficulty with any content area, we'd sit down and talk about it. We sat down and wrote exams together. We looked at everything together. We had a really good relationship.

There was no talk-down kind of administration; there was a collective effort by the whole department, and the students understood that. They caught on to that, so they would not put down one teacher in the presence of another teacher. If a teacher [was] having any difficulty in their class, they didn't have a problem calling me in, so I could stay with them during the class period and then talk about things, and [this] helped the students through that stage. It was unique. If we had a system like that here in our [U.S.] schools, it would be interesting.

The administrators were not separated from the teachers. The principal also taught a class, [and] the vice-principal also taught a class. All the heads (the chairpersons of the departments) were teachers, so there wasn't much separation between the teachers and the administrators. It wasn't like we had a team of administrators and a team of faculty. We were all together; this was a collective business that we were all in, and that made it very interesting. It's kind of a unique experience, but it was wonderful.

If a student had a problem, they didn't have a problem going to whichever teacher they thought would help them, and the teachers understood that. If somebody was experiencing difficulty in a math class, they could go to any teacher who they think could help them. The teachers assumed the position of leaders in the school. It wasn't like I'm a math teacher so I deal with math. No: I'm a teacher in this school, and I'm here to help every child in this school. That was the attitude. Even if I [am] not the student's teacher, they had to give [me] the same respect they would their own teacher, and if the student had a problem, whichever teacher was around was responsible for helping the student.

In the classroom, the students were able to talk freely most of the time. They voiced out their opinion. In fact, the strange thing about it [was that], there was no secret in the student body, which made it very good for the administration. It helped us to help them. If one student [was] experiencing any difficulty, we would know about it. It wasn't like the problem would go on for a while and the student doesn't have any recourse, because the other students who knew about it would let us know about it so we could help them. So, it was more like one big community, which makes it very different from most schools. It was the school's philosophy that, "Anybody who comes here is capable of doing this work, whatever it takes," and so that helped. It molded both teachers and students and everybody together to work together. I loved it.

4.5.7 Kofi's daily routine in Nigeria

I wasn't driving in Nigeria; I didn't live on campus either. I walked with the students; we all walked to school. I had some friends [who] lived in the same building that I lived in, and [one of them] had a couple of cars, so many times he would take me to school. When he had to go to his office early in the morning before I go to school, then I would walk with the students. A couple of my friends were cops, and they had motorcycles, so they would come after school and park, and bring me home, so I had so many rides: I didn't have to drive.

A day started with just routine: getting ready for school and going to school. School started at 8:00, so I normally left home at about 7:30. It was only about 15 minutes' walk from school, maybe a couple of minutes' ride. I usually got to school and started out at my office. On a typical day, my classes began in the third period. I had first two periods dealing with administrative stuff, and checking to make sure every teacher was in their class, and instruction was going on in every class, and if any teacher needed support, I'd try to be available. That was my first two periods. There were eight periods. A typical teacher taught all eight periods. School was from 8:00 to 3:30, I think. We had a lunch break. After the first two periods, I'd go to my classes. I'd have four periods, and then I'll have the last two periods off, and then I'd do the same thing; go through the same routine [checking on the teachers].

When school was over, I'd get a ride home usually, or sometimes I'd walk and then come home and change my clothes and go out. [With] the same friends, we would spend some time at the recreation club. I was a member of the club, so we would play tennis, ping-pong and just spend time together in the evening, and then come back home. A typical day was more like that: routine. Occasionally, I would take some time and write some stuff. I would go in early—when I really wanted to write—I'd go in about 7:00 a.m. From seven to eight o'clock, I would do most of my writing, and then after that, school activity begins.

I didn't give any homework. Most of the homework was more like qualitative work. It's not like you take your books home, do this work and bring it to school tomorrow. Much of the work was done during school. The fact [was] that the kids had to walk to schools, plus books were so expensive that students did not take books home. The few books that were available had to be used during school, so I think that has really impacted on my homework assignments.

I don't normally give homework assignments to my students from their books, even now. I prefer to do much of the work in class because what I've observed is that [when] many students go home, their parents have no knowledge of the content. In the class, it may sound like, "This is easy, I can do it," but when they get home, and they have to sit by themselves, they can't do it. They end up frustrated, spending all night trying to do the work that they couldn't do. They come to class the next day frustrated, angry, [and] sometimes they even skip the class because they didn't do their homework—not because they wouldn't do it, but because they just couldn't do it. So when they come to class the next day, they come in with a different attitude. So most of the time, I prepare for them to do work in class, so we do a lot of class work, where I'd be available to help them.

Same way back in Nigeria, there was not much homework, because most of the kids go home and they have to take care of their home—domestic responsibilities were very important. Most of [the girls] had to cook for the family; take care of younger brothers or sisters; go to market and sell goods. They were very enterprising, and so most of the families had businesses. When the kids came home, they had to go and help in those areas, and that's one of the reasons there were no homework assignments. They did enough at home trying to maintain the lifestyle.

Kofi's comparison of native Ghanaian and American schools

This is a topic that Kofi discussed at length in several different contexts. He noted that there were several important differences between his educational experiences in Africa and America. These are discussed at length within the contexts of the next chapter.

4.6   Summary

In this chapter, some background and contextual information about the author and each of the participants of this study were provided. This information, captioned pedagogical biographies, was included in order to help buttress and provide contexts for the later chapters. Emphases were placed on the international teachers' native socio-cultural influences, their early perceptions of teachers and teaching, and recollections of their teacher education.

Also included were their teaching lives in their native countries. These focused on descriptions of their native schools' physical environment, school organization and relationships, and daily routines. These were used as the basis for comparing their native and American schools.

This chapter indicates that international teachers should expect their past educational experiences to have an impact on them. When cross-cultural educators relocate to new teaching contexts, such past educational influences may be viewed as the infrastructure for reflection and resolution towards a better instructional practice.

Chapter #5

POTENTIAL TEACHING ISSUES FOR INTERNATIONAL TEACHERS IN AMERICAN SCHOOLS
International Teachers' Stories and Discussions

As the saying goes, "It is possible to predict the future by reviewing the past." In the context of this book, it is possible to predict possible issues of cross-cultural, international teaching by inspecting the experiences of others.

The transitional issues of the international teachers featured in this book may be categorized into three types: support systems issues, knowledge gaps, and knowledge shifts. In chapter one, support system issues were discussed as including the basic physical and psychological facilities the teachers needed in order to function comfortably in their personal lives. To the extent that one has difficulties acquiring these support systems or finds them absent altogether, one is likely to see a corresponding impact on his or her teaching effectiveness.

As the terms imply, knowledge gaps and knowledge shifts suggest that there are certain knowledge differences of which international teachers should be aware. They are therefore expected to make concerted efforts to make a "shift," or compensate for those differences by learning and reviewing their practices to suit the new environment.

5.1 Knowledge Gaps: Introduction to Trans-National Educational Issues

In this section, the knowledge gaps of the four participants will be presented in a true-to-life format. Here again, the voices of the participants are employed by directly quoting them where possible. This section describes real-life transitional issues in some United States high schools.

The participants are discussed together and yet distinguished from each other, and their transitional issues presented according to specific themes and sub-themes, where possible. This system, it is hoped, will enable the reader to make easier cross-references to the background information of each participant in the previous chapter, where necessary.

5.1.1 Mary's systemic knowledge gaps

Having taught for several years in several countries, Mary was naturally inclined to compare her current school system to that of her previous ones, especially her native English system. In terms of the way her American school's science department was organized, she noted that,

> In a department this [big], we would have technical help, more lab spaces in England, and probably slightly lighter time-table than we get at the moment. Science teachers here don't get any lighter timetable than any other teachers, even though we have to prepare and clear up and do lab stuff…. Since we don't have a lab technician, a lot of time is spent putting materials together for labs and then clearing up afterwards. So that is one big difference: technical help.

The absence of laboratory technicians, which several other countries do provide their science teachers added to her transitional difficulties. She also noted that work ethos was different between the British and American educational systems:

> Interviewer: What happens after school after you're done with your classes?
>
> Mary: I usually deal with my email. I keep an eye on it during the day.
>
> Interviewer: So, you think teaching here is [more] demanding?
>
> Mary: [It] seems to take more time, and the more you give, the more you get—but the work ethos in the States is very different than the work ethos in Europe. Americans work too hard from the start; they never take breaks. They seem to work longer days… the work ethos, let alone educationally, I find very different. There is no cut off; it seems to spread. You know, people don't say well it's five, I'm going home to be with my family, do some shopping…people don't tend to do that. It just seems to spread. [So] Americans are certainly very hard-working compared to most Europeans.

5.1.2 Joe's systemic knowledge gaps

Joe, with all his previous international teaching experiences, was not immune to the differences that existed between his previous educational systems and that of the United States. He observed that the general curriculum of United States schools was "college preparatory," whereas in Britain, the schools were more stratified, with only a portion them being "college preparatory."

On being asked to describe some of the immediate differences he noted between the educational systems in England and the United States when he first began teaching in the United States, Joe said that:

> England is a big exam orientated structure. The United States isn't. It could be more so, but it isn't, so that drives the curriculum: got to get these kids through these exams. One of the major differences I see is, in the British system, the kids get their [final] grades in the Summer... whereas, typically in the United States, they know about the college [they are admitted into earlier in their final grade year]: It's an internal grading system, along with SATs or whatever, but they know which college they're going into by Christmas, and so they typically slack off.

An interesting point was made concerning the nature and content of the subject matter. Joe noted that

> There [are] structural differences between chemistry here and chemistry in Britain, and if you look at the average American textbook, you'd find a very small section on organic chemistry. Grab the average British text book you'd find a larger section on organic chem... If you get an English chem book out, you'd find the anode is always positive and the cathode is always negative. You get an American textbook out, and it's sometimes negative and it's sometimes positive. Both are correct.

Joe, like Mary, also mentioned the significant absence of laboratory technicians in the United States high school.

5.1.3 Inga's systemic knowledge gaps

Teaching in a foreign language is one thing, but knowing which class period it is could add to the stress. Right from the outset, there was a systemic problem for Inga to figure out. The common class period in American schools lasts for 50 minutes. The school day or week may also be divided in very innovative ways. There are various ways of apportioning either the day or week, or a combination of the two. Two of those schedules are called block and rotational schedules. In a block schedule, students may essentially meet for about 90-120 minutes per subject every given week day, instead of the normal 50 minutes.

Noting that some students may not have their best learning times during, for example the beginning or last part of the day (because they may not be totally mentally-alert), the idea of rotational schedule was introduced. With this, students would not have the same teacher (and hence subject) at the same time of the day. With this system of compensation, one subject does not suffer. Monday (Day One) begins with the first period classes and ends with the last. Tuesday, (Day Two) begins with the second period classes and ends with the first, and so on. Although this sounds simple, it could be very confusing initially, depending on the combination with other schedules within a school. Both new teachers and new students in the school may need several weeks to get adjusted to them. Inga was not spared from this chastisement. Talking about her school, she lamented that

> They rotate: they have a rotational system. You basically have the morning and afternoon blocks or A, B, C, D, E, and they have one day— like "A" has Monday morning first, Tuesday second, Thursday second last, Friday last. So you get the four periods and it's highly complicated, and it took me a while to figure it out.

Interviewer: So is it like on Tuesday, the B-block has first period?

Inga: Yeah, and actually on Tuesday, B-block has first and they don't have class on Wednesday. They have last on Thursday, second last on Friday, second on Monday, so it goes and then cascading…

On the other hand, Inga found that her current school gave her more freedom at several levels. She translated this sense of freedom in her current school as respect for the teacher as a professional. To her, this was something refreshing. She elaborated, with grading student work as an example:

> [In America,] I don't have so many rules I have to follow about how many tests I have to give. In Germany they give you at least how many [tests], how you have to weigh them, and the grading part, etc. I don't have this. I have more freedom in saying, if I see that a student shows a lot of interest, effort, to give him a grade—also to force the student by saying, "This is not the way I expect you to work so I'm going to grade you down on this, and I'm going to put it down."

Although this may sound contradictory to what Mary may have noted, it is vital to know that these are people coming to teach in the same school from different countries. Therefore any differences they observed should be viewed in their proper contexts. Again, depending on which school one is teaching, there may be different policies in place regarding homework assignments, grading, etc. In general, however, grading should be consistent across the students, or students may be expected to appeal, depending on the classroom and school environments.

Another systemic difference Inga noted was that in Germany, less meaningful letter grades were sent home. A lead teacher who may not know a student very well was the final arbiter on the grades, making such grades less informative:

> Also the way you write report cards: you don't want to give them a letter. That basically doesn't tell much except that it's an A+ or an F. That [just] tells you, "Oh my gosh…" [or] "Yeah that's good," but even then it depends so much on the teacher and so much on what you teach…. The leading teacher of the class writes a comment on the student and the others say whether they agree or disagree with this.

On the other hand, in the United States, Inga noted the teachers are more in control, and had the opportunity to provide more meaning for their students' grades:

> …but here, I have to write a comment for every student, so I give my input. I can describe what the student does, what the level is, what that grade really tells about the student. [The student may be putting in] a lot of effort but [maybe] he has trouble understanding. Or, if somebody is lazy, but so bright that they're still getting a good grade; or somebody is bright but so lazy that there's no chance of getting a good grade—Just trying to give a little more input than those [basic letter grades].

As may be hinted in Inga's statements above and elaborated in later sections, report card days in American schools are busy times for teachers. Some students would pester a teacher for a better grade, if they could, and some parents may like to know why their children were given specific grades, especially if they are low. Teachers should therefore be ready to defend any assigned grades to students.

In chapter two, it was mentioned that teaching in America is still struggling for recognition as a legitimate profession. Interestingly, however, Inga thought that one underlying difference between her German school and the American one was mainly in the differences of their structures; the fundamental structural element being respect for teachers as professionals:

> You have to have a certain structure, and here [in America] I think the parents and the administration trust a little bit more that the teacher is a professional; that you basically should know what you're doing—and, yes, you can be asked why you did this or that, but not in a way that's attacking, but just in a way that you question somebody because you want

to learn about the idea [behind what they did].

An inferential statement that could be safely asserted is that in America, if a teacher is known to be effective in the classroom, he or she can operate with great confidence and freedom, provided he or she is operating within professional guidelines. Such teachers can easily become insulated from the personal whims and caprices of students, parents, and administrators who are the primary stakeholders of American education. Tough, but effective teachers may also win the respect and support of such stakeholders, and are viewed as an asset to any school. This is a topic that will be discussed in the next chapter.

A summative statement to encapsulate Inga's comparative views of the two systems would be that, in the Unites States, teachers have

Greater freedom, more trust from people. It's not an issue of how old I am, how many years I taught before. It's, "Do you want to do the job?" "Do you want to put in the effort?" And then you can do it. In Germany, it's more hierarchical. [There is] just more opportunity [in the United States].

5.1.4 Kofi's systemic knowledge gaps

Asked if he observed any significant differences in school organization between his Nigerian or Ghanaian schools and that of his current United States high school, he pointed out that there were several significant differences. When asked to mention some of the striking things he noted soon after he began teaching in the United States high school, he mentioned curriculum differences as one of them:

The other striking thing is that I found that the school systems here were very different than those back in Africa by the way they're set up. The requirements are very different. The way the courses are set is very different.

Elsewhere during the interview, he elaborated on his perception of the curriculum difference between the Ghanaian schools and his current United States high school. He pointed out that there existed a

Big difference, big difference! The semester system, the course structures; I mean how the courses are taught. I mean, back in Africa, you take a course like say chemistry. You take it in high school, and you take it in your third year, fourth year, and fifth year, and you take physics and biology concurrently. Here, it is very different: You take your biology without chemistry, then you take chemistry one year, without biology, then the next year, you take physics, without chemistry or biology, and so it's like the courses seem kind of disjointed.

The natural consequence of what appears to be "disjointed" coursework in the U.S., in Kofi's opinion is that

A kid leaves a math class and comes to a physics class and can't see why you will be using math terms to explain a physics problem, and that has to do with the very nature of the curriculum set up. So the kid feels that once they finish with a particular course, they don't have any obligation to use it again. So it goes, whereas in our system [in Ghana], if you do this, you do it again next year, so its progression. So you feel that every year, there is a requirement of you to know what you did the previous year, unlike this system here; that doesn't apply.

He further proposed that some of this consequence could have a dire effect on some students:

And that is one of the reasons why many students are failing these graduation tests, SAT's, and all of these, because it is not progressive. We expect that that's what will happen; that they [the students] will think of it [the curriculum] as being progressive, but we haven't the methodology or the system for them to actually feel that it is progressive, and we expect them to make the coordination [of the different subject areas], but its not there.

Kofi then went on to provide a personal example, to justify his stated conviction:

I worked with about three students this Summer who had graduated, but they failed to pass the graduation test so they can go to college. And all I did with them was go through the biology, and all of them passed; I mean just like that.

Interviewer: Because it has been a long time...

Kofi: Yes, its been a long time: They took biology in their freshmen year—at a time when they didn't even care about high school, and they got serious about their junior and senior years, and bio[logy] is long gone, and there is no way to go back and review that. And that's a big problem.

Another systemic difference Kofi noted was the absence of laboratory technicians, a point shared by Mary and Joe. He emphasized, as Mary, the point that laboratory technicians relieve science teachers of certain extra work. Besides this issue, he also grieved over the bureaucratic inertia that, in his estimation, belabors the United States teacher:

> Here what I find is that the teacher is overloaded: What we find is that a lot more teachers don't really put all their energies into teaching because of the other distractions; paper work, administrative duties. Teachers have to be on duty out in the hallwa s, police the kids, take care of discipline problems, even supervise the kids in the cafeteria.

Kofi had a point of divergence from the previous interviewees, who all belonged to the same, relatively more prestigious private school. He noted the virtual absence of time for planning and reflection for the American public school teacher, since there is practically no extra time available to him or her. For Kofi, it was not so much the fact that students were intruding in his classrooms, as in Mary and Inga's case. Rather, in his case, the absence of planning and reflective time was due to the official duties teachers had to do:

> Even though most teachers have a planning period, you can hardly plan anything in your planning period because there is so much to do that is not related to the classroom, so a lot of teachers are burnt out before they get to class. So in front of the kids, they have to really come up with a second wind to really give their best. That's what I've observed here.

Finally, he also noted a general difference in the structure of the school systems he had experienced, although he did not explain how that affects the teaching and learning processes:

> Then the school environment here [is generally different]. Most of the schools I've taught in [Ghana during teaching practices and later in Nigeria] were boarding schools, and so to find out that all the schools here are day schools and the students have to be taken back and forth by buses—that was different for me.

For many international teachers, another significant difference they may find in American schools is that teachers have their own classrooms, and stay there during for the school day. In many schools, they may even have a key to their rooms. The students, instead of having permanent seats in a classroom, are rather the ones who move around the campus to the teachers' classrooms. International teachers should therefore expect to have their own classrooms, and manage their rooms; keeping a poster board, electronics, science laboratories (for science teachers), ordering teaching supplies, and such issues.

From the accounts of the four teachers above, it is reasonable to suggest that international teachers should expect some amount of differences between the nature of schooling and school organization in their native countries and those of the United States. These differences can be dealt with effectively with open-mindedness and curiosity about the new system.

International teachers should insist on finding out what their teaching responsibilities would entail as soon as possible. They should make sure that they have had adequate orientation to such issues from mentors or administrators and make plans accordingly, well in advance.

5.2   Assessment Issues

In America, testing has become one of the biggest topics in education-related conversations. As previously indicated, the history of American education is rife with issues. There are racial issues, class issues, ideological issues, and several others. The school, being a reflection of the general society, is one of the places where ideological wars are fought. Ever since the Civil Rights Movement of the 1960s and 1970s, educators have become even more acutely aware of this fact. Bowles and Gintis (1976) were strong voices on this issue in the academic circles. They asserted that

> The structure of social relations in education not only inures the student to the discipline of the workplace, but develops the types of personal demeanor, modes of self-presentation, self-image, and social class identifications which are the crucial ingredients of job adequacy. Specifically, the social relationships of education—the relationships between administrators and teachers, teachers and students, and students and students, and students and their work—replicate the hierarchical divisions of labor. (p.131)

As in most societies, testing is used to sort students into academic ability groups. The American public has a very strong emotional reaction to what is generally captioned "high-stakes" testing—especially where they believe that many of such tests are culturally-biased and therefore either create or perpetuate societal inequalities. (For more on this topic, see C. H. Persell's book, Education and Inequality). Cross-cultural educators coming to teach in America may benefit from understanding the general American sensibilities to the issues of assessment in teaching.

5.2.1 Mary's assessment issues

If anything initially irritated Mary about the American Educational system, it was the issue of grading student work and its philosophical implications. These she found to be very different and difficult to accommodate. Talking about her American students:

> If you do everything you're asked, you should get an A, but that doesn't leave any room for maneuver. I never give A+s: It's crazy. I just don't see that at all—and because it doesn't exist... Where does that leave the really excellent student who really gets it right and puts a lot of effort into it? Where does that put them? [In America], they get an A unless they do something wrong... whereas in the UK, a C used to be average. You do what you do, you get one [or] two marks here, then you get your C, and then you got Bs and As.

With the above philosophy of grading, Mary experienced some initial issues and reactions, including:

> Kids complaining grades were too low. When you put grades on the report card, you have to be able to justify them—and there were just a lot of complaints, so I just sat down and realized that I was just grading a little bit too tough—and I would not let my principles get in the way of the kids getting in the university.

She found a compromise she could live with, as she noted: "So you try and make a balance that you think is fair."

Mary also mentioned that, not only students, but parents were concerned about their kids' grades, adding to the problem: "So you have these different criteria that you're using and that can cause problems. Parent expectations of their kids...can be very misleading," she reasoned.

In a way, she empathized with her American students by saying:

> I think that students are under a lot of pressure to succeed, to get their SAT score, and I would not make their lives worse because they'll burn out. But students have to be accountable for their own behaviors and so making up of tests and second chances are OK. ... Sometimes, holding a hand that needs help, sometimes you have to slap the hand instead of holding it. That's a judicious decision that you make.

Another philosophical difference Mary mentioned concerned the importance, and therefore the weight of examinations in the curriculum. She mentioned that her final exams accounted for 10-20% of her students' final grade—and she did not think that was enough. In America, one philosophy concerning assessment is that students' final grades should not depend solely or mostly on final examinations. They believe in the "continuous assessment" model: a constant monitoring of students' cumulative grades over certain periods of time. One justification for this is that if a student is having difficulties with his or her school work, it would be noticed early enough to intervene and implement any necessary remedies.

Another justification for the "continuous assessment" model is that the moods and attitudes of students can affect their test performances. Such moods and attitudes may change in response to differences in the environment, the emotional state of the student, and other internal or external factors. For this reason, the generally accepted measure of a student's true ability is his or her cumulative work throughout the semester. Once a semester is over, students in schools with block schedules have the opportunity to start all over again, with a new teacher, new colleagues, in a new environment—as opposed to long the year-models found in several countries.

A point of interest is how school work is done in America. Most of the student's grade is assessed from homework, projects, quizzes, and end of unit tests. The idea of homework is to get the students to do a follow-up on the school work, and possibly recognize areas of difficulty. In many cases, students will do their homework with some help—either from parents or colleagues or, in some cases, other teachers.

Besides, group work or cooperative activities are also encouraged in American schools. For this reason, students may not a have problem asking their colleagues to help them to solve a problem in, or outside the classroom. If they truly come to an understanding of the solution to the problem, then using cooperative learning strategies would have justified its place in the classroom. (See Jack Hassard's The Art of Teaching Science for more on this topic.) Although there are various means to assess one student's contribution to the group work, it may prove to be a psychological leap for some foreign teachers to accept all the assessment norms and practices in American schools. As Mary hinted,

> The big issue for me was the grading and the marking and how important tests are—tests and quizzes. There's a difference between a test and a quiz but I don't know what it is. I still don't know what it is. I grade them the same, and that's something that used to upset students, and I'd say "No, you sit down and do this on your own. This is your piece of work, coming from your mind, in your brain." It's not difficult work and it's not done by committee as opposed to assignments, which is a different issue. I explain why I do things. If I'm wrong then I'm prepared to change.

In the end, Mary mentioned that she partially yielded to the American system. She continued that:

> You have to be flexible, and you can't be mean-minded, and you mustn't take it out on the kids. Just because you have a different idea doesn't mean it's the right idea under this environment.

To summarize it all, she said that,

The grading system in American schools is very different from those in
Europe, and I found that very difficult to adapt to in the beginning. I tend
to compare [Britain] to the States; compare [myself] to American
teachers, you know. [Grade] A is very unusual for me. Not everybody
gets an A in the beginning—I work towards it now. [Final] exams are
very important [to me], but not considered to be so important here. They
have less weight on the final grade.

5.2.2 Joe's assessment issues

Although this theme was of a great concern to Mary, this is one area that was
glaringly absent in Joe's initial descriptions. In a follow-up interview
however, Joe made the following indications, in support of his fellow
British, Mary's assertions:

Grading or assessment is markedly different, with the focus on external
exams scores in Europe and little to no emphasis on internally awarded
grades, as these [internal examinations] are as difficult to moderate, and
with few really precise criteria available. [Also], the theory that 90% [and
above] is an A, is fairly alien to us: [In Europe], it all depends on the
degree of difficulty of the test.

5.2.3 Inga's assessment issues

On the issue of assessment, Inga also indicated that she noticed some
differences in the mode of assessment:

In Germany, you have grades going from one to six: one is best, six is
worst. Getting a one is very rare. Getting an A in America is not rare. I
had students getting an A-minus and asking what they could do for extra
credit to make up that A-minus. You have to learn to be more generous
with grading over here. What you learn [in Germany] is that only a
really extraordinary student should get a one [or an A], not just a student
who does everything you expect them to do, as in America.

Inga explained the philosophical and cultural infrastructure of the
German educational system, which may inform their assessment
expectations. She mentioned that Germans are stricter in, for example,
geometry. For her, this also laterally translates into her "obsession" for
proper drawings in physics:

What I'm thinking of is using a ruler: If you study geometry in high school in Germany, geometry means you draw something with a ruler and a compass—Greek traditions still in there, nothing else.

Interviewer: So, obsessed?

Inga: Yeah, people will call it obsessed. I didn't draw a single straight line without a ruler, whether this was over a square root or whatever... I [still] have my German ruler. They [my students will] get a white board with a grid next year. The German ruler is really good because you can draw parallel lines, you can draw perpendiculars, and the students know it. The students know I [used to] get upset. I don't get upset anymore. It's more in a humorous way saying, "Could you please sharpen your pencil?" "Could you please use a ruler?" I think if I [were] an English teacher it would be a problem, but being a science teacher, I think I have good reasons to say they should do it...

Another interesting, related point Inga made concerned the discipline of handwriting skills in German schools. She noted that this was not only expected, but it had to be well-done and, depending on the grade level, be done with fountain pens. Even parents expected that:

I can still see my mom ripping out pages for writing like in first grade or something. ... Keep the habit of using the ruler, using different colors... When an American student comes to my classroom, they usually bring a pen and a piece of paper. When you go to a German classroom, usually you bring a fountain pen because in eighth grade, you're not allowed to use something else.

People believe you get a better handwriting if you write with a fountain pen, so until like fourth and fifth grade, you get grades on your handwriting, so you practice handwriting, and I actually believe it because usually, it depends on the pen. You have very good pens right now where you can really write smoothly, but the fountain pen is still a different thing.

For Inga, the issue of assessment had a natural connection with the issue of discipline: One had to work diligently to merit the award of excellence.

5.2.4 Kofi's assessment issues

Without a surprise, Kofi found grading to be a major area of separation between the United States and Ghanaian (and also Nigerian) school systems. He mentioned some experiences, which related his own family, and other African students. He described two major areas. The first one concerned the total weight of exams making up students' final grade, as Mary and Joe also pointed out. The second area concerned the translation of foreign students' grades (being transferred through transcripts).

On the issue of the weight of exams, he had the following to say:

> Back home, when I was in school, the emphasis was on tests [or examinations]. The test made up a majority of your grade. Here, it's not like that. Tests make up no more than about 50% of any course. It's only in math that you have that high percentage of tests. In any other course, the tests may make up maybe about 30%, and now the county [i.e. his current school district] has stipulated that everybody will take a final exam in every course, and the final exam was 10% this year.

He also mentioned the cut-off points for the various grades; a point which hit home for him (concerning his own daughters) and many others who frequently asked him to interpret grades for African immigrant students:

> I have had to write up for my daughters, and I have had to write that the interpretation or translated certificates—transcripts for several Ghanaian and Nigerian students, because our grading system—is very different from their grading system here. Back in Ghana where my daughter was, she was in private high school. [Grade] A was if you make anything above sixty-five percent, so she came here with her grades that were in the seventies, and they translated all of them either as Cs or Ds.

He went on to describe what action he took in order to correct this discrepancy:

> ...You see, and so her report card came, and her GPA was about one-point-something, so I had to go and meet with the counselors and explain to them that, "Look at the letter grade that says "A," but the numerical grade is seventy-two, and here seventy-two is a D. And I had to explain to them that these are two different systems, and you can't make that direct translation.

Although this was the system back in his native country, Kofi still found himself giving out grades more in line with the United States system. He attributed this to the fact that he attended two American graduate schools, and had therefore had the opportunity to learn and operate within the general assessment philosophy of American schools:

I think that what has helped me to adapt to the system is the two graduate programs that I had taken here. So I was more in tune with the system here, rather than if I had just transitioned directly from home and come here, and then started [to teach] in the school system: It would have been very different. So I was more in tune with the basic system here, so it helped. But I think I am prone to give an A for a good effort than maybe some other teachers.

5.3 Communication Issues

International teachers coming to America may roughly fall into two communicational competence groups: the "internally-proficient," and the "externally-proficient." Those in the first group possess all the communicational tools to independently teach their students without any external help. Although this group may have certain problems, including different accents, idioms, and expressions, they can get by in the classroom by explaining things in other ways. In short, "internally-proficient" international teachers have a natural fluency, and possess the capabilities to employ the flexibilities of the English language. On the other hand, "externally-proficient" teachers may, to one degree or the other, fall short of such capabilities of using the language. They may therefore need some form of help in order to become effective communicators—and, for that matter, teachers.

Communication barriers have been described as a major issue in international or cross-cultural education. Fortuijn (2002) observes that "the problem of language is a problem of understanding." (p. 266) He continues that language involves "finding the right words, the right idioms, and the right nuances; it is a problem of pronunciation and audibility, tempo, tone and tune." (ibid.) He notes that even people who speak good English may have problems with idioms and nuances. Therefore, even if they are good teachers in their native languages, pronunciation and audibility become problems in international teaching.

Touching the issue of accents, Fortuijn further points out that accents may be national or regional, and that there are several types of English, including, but not limited to British, American, Australian, or other English. Confusion of non-native speakers by choice of words and pronunciation is therefore understandable. He provides an example:

In particular, Americans speak with more differences in their tune— speaking Dutch in this way is considered to be excessive or hysteric, especially when women speak in this way. To be taken seriously, one has to find a balance between monotony and exaggeration. (p. 267)

Ladd and Ruby (1999) cite an example of a graduating foreign student senior who visited a professor for a check on his coursework. The professor's comment was, "You have quite a few electives," to which the student became panic-stricken and replied that "No, I have quite a lot of electives." (p. 5) They also mention the American phrase, "Get out of here," which literally means "leave," but figuratively means "You are joking." They therefore caution the use of such idioms with non-native students. They suggest that when using idioms or forms of speech that cannot be understood from the individual meanings of their elements, instructors should be careful.

Clyne (1987) makes the observation that German communication patterns are different from Americans'. In academic discourse, Americans generally would inform their audience exactly what they are going to say in detail, according to "advance organizers" (p. 229) (generally introduction, body, and conclusion). Therefore, if they digress from the main point, Americans would warn the audience of the digression. Germans on the other hand, are less linear. They would simply digress and expect the audience to follow. Again, they would simply launch into their examples with just a change in inflection as the marker or signal to their audience (Kuhn, 1996).

Kuhn (1996) also observes that, whereas Americans generally value good presentation skills, such skills are not necessarily seen as desirable features in German academic teaching. Rather, more distanced, humorless presentations are considered more appropriate.

White (2000) reiterates the potency of certain popular axioms, such as such as, "A picture is worth a thousand words," and, "It's not what you say; it's how you say it." (p. 13) She proposes that non-verbal communication is important in establishing credibility and leadership, and that these are two traits that excellent teachers exhibit. She also mentions six non-verbal factors which relate to effective teaching as being eye contact, gesticulations, paralanguage, posture, clothing and environment, and overall facial expression. Each of these factors is replete with issues that may concern the international teacher.

On the issue of paralanguage, White suggests that pronunciation is a vital factor which elicits student respect and confidence in a teacher, and that some amount of eye contact is optimal for effective teaching. In situations where the cultural traditions of an international teacher do not permit a female to look into the eye of a male, one could foresee a potential problem.

5.3.1 Mary's communication issues

Mary, being British, naturally had an unmistakable British parlance. Therefore she soon noted that, "when people say 'come around' or 'we must go out' or 'keep in touch,' they don't necessarily mean it," and that was an "odd thing" to her. However, it was in the classroom that the language differences became more interesting, since she and her students were the captive audiences of each other. There were several levels at which communication proved to be of particular interest, from differences in spelling and expressions to differences in the meaning of words.

At the word-meaning level, she thought that the communication gap was fairly significant. She provided an example of that:

> You do get in trouble sometimes with the faculty if you are talking about important issues. One very important word has a different meaning in English. In American English it's "quite"--q-u-i-t-e [spelling it out]. In "English English," it means, "It's OK": quite average, [as in,] "I feel quite well; I feel OK." But in American English it means good; excellent. So if a fellow English-Brit said to me, "You're quite good at your job," it wouldn't really be a compliment, but if an American said it to me, "You're quite good," it would be a compliment; it would mean you're very good.

Mary elaborated on how such an expressional gap could be a problem, not only in general communication, but also in the performance of the teaching job in America, such as talking with parents and other colleagues:

> …And that single word has caused more problems than I could describe to you, because I would say to someone, "Yeah your child's quite good. He's behaving quite well," and I actually mean in English "quite": they're OK." They think I mean in American "quite," which is "very". It takes a long time to find where you're crossing. It took me a long time to find why we were misunderstanding each other, and then I realized it's that word "quite." Somebody told me you're quite good as a teacher and I was offended… I thought I must be better than that. It's a linguistic thing, but a simple word like that can make a huge difference.

In terms of teacher-student relations, expressional gaps were obvious, but Mary mentioned that she survived, employing the weapons of humor and respect:

Interviewer: So are there occasions that they use expressions which you don't understand?

Mary: Yeah, but I think that they would try to do that. Me, I don't try to do that. I just speak the way I normally speak and use phrases, and try to use analogies or similarities to explain things that are familiar to me. I might just do it, but kids always want to be different. They don't want people to understand what they're saying, so when they're just chatting they will use phrases and I must say, "I'm sorry, I don't know what you mean; you have to explain that to me." Again [with] that kind of respect, the differences seem to work. But again don't forget I work with older students so it's easier. I don't know if you'd get away with that with an eighth grader.

Mary used humor to lighten up her classroom, and relationship with her students:

Just making mild jokes. One of them comes in late, I just look at my watch and say, "Oh, how good of you to come! Thank you." Or, if they fall asleep, I'd say, "I'm not keeping you awake am I?" and things like that. On the whole the language difference isn't profound.

Spelling was also the subject for an interesting commentary. On being asked, "...how about when you have differences in spelling?" Mary enthusiastically went on:

Oh, how do I do like colo[u]r? Yeah, I spell it my way. I spell h[a]emoglobin my way. And I say you don't get the [letter] "a" in it. I don't care how you spell it. Just spell it the same way every time, and I'd say I'm not changing because I've been doing this for too long, and they laugh about that. C-o-l-o-u-r [spelling it]; Colour is one. Humo[u]r.

Yeah, hemoglobin. Things like [o]estrogen…which doesn't have the 'o' in front of it. All sorts of things like that. But it's OK. I don't think it's a problem as long as they appreciate—you know; it's not a spelling mistake.

On the whole, Mary believed that the students were aware of the differences, and thought that her students' attitudinal responses were positive to such spelling differences:

I think they have enough sense to know what's going on. They might ask if that's the way you spell it. I'd say that's the English spelling. "English English." In American you simplify it and use the "a" or use the "o," whatever the difference is. And they say it's fine. Some of them will spell it their own way. Some will spell it my way.

On her part, she thought that "consistency" was the operative word for academic engagement in assessing student spelling:

For all that, my attitude is, I don't mind how you spell it. Each is equally OK as long as it's in the right context. Just spell it the same way every time otherwise if you write it down, somebody would think you don't know what you're talking about if you change the spelling every time. But that was it. That was how I did it.

A solution to the spelling difference was in part solved by the use of computers, although she sometimes intentionally tried to make the educational point of letting the students sort some words out by, and for themselves:

Program is another one. We spell it m-m [programme] and an 'e' at the end. The computer corrects a lot of that for me if I'm writing it down but sometimes I deliberately override it and put the English down. It's a small point but it's quite important for the students to know that this way is not always the only way.

Mary did assimilate the American lingo: After five years of teaching in the American school, she notes that, "I use the words they understand." On being asked is she still used her native words, she replied that, "I do sometimes, but I correct it. But they know what I mean by that because I've had these kids before."

Interviewer: So you are re-educating the kids.

Mary: Yeah, and they're reeducating me. It's a two-way process really.

Mary also acknowledged that linguistically, "Brit's have a reputation for being sarcastic," and with this seeming language problem, "You can actually use the differences to make a bond if you use them correctly." In the axiomatic co-mingling of velvet and iron, Mary, a master teacher, fluidly harmonized sarcasm and humor, in order to reach her students.

5.3.2 Joe's communication issues

Parlance is one thing that follows people, and so with even the least possible luck, one could easily make Joe out as a British when he spoke. Having lived in Britain until adulthood before traveling globally, Joe still retained his unmistakable British parlance and accent, just like Mary. It is therefore a foregone conclusion that this became a subject during the interview. Joe was interested in, and particularly sensitive to the issue of students' emotional response to British sarcasm, as much as Mary, as he cautioned that:

> The kids get a bit put out by British sarcasm; that's certain. It takes a little while to adjust to me and me to adjust to them. But once they become familiar, I think everything settles down, but I have to be more sensitive to their feelings.

An example of this sarcasm was inadvertently generated as a kid was trying to joke with him during class:

> I had one kid say to me, "What would you say to me, Mr. Key, if I said you suck?" I said "I'd presume you'd give me instruction on how to use a drinking straw." (Laughter) He was angry. He [then] just burst out laughing and the rest of the class laughed. As a Brit, [you suck] is not part of my vocabulary. The way that it was said told me that it was inappropriate.

Another example was his getting used to common, everyday expressions on arrival in the United States:

> The typical American greeting, "Have a nice day" or parting comments was totally foreign to me, and I didn't like it at first because it was said by people I hardly knew, who seemed to me to not care whether I had a nice day or not, and so it was false affection—and so to me it was bordering on sarcasm. So it took me a while to respond, and it wasn't meant in that way but that's how initially I felt it was meant. So it took me a while to be able to respond more positively to that.

This is an example of "expressional gap" mentioned in Mary's discussion. Joe also emphasized that, linguistically speaking, the English are more direct in their approach:

> There are cultural differences and I would be more prone to play it straight in England. If someone has performed poorly on a test, I would probably say "You did badly," full stop! "This is rubbish," full stop! Whereas here [in America], I might phrase it more delicately.

In terms of differential parlance and word meanings, the following ensued:

> Interviewer: You were using a term, "full stop," which over here means "period."

Joe: You're talking about words?

Interviewer: Yeah, do you encounter some of these issues in the classroom?

Joe: Yes. Not only could it be that, it could be, again, the age difference. The "in" words [of popular usage] change, and as you're younger, you're more likely to know the "in" words with teenagers than as you get older. I remember for example, in Germany, this student came in—she had just been playing basketball—and I said to her, "You look hot," meaning. "You look as if you overheated doing so much exercise," and you see, that was inappropriate to say that to her [since the current usage of that expression meant that she looked sexually attractive]. So, it can go [with] age as well.

On the issue of such language differences and what impact they have in the classroom during teaching and learning, spelling came up again, as in Mary's interviews.

Interviewer: Do you find any of these expressions being an issue sometimes in the American classroom?

Joe: I might have to rephrase something, but I think I've been around Americans long enough to get most of them sorted out.

Interviewer: So when you begun dealing with this kind of issue...

Joe: It was harder, yes and British spelling versus American spelling [differences, but better nowadays]....

5.3.3 Inga's communication issues

The communication issues recounted by Mary and Joe are different in nature from Inga's. One could describe Inga as an "externally-proficient" English speaker. Inga was aware of that, and did not mince words admitting that she had initial communication issues. She had previously confessed to the fact that she had never taught in English before. Her positive attitude however, made it possible for her to function well in the American science classroom.

In the course of the interviews, she described her linguistic issues on different levels. For a start, she had learned British English in Germany. That introduced its own issues, and this was further complicated by certain

English words having different meanings in German or vice-versa. She described an example as follows:

> The biggest problem is that you have some words... where you have two words in English and only one word in German and vice-versa, so I sometimes write a word and I understood it and I misused it because I wasn't sure about the second meaning. For example, like in Germany, you only have one word for "speed" and "velocity," so you have to talk about the "vector character" all the time, so I ended up talking about velocity and that velocity is a vector so we have to give it direction... The definition of velocity... is nice when you figure it out, because it makes it easier [to know the correct words to use].

Inga gave other examples in the same vein:

> ...sometimes, little words like "vaporization," "evaporation"—getting them straight is sometimes [difficult]—just in the class situation, the teaching situation. If I sit down and put it on paper, it's pretty clear which is which, but just being busy teaching, I sometimes mix them up.

Inga then talked about the absence of a German direct equivalent term for "acceleration."

> That's a classic. I actually like it because it's hard in Germany to tell the kids that, you know, "Change up" (speaks in German), which is a word for "acceleration," because it's not; because only if we have it as a vector point of view, then the change is an acceleration. That makes it so complicated to explain to an eighth grader what it is.

Before the second interview was over, the interviewer's curiosity about how the language barrier would influence the ease of providing tangible, instructional examples was raised. Inga retorted that although there was a mental barrier in the switching of languages, especially during her teaching activities, pre-though-out, relevant examples do suffice. Diagrams and photographs may all help to drive home the point in the classroom. If possible, a teacher may invest in a dictionary with good photographs, diagrams, and illustrations. The following exchange may illuminate this point:

> Interviewer: In the classroom scenario, when you're talking with them about various things, how are you able to reach them by giving [relevant] examples, etc.? What kind of examples do you normally use? When you're thinking about examples, do you think of German examples or American examples?

Inga: That is the issue. If I think of a German example, I have trouble translating it. The problem is, as soon as I switch the language in the head, the English is gone. The prepared example—I usually think about them before, and then it's not a problem. It's just when the students sometimes come up with something and I just get a very specific German word in my head, then that might cause a problem for like a minute or so, then I have to switch back. That's quite hard. Usually, I just put it down and say, "We'll talk about that tomorrow," and I try to find a picture of something or diagram—which is not a problem in the time of the Internet—that I can show them and talk about it.

I usually have a dictionary here, so if it's something I think would be in the dictionary, then I just look it up. That's not a problem with our students because they're used to it. They have so many things that they look up. So it's not that you're not a good teacher if you need to look them up.

As with Mary's situation, Inga also experienced the issue of spelling, because she learned British English:

I learned British English in Germany. I completely adapted to the American one just because we use Microsoft Word and it gives you the spellings and you get used to them, but that British textbook [we are using] completely messed up everything.

She provided an example of how confusion could have arisen, and how a dictionary at hand was always a good idea:

One of my language issues is that I have a British textbook and I get confused about spelling—and IBs [programs] are actually British—so one day I put two problems on the board and I had "traveling" spelled once with one "l" and one with two "l's,"… and we all didn't know anymore which was correct, so we had to get a dictionary.

Granted all of the above, Inga made progress, largely because of her personal attitude. She was very aware of her limitations and, because of the kind of relationship she had established with her students, was able to learn from them:

My English got better, so they didn't have to correct me that often. I had good luck because in the senior class I had three or four kids who spoke on a native level, German, so I think they trusted me that I know what I'm talking about. It got easier in many ways, harder in other ways.

5.3.4 Kofi's communication issues

Very much like all the other teachers, it did not take much to recognize Kofi as having a foreign accent, although he was well-spoken in British English. It therefore came as no surprise that he had similar issues as the previous interviewees in this book. He mentioned that his issues related to accent, expressions, and differences in word meanings. Kofi emphasized that his local language was "filled with parables" and figurative expressions. Therefore, as opposed to the relatively more "direct approach" to speaking, his native language used the "indirect approach" to address each other. That was an issue for him to be cautious about, as he communicated.

As regards accent, Kofi noted that that was an initial problem in the classroom, and provided an example how this played out:

My first week in class, a number of students kept saying, "You have a beautiful accent." So I found that some of them were concentrating more on the accent than the material I was trying to impart to them. I had the same experiences with the faculty and staff.

That was the positive side of things. On the negative side:

There [were some] of the kids who would say, "You have an accent and you're teaching chemistry?" And the kids shouted, "You have an accent. I don't understand what you're saying," from the back of the classroom. Stuff like that can be disrupting in the class setting, so you have to be really tactical about how to respond....

To such kind of disruptive questions, he recalled what he did in one instance:

I remember one time I had to tell one student who said, "You have an accent"—I asked "Where are you from?" He said "I'm from Georgia." I said, "You have an accent too," and the whole class laughed. He said, "No, I don't have an accent." I said, "Have you heard a New Yorker talk before?" He said, "Yeah, they talk kind of funny." I said, "That's what..." So I had to let him know that everyone has an accent. It's not a bad thing to have an accent because everyone has an accent. It depends on whose perspective you're looking at. If you talk to me, I'd say you have an accent, vice-versa. And it's true we both have accents.

Although the above instance may appear smooth-going albeit rather insipid, Kofi noted that this kind of classroom dynamic did sometimes elicit both emotional and tactful responses from him. In making such responses, Kofi would call on the teacher to observe "caution" and exhibit professionalism. He said that,

> You have to be really willing to see yourself as a helper for the students, otherwise it would have generated serious discipline issues, especially for those of us from a culture where students could not under any condition scream at a teacher, to a culture where anything goes: Everybody has the right to do anything they want to do. So you have to be really tactful in dealing with issues like that.

In the vein of Joe's, Kofi also mentioned some local expressions, which were different in meaning from what he was used to. It therefore took some time for him to get used to them.

> There are some expressions that are local, and there some expressions that are foreign to the American culture. For example, when a student once said to me, "Can I go the restroom?" it did not occur to me that the restroom was what the toilet was, so I asked, "What's wrong?" and he said, "I need to use the restroom." And one student said, "He needs to use the bathroom," and I said, "Oh, OK." You know, it connected! But restroom was not a common vocabulary to me at the time.

Just like the previous interviewees, Kofi managed to survive in the school. For him, the weapon of choice was the use of anecdotes to drive home the point that normality is relative. With that, he was able to teach the students that familiarity breeds the illusion of normality, and that students had to be cautious about making the assumption that their local terminology is ubiquitously admissible:

> I shared a story with my students about "hotdogs" [a kind of rolled meat in the United States] and they realized that... there are certain words that you use that you think that everybody ought to know, but not everybody knows, and there are certain words that I use that I think that everybody ought to know that they do not know. So feel free to ask me, and when you say something that I am not familiar with, I will ask you, and I want you to ask me.

This sounds very much like what the other teachers were trying to tell their own students. Having done this, Kofi placed himself in the shoes of the rest of the teachers in this book: "I let them know that this is a teaching environment, and it's also a learning environment. So I am willing to learn from them, just as much as they are willing to learn from me. So it helped greatly."

Although he was the teacher to these students, he was also willing to be their student.

5.4   Communication Help for Foreigners

For the international teacher, it suffices to know that there are several types of English—and accents—depending on one's national origin. A very seasoned international traveler could possibly tell the continent a person originates, and possibly one's nation or even tribe, after a few sentences. There are, however two main influences on the English language; Britain and America. Most Europeans, Africans, Asians and Australians are likely to speak the British English, and people from the Americas may be more influenced by the American parlance and accent. One may therefore arguably say that there are two types of English: the British and the American.

These two types of English do have the same basic forms, but still have significant differences such as the finer aspects of grammar and punctuation. This becomes obvious when dealing with different academic journals which specifically require either form of English. Therefore, even if one speaks the British English language, one may still have some issues about which to be concerned.

The issue of accent in America is not a simple one because specific accents have their own status. Thus, even if one spoke British grammatical English, those with British or Australian accent are more likely to find favor and acceptance than those with East Indian or Vietnamese accents, for example. Even among the America-born, as noted below, many people with southern and other strong accents seek to reduce it by taking accent reduction classes in order to promote their professional outlook.

There are several agencies in the U.S. which may help people with language (English) mastery difficulties. Some of them are discussed below.

5.4.1 Churches

In large American cities (where most foreign teachers are likely to end up, and the rest in rural towns), many churches provide free English-teaching services with volunteer members. Although the arrangements may differ, one could expect to have "conversational English" meetings once or twice a week. The main missions of such church activities are to help acquire new members, and also reach out to the members of the community. Some churches may therefore use the Bible as the basis of their conversational lessons.

5.4.2 Local schools

Most American schools, for various reasons, are proud to indicate that they have international connections. In this regard, many larger colleges and universities have special units which just deal with international students and faculty (in the larger universities). In order for international students to get admission into American schools, they must take, and score well on the TOEFL (Test of English as a Foreign Language) test. Many of such school units also have programs which help students to prepare for such tests, if such students are already in the U.S. Foreign teachers could take advantage of such programs in the area schools—for a fee.

In cosmopolitan cities, there are several international business professionals who seek to "better" their accents. In fact, there are several America-born business people who seek to change their own accents to that of the mid-western states, (which is considered the American standard especially for newscasters). Such people believe that it makes them appear more "professional," and therefore promotes business. In response to this market, some of the larger universities offer "accent reduction" programs. Such classes may meet about two hours per week, for about 6-8 weeks.

5.4.3 Books and audiovisuals

One could also take advantage of certain books and audiovisuals, such as cassette tapes on the market. All one needs to do is to visit the Internet and do a search for "American" and "accent," and one would get a myriad of information about what books and audio products available. One such search generated hits including: <u>Speak American: A Survival Guide to the Language and Culture of the U.S.A.</u>, in a book and cassette format, by Dileri Borunda Johnston (Random House, 2000.) Such information could be useful for locating useful resources.

5.5 Textbook Issues

Textbooks are at the heart of teaching in America. In most schools, the selection of textbooks is taken seriously, and is done by special, Textbook Adoption Committees, for several reasons. First of all, the contents of textbooks are ideally expected to be suited for the current curriculum of the school district. Secondly, and beyond the obvious content matter, textbooks could sometimes be viewed as politically-, racially-, or religiously-charged, and the list goes on. For these reasons and others, many American public schools may be expected to select their textbooks with some caution. With that said, there are sometimes some other issues for consideration, as was to be discovered by the international teachers featured in this book.

5.5.1 Mary's textbook issues

If there was one thing that got on Mary's nerves, it was the careless use of textbooks by her students in the United States. On this issue, she quickly took action. She elaborated on what transpired between her and her students as follows:

> One of the other major issues I had when I first came was textbooks. I saw a lot of my senior students [during] my first year highlighting the textbooks—and it never crossed my mind that the kids kept the textbooks. They're supposed to pay a book fee, which doesn't anywhere near cover the cost of the text—and biology and science textbooks cost a fortune. I just said, "Don't do that. They are not your books to do that,"—and that was a major flare-up, because half my science budget every year was going towards textbooks that the kids never returned, and it was a major turn-around for me to say to the students, "These are reference books, they are textbooks. If you need anything out of the book, I'll give you a picture or photocopy out of it. Don't mark the books."

She further remarked that this was not an easy policy to put in place, as she found herself in some kind of conflict with parents:

> And I had confrontations in class about that, and confrontations with parents about the textbooks. I just said, "Return the books at the end of the year. You have to return the books." We gave them a book at the beginning of the year, and they kept the textbook." They thought it was for them forever.

At this point, Mary was interrupted by the interviewer: "You use the term reference book...," to which she continued,

> They [should] use it as a reference. It is not their notebook. They don't write in it... Reference! There's plenty of photocopying facilities in the school, if they want a diagram or drawing or something. I would say, "We're lending you these books." It was a major policy shift on behalf of the school and the parents didn't like it. The book fee was something like fifty dollars, and one of those is sixty dollars because I had to import them from England, and it was a huge drain on the science budget when we lost all the physics, chemistry, bio text books.

Most of the kids threw them away, anyway. They didn't want to keep them, or if they handed them back they were so badly marred, nobody else wanted to keep them—and now everybody does that [returning the textbooks], but I was the first one to try and organize that. It was a complete waste of money and laziness on behalf of the kids. They would never take notes. They would just highlight the textbook. It was never constructive thinking.

America is a very wealthy nation by any standard. Even some of the poorer schools may have certain enviable (but not necessarily educationally useful) resources. Mary eventually confessed that her thrifty worldview concerning the use of resources was influenced by her previous experiences in other countries, where the students were poor, and their schools had to ration resources. She made some statements to explain this point, including the following:

One of the big differences is we have enough books for everybody here, and my other school in England we had three kids to one book. There just wasn't enough to go around.

Back home we expect kids to take notes; have a notebook. I'd give them notes, we'd work in the class, and they'd use the textbook to read in advance, research an essay, or as a support to what I'm doing with them.

Interviewer: So you had to leave the books in the classroom?

Mary: Yeah, I had one set of books for all my classes and it was one to three and basically if I want or need anything like books and equipment, I could go and get it.

The [American] school would provide you with that because the parents would help. And so certain teaching resources [are a] huge difference in what's available and what wasn't. I tend to be a bit frugal. I think my experiences at my old school are reflecting on the way I behave, so I won't waste money. I make sure I get what I want, but I don't pay a penny more for it than I have to, because I'm used to controlling a budget and not having a lot of money. Sometimes it surprises me how much things like photocopying [are so cheap here.] You want a photocopy? Here it is! You used to have to pay for photocopying. Things like that will help support your teaching.

Regarding her American students, Mary remarked that although "The kids: they don't feel privileged, but they are."

5.5.2 Joe's textbook issues

With regard to textbook issues, Joe mentioned that the obvious differences had to do with the areas of emphasis. For example in chemistry, he noted that:

> If you look at the average American textbook, you'd fine a very small section on organic chemistry. Grab the average British textbook you'd find a larger section on organic chem ... If you get an English chem book out, you'd find the anode is always positive and the cathode is always negative. You get an American textbook out, and it's sometimes negative and it's sometimes positive.

Although the content matter may not be significantly different, it may still be advisable for international teachers to carry with them sample textbooks for personal reference. This may help them to verify any information in their current American textbooks, where different, thereby avoiding personal confusion. It is also helpful to have such a resource to show students (and other American teaching colleagues), since a new teacher may, on occasion have to "prove him or herself."

As has been hinted earlier in previous narrations, trust is an important issue for the teacher, and may be even more so for the new foreign teacher. Inga, for example, recalled that, being a German teacher with some initial language difficulties, it was nice that she had some students who spoke German proficiently. Through them, she could provide her class the assurance that she was competent in her subject matter:

> I had good luck because in the senior class I had three or four kids who spoke on a native level, German, so I think they trusted me that I know what I'm talking about.

The simple reason is that, although most foreign teachers have very strong background in content matter, students may not be aware of that, and may (rather joyfully) challenge the "facts." Having a textbook which "proves the facts" will help to absolve the teacher and ease any unfounded suspicions.

5.5.3 Inga's textbook issues

During the three interviews, Inga did not indicate that there were any issues with her textbooks. For this reason, a follow-up interview was done in order to find out more about it. She did answer that, owing to the IB curriculum, it was difficult to make a comparison, although the typical German textbook was more content-oriented:

> Inga: That question is hard to answer. I have British and American science books. And I use mainly an American college book because there is no reasonable IB physics book out there. In Germany we have very specific books going with our syllabus. As this is not the case for IB, comparing is hard. I also only taught up to 10th grade in Germany, where the books have to be very different anyway. Anyhow, the college book that I use in class could never be a college book in Germany, because that is stuff covered in high school.

The above statements reveal an interesting point about the contents of the American curriculum. In line with what some curriculum critics have characterized as "a mile wide and an inch deep," American college textbooks may only begin to cover, in depth, what other nations' school systems may have already covered at the secondary school level, especially schools with sixth forms (being the 6th and 7th years in high school in the British system). Many African, European (Russian), and Asian (Japanese, Taiwanese, and South Korean) students have personally attested to this fact in my conversations with them. In fact, students who skip sixth form education can comfortably succeed in American colleges for this reason.

5.5.4 Kofi's textbook issues

In harmony with the previous sections, Kofi found the textbooks he currently used to be of very little use and especially lacking in appropriate content. He confessed that he was inclined to compare them to what he used in his own high school days in Ghana. Notwithstanding his own bias, he cautioned that teachers should be aware that the general intention of American high schools is to prepare and produce students for college. The problem, however, was the "lack of content" in the textbooks, which denied the students of the requisite knowledge for success when they arrive in college:

> ... [The high school course may have] had no content, and that's the problem that many of the high school students are facing when they go to college. The college curriculum is still content-based [in] foundation, I mean, just general chemistry [course in] first year is still content-based. In the high school, it's not!

He also noted that the lack of appropriate content in the textbooks was compounded by the fact that they did not harmonize with the curriculum requirements of his school system. For that, he voiced out his opinion several times:

> They [the curriculum requirements of my current school system and the textbooks] are two disjointed programs, and I think I have voiced this out at several teachers' science workshops. [Interestingly] the [curriculum] was defined as a great program for the county. The only problem is that there are no textbooks that follow the [curriculum].

He found this problem at "at every level in all the sciences." For this reason, he reasoned that teachers had the additional responsibility of having to become extra resourceful in order to provide appropriate content matter for their students, and satisfy the curriculum requirements. For the fresh, inexperienced teacher in the U.S., he thought that this could be a difficult proposition:

> The textbook is literally helpless when it comes to the curriculum, so teachers are having to come up with alternatives, and so it makes it very difficult for first year teachers and inexperienced teachers to really teach a good lesson to the students, because the textbook does not support the course structure or the curriculum.

He provided a personal example by noting that, owing to the incongruity of the textbook with the curriculum, he had "not been able to issue any textbooks to any of [his] classes." He taught his students with personal notes and other supplementary materials he had collected.

In conclusion, Kofi would note that,

> Teachers have had to be really more resourceful. It puts a lot of demand on the science teachers particularly to be more creative and to adopt [and] steer the students in the direction that they are to go to be properly prepared for college. So there is that gap.

5.6   Teaching Method and Related Issues

The relationship between student attitudes and teaching methods approximate natural pairs. Students who have good attitudes are easy to work with, and one could cover more material with them, using an effective and yet easiest instructional approach: the lecture method. This point is very crucial for any new teacher entering the U.S., since American students in general would find ways to communicate to the teacher if they do, or do not appreciate his or her teaching method.

It is very common for American students and parents to send notes of appreciation to the teachers for helping students to achieve in school, or get through certain situations. On the other hand, a teacher may experience a difficult classroom situation, depending on the nature of the students in that class. Teaching method and related issues will be found to be very important for international teachers' success. This is a topic discussed at length in the next chapter.

Here again, it is useful to learn from what others faced, and how they managed the issues.

5.6.1 Mary's teaching method and related issues

In her American, private school, Mary noted that,

Because the kids are better behaved, I can lecture. I don't have to resort to educational tricks to keep the kids occupied, which I used to have to do at my old school: They had short attention span. These kids [in my current American classes] tend to be a lot more focused and committed toward their course. So they're prepared to work.

Mary explained what she meant by "educational tricks":

I resort to tricks like, "I'm going to give you a test in ten minutes. Read this. I'm going to test you on that… Other examples included, "color things in, or cut and paste or crosswords, or "Let's have a quiz."

These were rather educationally-unproductive activities she did, in order to pass the time in a difficult classroom situation. In a productive classroom, there was mutual "trust," which also reflected on the nature of her instruction.

A point worth noting at this juncture is the relationship between the rigor of curriculum and teaching method. Although the term "rigor" may have various definitions, it is used here to point out that teachers are expected to keep up with their curricula, especially with current education reforms. Several states have educational standards or curricula which they expect their teachers to follow closely. For this reason, teachers may have to be rather rigorous in their pacing and coverage of content. This means that the learning objectives for a given subject are more than those found in several industrialized nations. American teachers therefore need to be very innovative in order to meet the demands of rigor in the curriculum, and at the same time, stylistically teach to the suit attitudes of the students.

When she was asked how the rigor of the curriculum influences her teaching techniques, Mary responded that "speed" became the operative word; an endeavor just to cover the material, not necessarily concentrating of the teaching process itself:

Yeah, it did; not for the better. I have a lot of material to get through, so the only way I can get through it is by lecturing, and lecturing requires commitment on both sides: me to get it right and the students to listen— and that's where the trust comes in. They trust me to deliver the right info at the right time... [So] they tend to be a lot more focused on what's going on and will cooperate with me to get to the end point, because they do take ownership in their own education on the whole.

The atmosphere of Mary's classes, besides her teaching methods, was driven by what she perceived to be the behavior or attitudes of her students. She noted that her teaching style in certain past situations, "tended to be determined by the need to keep some sort of discipline in the classroom." For the classes comprising students who "reluctantly" attended school, and therefore had attitudinal problems,

Lessons had to be so much more carefully controlled and constructive, and I'd find that I'd have my materials ready and keep going as much as I can, and have my break if I think it's appropriate to do that.

[Lessons] tended to be highly structured. I always had plenty of work for the kids to do, no doubt I made breaks. Everything was tightly controlled for me: It was the only was I could maintain security. It was different in the lab. You had to be careful of the kids playing with the gas tops, playing with the equipment....

She compared her particular British students who were rather problematic to her current students, who were relatively less so. She delineated the major factor for their differentiation as being that, "it was just the case of kids being in school because they had to be there, and that changes the nature of the way you teach."

Another factor controlling teaching approach she observed was class size. To the contentment of the reader, American schools are probably likely to have fewer students than elsewhere in the world. Besides that, there are current educational reform initiatives in American schools. One of the objectives for educational reform is to further reduce class sizes.

Depending on the school district and resources available, one may expect to have 25-30 students in typical high school classes, and slightly fewer in middle schools. Specialized classes, such as Special Education may have as few as 5-10 students per class, and 5-15 for Advanced Placement science classes (roughly equivalent to Advanced Level or the International Baccalaureate in the British educational system). Again, the class sizes may depend on the number of students available within the school district, thus explaining the wide range in numbers.

Mary indicated her contentment with her American school's relatively smaller class-sizes. The typical American teacher, however, holds the sentiment that class sizes are still too large. Their concern is that it is more difficult to control classes which have too many students (especially when teaching American students who generally expect a more democratic classroom, and may need more personal involvement in the learning process). Coupled with this is the expectation that teachers use different instructional approaches in order to reach most, if not all their students (see more under Differentiated Instruction). On this issue, Mary observed the following:

> Also class sizes make a difference. My class sizes have been reasonable [in America]. If you spend a large proportion [of effort]—sometimes 90% of my effort and concentration would be spent on 1% of the class [students], and that would be discipline—just trying to get the kids to stay in their seats or to stop talking or do some work. ... I find that that's not an issue here [in my current United States school], but it used to be an issue in England, in London.

Mary did not hesitate to make the point that, although she was an international teacher, she was still able to provide useful and relevant examples to drive home her lessons:

> Interviewer: In dealing with classroom situation when you're trying to relate an experience to them, how do you bring practicality to theory? For example, when you're citing an example, how do you do that? Where do you fetch your examples?

> Mary: Where do I get them from? I think carefully about using examples in science because if you use the wrong kind of example, you can give the wrong impression, and so I tend to use the same ones. At the end I always say, "Does that make sense to you?" "Can you relate the example to the theory?" If they say "No," I say, "We'll have another go." If the kids are very open—and I appreciate them being open—I'd say, "If you don't get this, please say so and we'll do it again."

Mary was intentional and directed in the use of her examples because she wanted to broaden the horizons of her students:

> But using examples, I'd say for instance, "In England, you might find this happening," in ecology for instance; I would try to use different examples from around the world... I want the students to realize there is something

going on outside the States, so I will try and explain, "In Germany they did this, in Portugal they did that." Mr. Keys [another international teacher in her current school] would talk about Africa and tell stories about Africa. I would tell stories about Asia—and I've traveled to Korea and the Far East—and whatever and just try and bring it in; that it's not just the States…

The very idea of being an international teacher also means that one has the natural asset of knowing about different worlds, and therefore different perspectives. It may therefore come in handy to lean back on one's own native knowledge to make sense of a lesson, and simultaneously broaden the students' global outlook on the subject matter.

For advice on how to cite examples, Mary would say, "Play it by ear. You have to be careful with that... It's nice to have some background experience to fill the students in." She went on, illuminating at length, an example on how she made global relevance as the interview progressed:

> An example we faced the other day was, we needed to look at AIDS-HIV infection, and of course being in the States, that refocuses to a large extent on huge fund-raising efforts. And when I told them where the AIDS problem is really huge is in Sub-Saharan Africa, they really hadn't considered it. To them, HIV and AIDS is an American thing because only American rock stars and film stars used to die from it, and it was like, "Oh, you can find it somewhere else? The infection is huge, devastating." I just couldn't express it enough, and I actually said to them, "When people talk about AIDS and HIV cases, please don't be limited to "AID Chicago" or the local thing; think globally. And we talked about the effect that HIV infection has on the infrastructure: people dying; businesses closing down; all sorts of things. I really think they hadn't considered that. Just one example of trying to get them to think outside the States.

Mary provided another example, which would conclusively drive home her point:

> When we were doing pollution and were looking at acid rain and global warming, they really weren't that concerned … it wasn't until they looked at some statistics [then] they realized it's more than just leaving your engine running in the car or leaving your air condition running, etc. We compared populations and pollution—and I don't think a lot of these kids think beyond the U.S. Kids are naturally selfish anyway, but they don't realize the effect the U.S. has on the rest of the world.

5.6.2 Joe's teaching method and related issues

Joe agreed with Mary in asserting that student behavior in the classroom influences teaching style. He noted that in an inner city school in England, certain swear terms may be heard frequently. Consequently,

> One of the things you have to maintain in your classroom is discipline, and some of the best teachers I've seen for handling troubled teens have sworn a lot; a heck of a lot. That would be totally inappropriate in many classrooms. The bottom line for me was that in the particular classroom where they were using that type of language, they were getting the kids to do a lot better. So was it justified? In my view it was.

Another point Joe made was that, a teacher is only as good as the caliber of the class being taught: "So I can do the lab as badly as the worst student in my class." His reason was that in his current school (where he has more trust in his students), more of his time was devoted to ensuring that things worked well, thus ensuring more successful teaching and learning.

5.6.3 Inga's teaching method and related issues

Inga did mention on several occasions her dislike of the high number of students per class in her previous school in Germany, and how that affected teaching method. She mentioned that where there were too many students per class, it was more difficult to do more thoughtful, student-centered activities, and vice-versa. She was content to have small classes in her current American school, in which she could use inquiry-oriented methods:

> I had only one class which was small enough—a project class, where they started teaching physics in 7th grade [with] only 12 students. We really could do lab work.

> I had a group this year of five in high level physics, and its wonderful, because you sit around a table and you say, "Let's [do] something!" And they go out of the room and get the equipment that they want, to put something together. They get the generator, and they just basically do so much things on their own, because you see what they are doing, and they know each other so well, and they learned to work well with each other over the years—And for me, it's perfect, in that sense of class size.

In the situation where there were too many students per class, the inquiry orientation gave way to cook-book approach to teaching:

In the big classes, yeah, I think teachers are quite happy if students just sit and do what they are told to do, and they don't teach you much about being responsible for your actions, because they take the responsibility by giving you instructions....

Very specific instructions, not just giving you instructions saying, "Go and look what you make out of it." Just giving you detailed, step-by-step instructions of what you are supposed to do, and if you follow you're fine.

Although the cook-book and all-lecture teaching approaches may be found in many American schools, such practices are being discouraged by the current education reforms and practices. Foreign teachers should therefore refresh their memories of the different teaching approaches available. In part, effective teaching or instructional practices may help to minimize behavioral problems in the classroom, as the students are more likely to be constructively engaged in the teaching-learning process. A section on instructional practices effective for teaching is included in this book.

5.6.4 Kofi's teaching method and related issues

Kofi described his teaching methods as being partly determined by the availability of resources. He commented that he personally favored a "hands-on approach" to teaching and learning. However, in the situations back home where there were limited resources, he resorted to the lecture approach. When, during the interviews, he was asked: "So do you think there have been any changes or differences made in the way you teach, compared to the way you used to teach back home?" He had the following in response:

Oh, yes. A lot of changes and differences. Here [in America], I found that because we have the facilities and equipment, my teaching style is more hands-on, participatory, and very little lecture, whereas, back home it was the other way around. My style has always been participatory, but because of lack of equipment, I've had to do a lot more lecturing than I normally would have preferred, and so this system here [in America] is good for what I normally would be doing.

As has been noted before, the international teachers may find themselves having to modify their teaching styles—not so much because there are more resources available in American school, but that multiple teaching approaches are demanded by the nature of the American teaching profession—in order to reach a diverse student body.

Kofi also used a lot of anecdotes or stories during his teaching lessons. He was inadvertent and eloquent as the stories came, during his interviews. He alluded, in several instances to the idea that his delivery method was in agreement with his African traditional background, where the language is flavored with proverbs and stories. To him, this was a way to more effectively relate to his students and concurrently win their attention. In that respect, Kofi said that:

> Back in Africa, most of our speech, even our language is filled with parables. We hardly speak directly to a person about their faults. We tell it in the form of a parable. That's very different here.

Although Kofi found speech patterns to be different in the United States, that did not deter him from the use of anecdotes to reach his students. He indicated that this was a common occurrence in his classes, as he purposefully tried to make both the students' and his own presence in his classes relevant—since many of his students were struggling with school attendance and school work:

> I used to tell my students how I was the only one in my graduating middle school class who went to high school—out of twenty-one students who graduated from middle school—to let them know how privileged they are, and to let them know that because they have that privilege, there is an expectation on their lives: They can't afford to just fool around and think no one cares about them and that nothing can happen; [that] their lives don't really mean anything: it belongs to them. So I use that kind of approach to help them know that they are here for a purpose, and so am I.

He noted that, "You have to see yourself as a helper for the students." Therefore, during his instructional enterprises, he would focus his attention not only on academic work but also on the total welfare of his students:

> I also let them know it's important that they keep their minds on their schoolwork because it can make all the difference in their thought process and in their lives. So I probably do a lot more counseling—not officially—and I do a lot more one-on-one: I talk to the students individually many times. If I find a student is misbehaving in class, I call them aside and talk to them after class. Sometimes I let them know I'm there to help them; I see their frustrations and that they're trying to deal with them the wrong way, and they need help, and I'm there to help them, and many times it worked: Not all the time. There are some who have just decided, "I just don't like you and I don't care what you think."

5.7   Teacher-Student Relations

5.7.1 The nature of American high school students

The nature of American high school students may be initially elusive to international teachers for several reasons. First of all international teachers are likely to compare their American students to those in their native countries. That would be a major mistake. Although their overall cognitive developments may be comparable, their socio-cultural developments may be worlds apart. This may be in line with the concept of cultural differentiation, which postulates that different cultures have different values and needs and therefore have different areas of emphasis and mastery.

To many foreign teachers, American students may appear to be relatively more socially mature for their ages. This is because American students may be found to be typically loaded with general (if uncoordinated) information. They are also relatively more aware of the issues of "rights"; issues with which people in other countries may become familiar only as adults.

American students are generally fully aware of their rights to the democratic freedoms that America stands for. They are aware of their rights to speech, religion, and education, to mention a few. If they smoke, drink, or are sexually active, they are more aware of their rights to engage in exactly those acts (or not), and would defend themselves under the protection of the American constitution. They are therefore much more independent, both of their teachers' opinions, and even their parents'.

Unlike many parts of the world, America is a place where there are ample supplies of employment opportunities, with some to spare for the youth. For this reason, many American high school students are also part-time workers, and oftentimes car owners. They are consequently financially savvy, and semi-independent. There may even be some high school students who may be found to be living on their own (depending on their ages and state). Some or all of the factors above individually or synergistically make some American students relatively more independent of their parents and other authority figures (like teachers).

Even not totally independent of their parents, many American students may become "latchkey" children, once they reach the middle or high school. These are children who stay at home by themselves after school until work hours are over, because both parents may have a financial need to work to support the family (Celente, 1997). They are so-called latchkey children because, in many American cities, children stay indoors, and may not venture outdoors without adult supervision. This is in reaction to fear of potential violence and other accidents within certain communities.

Although still exhibiting some typical adolescent traits, American students may still show certain surprisingly responsible characteristics for their age that may surprise foreign teachers. This mixture of adolescent behavior and maturity could be very confusing. Although many high school students, for example, may work and save up for a car, and may understand the business world (because they might pay for their own car insurance), they may still not relate to the adult world owing to lack of experience. Time brings on more maturity, as may be expected of any adolescents in any society.

There is also severe competition in almost everything from athletics to physical appearances (as models), to playing chess or the violin. Success in each of these competitions could mean a college scholarship with great financial rewards to the winners. The American student is therefore sometimes saddled with the burdens of physically training their bodies through often rigorous football, baseball, soccer, basketball, swimming, drill team, or any number of team practices. Through physical and emotional pain, many American students would still try to succeed in something, in addition to academic work: They are indefatigable in this respect.

In fact, academic work is just one of the things the American student may be engaged in daily. Unlike students in other countries around the world where all they may probably do is study—perhaps in a boarding school— American students are encouraged to do community work and create an impressive resume in order to qualify for some of the very competitive colleges.

In an edition of *The Charlotte Observer* (Jan 18, 2004, pp. 1G and 4G), staff writer Elizabeth Leland cogitated: "Why Jenny can't sleep: Today's competitive teens survive on a few hours' rest a night. Is this what it takes to succeed?" Jenny, a high school teenager (18 years old) took 5 Advanced Placement subjects, was the president of the French Club, president of the government club, and captain of the World Quest team. She volunteered at the public library at the weekends, at a U.S. Senator's congressional office on Fridays, and at Habitat for Humanity program. She was also a member of a U.S. Representative's Youth Advisory Council. According to the author, Jenny was "making sure her high school resume will help her get into a good college and eventually a good law school." (p. 4G)

Although distinct from some other American students in terms of her academic ambitions, Jenny is not exceptional as compared to her ambitious peers. In certain public schools, Jenny may be a representative of her classmates. After all, they are her competition, and are achieving similar feats! If not working for money, many American students are engaged in some form of extra-curricular activities. All these activities are both physically- and mentally-demanding. Although a very broad generalization, it is still instructional for international teachers to bear this image of the American student in mind as they enter their domain.

In short, American students are probably different from what international teachers are used to. According to a 2000 newspaper report, "educators from Mexico and the Philippines left because they didn't feel comfortable.... They were well-qualified...but many were used to managing classrooms differently and found U.S. students disrespectful." (Cook, 2000) Although this may initially pose as a problem, it is very possible to teach them through better understanding. This is because they have various strengths which international teachers could use as leverages to form better relationships with them, and consequently better instruction.

5.7.2 Mary's Teacher-Student Relations

Mary observed that there were great differences between her British and American high school students. She noted such differences in several instances of the interviews. One of the main areas where this showed up was in her own relationships with the students through in-classroom, and out-of-class relationships.

Mary mentioned that she stays in teaching because of her students. Notwithstanding, she realized all to soon that her American students had a very different view of their teachers, and felt very uninhibited to visit them for various reasons, on their own terms. To this, Mary vented about the amounts of time her students exacted of her: "Some students seem to think it's their time, not mine, and that's an issue that crops up every now and again." Owing to this peculiar problem, Mary had to resort to alternative arrangements in order to get her work done:

> In fact I often come into the lab on Saturdays, occasionally Sundays if I need to sit down and write my reports. I can't sit and write my reports on the computer during the day because some people [keep] coming in talking to me, and kids want help.

She also perceived some differences between the nature of her current student and those of her previous British school. For one thing, she observed that the American high school students liked to engage in conversations and ask more questions during classes. This was different from what she was accustomed to. In the course of the interview, these issues were addressed in great detail, as follows:

Interviewer: So dealing with attitudes: Do the kids normally talk back because there is the general sense that kids over here have some kind of freedom?

Mary: Definitely. It is different: They will answer back. I find that American students or students who've been to an American school are much happier to stand up and say things, like they would stand up in front of an assembly and speak and they have the confidence to do it. I have some British students: I can't get them to say anything in the class. It's like me. I don't like standing up and speaking in front of people. There's a natural reticence, certainly with Brits, to get to stand up and speak, but the Americans would either answer back or they would contribute, or they're happy to have a dialogue with you.

And it's a confidence [issue] I think. I don't know where it comes from, but we have noticed it—the other British teachers and I always agree that getting one of the American students to stand up to do a presentation [is easy], but you try to get a Brit to do it and ...they're much more reserved. And I think other nationalities are the same. I don't know about other Europeans, [but] some of our Asian students are quite reserved; some of our African students are quite reserved: They won't do it. They find it difficult to stand up and deliver. Whether it's a language thing or not, I don't know ... There's no reason for Brits not to do it, but they won't say anything. On the whole, they're quiet.

The sense of freedom of American students in a classroom comprising a variety of cultural backgrounds can create a peculiar problem for teachers coming from societies made up of mostly one culture. In a situation where one group of students are more vocal or active than others, it is important for teachers to be aware of strategies for leveling the playing field so that the learning needs of all the students may be addressed. Mary, in this regard, provides a look at this issue, and how it could manifest itself in class:

I have to sometimes stop some of the home-based [American] kids from butting in and asking questions, and I'd just say, "Just wait your turn," and then I'd take questions in order. It was like that the lesson I just had. I was going to ask them questions about their exam, but they wouldn't stop asking questions. [So] we didn't do any review. I was going to review with them. They were just asking so many questions about things and butting in. I didn't get any work done. Sometimes you have to stop that. It's a comfort level—asking questions, I think.

In the situation above, taking students' questions in an order may be helpful. Mary could also have reserved all the questions for later in the lesson. Another option is to have all questions written on a piece of paper and either placed in a container, or passed forward. Depending on the amount of time available, she could have addressed chosen some randomly for discussion.

For what it's worth, Mary nevertheless benefited from her students' freer sense of conversation and more open relationship, since she did learn a lot from them, especially during her induction year:

> I needed the year to [learn to] work out how things work, who has the power in the school—because it's never who you think it is, and very often the students… they were the ones that told me how to get things done. They showed me how to use the library, photocopier, where the coffee pot machine was, where to get sandwiches at lunchtime. The kids were great. The kids here are great kids.

In her relationships with the students, Mary found herself having to justify her actions to her students. She noted that such justifications would not be necessary in a British school, since the hierarchical structures of the British society precluded such a social intercourse between an instructor and his or her students. For example, she stated that, "I am very good with discipline and control, so I didn't have a problem; I could also control kids with my demeanor and my voice," and, "They [the students] felt intimidated; I needed to do that. I was a successful teacher." However, when she relocated to her American school—a situation where the students had a greater sense of freedom—she then realized that,

> That heavy-handed type of control that I had was inappropriate. It took me a long while to realize that I could relax; I could actually smile; I could [converse] with the students, and it wasn't going to undermine my teaching, or my discipline or anything else, and that was one of the hardest things for me being in [a different] school when I started.

In fact, in America, it is not only the students who expect to have a "relaxing" classroom atmosphere: the administration may also expect it, depending on the school. Although an unspoken rule, more and more American schools are being run like businesses with the students viewed as the customers; more so in the private schools, but also in the more affluent public schools. There are the American sayings, "The customer is king," and, "The customer is always right." Teachers, through the conduit of "professionalism," are expected to make all students feel at home and develop a public relations approach to dealing with both students and especially their parents. This approach has its merits and problems. Brain-based research proposes that relaxed environments are positive for learning. Caution should however be exercised so that students who may not know how to comport themselves may not create chaos in the relaxed environment. Class monitoring techniques are valuable in this choice of classroom environment.

In the end, Mary emphatically noted that her relationship with a student "would depend on the student," and that naturally elicited a teaching style which "tended to be determined by the need to keep some sort of discipline in the classroom" if the need arose.

5.7.3 Joe's Teacher-Student Relations

In terms of teacher-student relations, Joe asserted that in England, particularly in the eighth to tenth grades, fear governed what they did to a large degree. The teacher was seen as an authority figure, thereby limiting teacher-student personal relationships.

Joe had less of a barrier to cross when he came to America. Even back in England, he was somewhat unconventional and iconoclastic, because that he was able to break the societal hierarchical structures in order to reach his students. To him, there was value in making a difference in the lives of kids who otherwise would have no future. Excerpts from his interviews may help illuminate this point:

> The hardest part is that I was a form teacher, which means I was in charge of the social development of a few of these kids, and they always gave me the bottom band, and keeping them out of juvenile court was the big thing, so I ran a fishing club... I used to write fishing articles, and for the money I used to get from that, I would subsidize them on a fishing trip, and we used to run it in a very democratic way, so everybody could get some subsidy. ... We'd have a committee to decide how much each paid, and everybody knew that if they mocked up, that was it; they were kicked out! So peer pressure—I never had any trouble with them on these fishing trips. They were great! They knew, and their parents knew that their son was safe when the fishing season runs up: he's not going to get in trouble, because, if he's out all night, he's not out doing drugs, not going to get in trouble burglarizing some house: He's all-night fishing, probably with me.

Joe told another story worth mentioning:

I remember in my bio class back in England. Because I had enough time, I had to do the home environment from a biological point of view, so I went beyond that and the normal biological: hygiene in the kitchen and bathroom, etc. and went into how to rent your own apartment, the difference between a mortgage and renting, what social services in the town could you apply for, what were your legal rights as a tenant.

Interviewer: And this was a biology class?

Joe: Yes, and some of the students afterward said that was the most important thing. The complaint that many of the students still had was that there was nothing they were learning in school that was directly applicable to them, and they could leave school and still not know how to open a bank account and how to set about renting a property.

It therefore comes as no surprise that when Joe continued that although he left England in the 1980s, he was still in contact with some of the students he taught and had some coming down to visit him in America.

Even under the toughest circumstances, then, Joe had found a way to deal with student behavior problems. He however did not claim perfection in this endeavor, since he had his share of discipline issues back in England, and resorted to other avenues for resolution. One of such was the use of humor in dealing with vulgar language in the instructional environment:

You can't react to every blasphemy that comes out. You tell them if they mind moderating their language. There are various ways with British students to get around that. You know, "Would you please add -'rying out loud.'" They would just look at me. They've gone "Oh, f--k--'rying out loud!" You know, [perhaps] they've dropped something and they didn't mean to swear, they've done it, and I'd say look, if you just add "'rying out loud," it's not swearing is it? "Oh, for crying out loud!" ("Fuck-rying out loud!"), and it's not said with malice. It's not a big deal. There's a difference between the language one accepts in a certain situation and the language one accepts in others, and how it's used. I'd rather [they] didn't swear, but swearing with venom; that's meant to hurt us. Some people swear a lot, some cultures swear a lot. Some cultures hardly swear at all.

In any situation in a classroom, if you could diffuse it easily and quickly with a laugh then get on with what you're doing, then that's best. I had one kid say to me, "What would you say to me, Mr. Key, if I said you suck?" I said "I'd presume you'd give me instruction on how to use a drinking straw." (Laughter) He was angry. He [then] just burst out laughing and the rest of the class laughed. As a Brit, [you suck] is not part of my vocabulary. The way that it was said told me that it was inappropriate.

In the United States, Joe was still involved in students' lives outside the classroom, noting that the soccer field for example was a place to build bridges with students: He therefore coached soccer. Without saying too much of it, he noted that, if a new teacher were coming to teach in the United States, this would be his advice, in terms of teacher-student relations:

I'd warn them that [in America], it's a more informal situation between students and teachers. You cannot deal with these students as they were used to in England. Their opinions are going to count more. I cannot imagine any case in England where a student would go and complain to the principal. That's likely to happen here. That's why you have to be a bit more careful. I still think good teaching practice is good teaching practice, so whatever systems they used in England with minor modifications would work here.

5.7.4 Inga's teacher-students relations

The theme regarding teacher-student(s) relations was the primary personal interest of Inga's. For this reason, in all three interviews, several of her responses took a tangent to connect with this theme. In agreement with all the teachers featured in this book, Inga immediately observed that there was no way to avoid American students. Her classroom was totally shared with the students; they came in and out when they wanted to talk about what topic they wanted, even during break times:

I have lunch with the IB students—which is good, but sometimes not good because they know where you are …. You can give them some lunch detention, which is sometimes quite nice because they then do their work here. I actually work a lot over lunch with the seniors, so we had like two lunches a week [last year] where we studied some questions.

On further questioning, Inga continued that she had good reasons for allowing the students to come in to eat in her classroom (which was also her office). (It must be noted again here that in American schools, students go to the teachers' classrooms for their classes.):

First of all, it's a physics lab, so we don't have any chemicals here. We don't have any dead animals, because it's not biology and they know as soon as we do a lab, there's no food in this room. So they come for lunch and then it's like a study room. It's the way the tables are here. They're like lab tables so it's not a big deal. It's not a problem unless they disturb anybody. Sometimes they come to just socialize; talk about something

Inga obviously took these relationships in stride, since she both accommodated them, and even had a preference for her students to be in her room. This can be seen in her description of the kinds of latitudes she provided them, and also the flavor of her conversations with them. In continuing the train of conversation above, she was asked:

Interviewer: You were laughing at a lot of things. How would you describe a classroom scenario when some of these things were happening?

Inga: I think it's crazy. I can't describe it. Students say I should be a comedian. I'm not sure if that's a good thing or not. I think the students, after a few weeks, get an idea how far they can go, and I'm usually open as long as they do their work. So as long as we have classes, they can bring something to drink. If it's in the morning they can bring a bagel or latte, [or] whatever. I prefer that they sit here and eat while they're working instead of complaining that they're hungry or really not working because their blood sugar level is so low that there is no way of working.

Interviewer: Would this happen in a German classroom?

Inga: No, never! Because if I [did that], I would get in trouble with my [administration]. I think it is way easier here [and] the students know we're all very different. So if I teach differently because I'm German then I teach differently because I'm German.

The last point above is worth noting and exploiting as an international teacher. Within professional guidelines, teaching colleagues and students do allow international teachers to invest their natural differences in the classroom, and may even expect it. Within reason, new teachers may enjoy such differences, and that may help to ease the pain of transition. In fact, foreign teachers may find the American public to be very welcoming of them as teachers of their children, since such teachers may expose their children to other cultures.

On the other hand, Inga also touched on issues of stereotyping, as she dealt with her students. Although she did not think that this was negative kind of stereotyping on the part of the students, this is something to be expected, especially for teachers who come from nations about which the students may be curious.

Interviewer: So you think the students expect you to be different from other teachers?

Inga: I don't think they expect it. I think when they come into the classroom thcy don't expect you to be in a certain way. Yes they do because I'm a physics teacher, so that's one thing that would never change because physics teachers are scary, but I think we worked on that a little bit (laughs) this year.

Interviewer: So they have no stereotypes [about your being German]?

Inga: Oh yeah, they have stereotypes but they're aware that they have stereotypes, because they talk about them. They work on stereotypes.

Interviewer: What kind of stereotypes do they have?

Inga: That they have to be punctual when they come to my class, which is not that German anymore, but I still can get upset about it.

Interviewer: So they don't think it's necessarily German?

Inga: They think it's German but we all adjust over time. Sometimes I'm not so sure.

Still on the issue of stereotyping, Inga then went on to address an interesting observation with her students, as they curiously asked questions about rather unexpected possibilities. To such questions, she saw an opportunity to indulge the students in some level of educational exposure:

There was one incident in the senior class—and I already taught them for six months—and, in the middle of a discussion about physics, a student asked me whether my grandfather fought for Hitler; and that was in the middle of the whole thing. And I stopped and said, "We can talk about this. We probably can talk about this now." So we talked about the whole thing; of what I knew about my family and what I didn't know about them. It was very interesting. It's actually something you usually don't talk often about, so it was a little bit awkward... We talked about what ideas they had and what they thought, and I think they talked about it in history class too. There might have been a connection, but it really came up in the middle of a completely different discussion.

As in the case above, foreign teachers may find a lot of Americans they meet—especially within the school context—more curious about them and their backgrounds or cultures than merely negatively stereotyping them. In fact, as is hinted in Inga's case, foreign teachers could easily make themselves valuable resources as specialists to their schools in several ways. For example, they could intentionally (or inadvertently) become the resident authorities on their native countries. The responsibility that comes with this is that one has to refresh one's memories of facts concerning their country or even continent. Foreign teachers are therefore ambassadors of sorts for their nations, and their actions, for better or worse, may become symbolic and representative of their nations.

Precautions in teacher-student relationships. Depending on the personality of the teacher involved and the school, students may take a special liking to a foreign teacher. However, a note of caution: Inga's case was a special situation, and she was teaching in a private school with several international students and different cultural expectations. In the public schools however, teachers need to be very careful about their relationship with their students, especially from adolescent ages and above. There have been several instances whereby teachers have been terminated from their positions because of inappropriate relationships with their students, even of the same sex. Even though the nature of many inappropriate relationships were clearly noted to be of sexual nature, it is sometimes very difficult to clearly define the rather nebulous limits of human relationships.

Many instances in the news have involved male teachers and teenage girls. However, there have been a few instances involving female teachers and their teenage male students. Owing to the seriousness and rather salacious nature of this issue, inappropriate relationships between teachers and their students do become news stories for both TV and newspaper reporters, and therefore a public relations problem for the schools involved. For this reason, the following precautions should be observed by teachers:

- Do not stay in any room (including your classroom, lab, or office) with only you and a student: Always keep the door open when you are working alone with one to few students.
- Do not affectionately touch (or hug) any student, especially of the opposite sex. If students do initiate such affectionate acts, offer only one side of your body, and disengage as quickly as reasonable.

- Do not permit any students into your house for any reason, unless they are accompanied by a responsible adult such as their own parents.
- When having to go anywhere with students, insist on having other responsible adults with the party.

Although some of the above measures may sound rather harsh, in certain rare situations, teachers may sometimes need to protect themselves from adolescents who may be seeking affection from an adult or an authority figure.

Inga's relationship with the students continued, in a progression from the classroom to her house. In her case, although she did have several students at a time in her house (and other adults such as parents may have been present, but not mentioned), it is nevertheless not the advisable thing to do. She hinted at certain inherent, potential problems with relationships with adolescents:

When you get close with students, they sometimes don't know where the line is anymore, on the other hand, if you aren't that close, it's hard to get them to work. So it went in this direction, especially the seniors: We worked [during] so many lunches. [After] Christmas, we worked Saturdays. We worked Sundays at the end because we all couldn't stand school anymore. We met at my apartment. I taught students around the table.

We studied because I had that two-year syllabus to get to them in a year. So there was no way if I was just using the regular time, so we used mainly the Saturdays for covering syllabus material and Sundays for practices.

Although she sometimes wanted time to herself, Inga's attitude was that if the students were motivated enough to ask for extra lessons, a good teacher should yield to their request. She believed that, "You're in the wrong job if you tell students not to come and study if they want to."

In the course of the interview, Inga could not help but make some observations about the differences between the students in her previous school in Germany and her currents students. This comment was generally in agreement with the observations made by Mary and Joe, concerning their British students:

They have a lot of self-confidence. They [American students] know a lot. They know how to talk; they are not afraid of talking to a teacher; they're not afraid of punishment of a teacher. [They can easily say,] "I don't want this or something like [that.]"

Whereas in the United States she would reason with the students and even admit it if she was wrong, in Germany, she was an authority figure, and treated the students as subservient to her:

Interviewer: Looking back, if you had a new international teacher coming from Germany to teach in your situation, what are some of the things you would tell him or her?

Inga: What I tell people when they come is that students want to come and learn and that they're very open. [Also], don't yell at American students.

Interviewer: So back home...

Inga: You have a different tone. You tell people what they're supposed to do, and here you have students saying, "No I'm sorry, I have a different opinion and I can back it up for one, two hours." You're kind of [responding], "OK, so you don't want to do this."

5.7.5 Kofi's teacher-student relations

Some aspects of Kofi's teacher-student relational dynamics were mentioned in the section above. When he began teaching in the United States, Kofi had a combination of different situations. Being the author of a chemistry textbook, he commanded the respect of several of his student and teaching colleagues. For this reason, he observed that he was all the more interesting, and his students were even more curious to learn more about him. He declared during the interviews that,

The days were usually good with the students. I enjoyed working with the students, so whenever they came, that was my highpoint. Once I get settled in class and the students are there, that's big time.

It is gratifying to note from this point that, granted all the inherent difficulties in the field of teaching in America, it can still be a satisfying job; a point shared by all the participants in this book, and many veteran American teachers.

Granted the moments of joy above, there were the certain issues Kofi had to deal with. For some students, he had to exercise caution, "otherwise, it would have generated serious discipline issues," "especially for those of us from a culture where students could not under any condition scream at a teacher." It is for this reason that if there were a Ghanaian teacher coming to fill his position in the United States high school, he would issue the following:

> First thing will be discipline. That will be my first advice: discipline. I will try to explain the differences in the cultures. I understand that Ghana has changed a bit: the kids are now more in control, and more able to speak out, but it's still within the cultural context. It's different from here. No matter how much Europeanized we have become, its still the same cultural foundation [in Ghana].

Kofi also reflected that this cultural difference would, at least partly, dictate the way a new Ghanaian teacher relates to his or her students.

> So, I will tell the person to be more tactful in dealing with the students. The reactions; how to respond to questions; not to take it as an attack or in a degrading stance, because when people don't understand your culture, they have certain presumptions and assumptions about your culture, so take that as an opportunity as a "teaching moment," as I call it.

On being asked if such disciplinary problems was something he would find back in his homeland, he retorted:

> No, you wouldn't find that kind of disciplinary problems, and part of that has to do with the culture. The respect for the elders goes right through our school systems, but here it's a very different culture; so many of the kids feel they can do anything they want, and tell you anything they want. They don't even have to listen to you, so that makes it very difficult initially.

Elaborating on the issue of student discipline, Kofi experienced a reversal of what both Mary and Inga noted between their native schools, and their current United States high schools. In the first place, some of Kofi's American public high school students did not want to be in school, as opposed to Mary, Joe, and Inga's. Consequently, that attitude translated into a classroom discipline issue. It was in this respect that Kofi noted:

> The toughest! The toughest thing I had to face was the fact that there were kids who didn't care to even be in the classroom... I thought it very strange. I also found that there were serious discipline problems. So not only do you have to be a teacher, you have to be more like a counselor and an administrator, all of that rolled into one. The demands on the

teacher—teacher responsibilities are far greater than just being in the classroom.

5.8 Teacher-Parent Relations

5.8.1 The political clout of American parents.

One of the strongest traditions in American schools is to have a Parent Teacher Organization (PTO), sometimes referred to as Parent Teacher Association (PTA). As discussed earlier in chapter two, American schools are one of the places where many social issues come to a convergence. For this reason, PTOs remain one of the most powerful forces in each school.

During the school year, at least one evening is set aside during the first semester in order for teachers to meet their students' parents, and vice-versa. Depending on the school involved, PTO nights may be well- to lightly-attended. Schools found in wealthier neighborhoods are more likely to have more parents in attendance and more involved, and vice-versa for poorer neighborhoods.

During PTO meetings, teachers are expected to show the parents what they are planning to do with the students in the coming year. Teachers may talk about their curricula, syllabi, textbooks, and find ways to engage parents' help with student work. This is also an opportunity for the teacher to inform the parents about the nature of the subject matter, and what to expect as the year goes on. Many parents coming to this meeting are specifically interested in making a personal contact with teachers, and how best to help their own children. Teachers are generally prepared to answer a wide range of questions, from specific student behavior (with individual parents) to grading schemes or formats.

Teacher-parent relationship is an area many international teachers will find to be very different from their previous educational experiences. In line with the idea that the student is a consumer of professional education services, there is also a very strong sense of parental (and hence students') rights within American sentimentalities. In fact, parents are represented on several school boards across the nation, and have a strong influence in the educational landscape, especially in the wealthier neighborhoods. In such situations, parents who are dissatisfied with teachers' or administrators' work may call for their resignation—and many have a success track in this endeavor.

As noted in chapter one, education in America is not a privilege, but a right: All citizens have a right to free, basic public education. Although private schools have the right to expel a student for misbehavior, local public school are expected to accept all students. School is funded with taxes within school districts—and such taxes come from adults, including parents within that community. This creates a sense of public ownership of the local schools.

There is also the general feeling that education is an avenue for social and economic progress (although this may be debatable in certain situations). Parents therefore have a sense of responsibility to their children, and this is generally shown in part, by exerting their influence in the classroom. More than that, they believe that they have the right to the best education for their children, and that they, ultimately, are the ones who pay teachers' salaries. Teachers are therefore expected to be responsive to parents.

5.8.2 Working with American parents.

American parents, in line with the philosophy of continuous assessment model, are likely to keep in touch with teachers in order to keep apprised of their students' academic and behavioral progress. For the foreign teacher who is already overwhelmed by the novelties of duties, finding a way to manage parents is vital. One way to manage such communication is to call parents by phone according to a schedule that works for them. For example, one may set two hours per week aside to call the parents of specific classes. It may take several weeks to cover all one's classes using this plan. It may therefore be a good idea to first contact all the parents of students with academic or behavioral issues.

Another avenue may be to send notes home to parents. This may work in the lower grades—since middle and high school students are likely to either forget to send such notes, or intercept them, if the contents are not in their favor. On the other hand, one may just wait until it is time to communicate "deficiency grades" to parents. This is normally done early enough in the semester: about the third week in many school systems. Concerned parents would therefore contact the teacher for necessary remediation actions.

The last avenue, which is very easy to do, and yet surprisingly effective, is the use of electronic mail (e-mail) for communication with parents. It is very common for American schools to provide e-mail addresses for all teachers. In some private schools, parents are supplied with hand-books containing teachers' personal information, such as home telephone number, address, and school e-mail address. Although many public schools are not as forthcoming with such personal information, the e-mail could be a good option for teacher-parents communication line.

One good way to have parents' electronic mail information is to solicit this information during the first days of school. One effective strategy many veteran teachers employ is to send home a copy of the syllabus (which may include the time-line for covering specific subject content). As a part of this syllabus, a teacher may include the discipline plan, and have a small area soliciting parents' home phone numbers and e-mail addresses. If this is done early enough (hopefully on the first day of school while the students are still operating on a formal level with the teacher), it is more likely that this information will be provided—and returned by the students. Teachers may then compile such information for later use.

This section would be incomplete, if the concept of parent-teacher conferences is not addressed. This is an important communication device in the American educational system. Although it is, in many cases, an intervention for relatively more severe and negative student behavior or academic deficiencies, international teachers could use it as a wonderful outlet to solve two problems: student laxity and classroom management issues.

Should the issue be the student laxity, and the grades of the student are suffering, it is likely that the call for the conference would be from a parent. In this situation, the teacher would come to the conference, which is normally arranged before or immediately after classes with parents. The student in question, and the school counselor or an administrator will also be present. The teacher should be prepared to offer good reasons why the student's grades are suffering, and prove it with records (from his or her grade book or examples of student work). This implies that good record-keeping is vital in the American classroom. As was previously indicated, the class grade book is considered a secondary legal document, and should be meticulously kept. At this meeting, remedies to the student's problems are also offered.

If the issue is classroom misbehavior—and it is conceivable that new teachers are more likely to experience issues with classroom management issues, and that such problems may be attributable to a few students in a class—the teacher would call for the parent-teacher conference. The same participants would be present, and the issues would be presented by the teacher. If the parents of such students are employed in the discipline process (and many are willing to participate for the sake of their children)—the teacher will likely discover a great ally!

5.8.3 Mary's teacher-parent relations

Mary, finding that teacher-parents communication was a new expectation of her new school, initially found things difficult. Although very understanding of parents' concerns, she was nevertheless protective of her privacy. She commented that:

> Accessibility is another issue of parents in the private school: feeling free to phone you up. Teachers' phone numbers are published. The first year, people would phone me up at home asking me to help out, and I really resent that, and a lot of people do. So accessibility of us as individuals to the parents is an issue that worries people.

She however understood the issue of parents' rights in America, and became comfortable with them keeping in touch with her:

> Part of our job here, again—which is something I found different and difficult—was that you have to call the parents and tell them if the child is not doing the homework, and that is something I had never done before, ever, or very little, other than parent-teacher conferences. So I do believe that some of the middle school teachers spend a lot of time on the phone talking to parents. A couple of parents e-mail me regularly about how their kids are doing—and I mean that's fine!

She also had a preference for the use of e-mails for communicating with parents, and had her reasons:

> Interviewer: That's interesting: the e-mailing issue: How do you feel about that? I mean, that is something that was non-existent back [in your previous schools].
>
> Mary: I'd rather e-mail than telephone because [with telephone], I have to stop what I am doing, and the e-mail you stack them and reply when convenient and go and get the info they need. When we do have parent conferences and parent events, many can get to meet the parents. Many of them are quite supportive. I mean, this is a private, fee-paying school, and they want to get their money's worth as much as anything else.

5.8.4 Joe's teacher-parent relations

During the interviews with Joe, the issue of teacher-parent relations was not addressed. Therefore a follow-up interview was done in order to find out what he thought about this issue. Joe agreed with others' observations that international teachers should expect more parent involvement in American schools:

I have found that U.S. parents attempt to get far more involved in their child's education, and are far more likely to complain about which books are read in English class et cetera. They also are more prepared to apply pressure to the teacher to raise the students' grade, and get involved in assisting in school life—especially sporting activities.

5.8.5 Inga's teacher-parent relations

Inga observed a difference between teacher-parent relationships in Germany and in the U.S. She noted that in Germany, there was very little communication within the school, both through the official and unofficial channels. There was also no expectation of praise or other forms of communication from teachers, which was partly a reflection of the general society. On the other hand, she found the opposite to be true in her American school. Her American parents expected to hear some positive comments, where possible, about their children:

> [In Germany], you can't put [praise] on a report card, and there's not so much communication between parents and teachers. Usually, when a teacher calls a parent, it usually is to complain about something, but calling a parent and saying that, "Your kid did an incredible job" is something, [for which] I think people would call you "nuts," so you don't do it. I remember you have like, "Back to school night" and things like this, and because of the way the German culture is, people aren't used to [a situation where] teachers come and praise.

5.8.6 Kofi's teacher-parent relations

Kofi described his parent-teacher relationship as very positive. He pointed out that, right from the outset, he became the subject of dinner table conversations because the students were curious about him and his culture. It did not take long for many students and parents to note his presence in the school, he observed. Even parents would find a good reason just to meet him and relate what their children had told them about his classes:

> After the first couple years, every kid, and every parent knew about Mr. Kofi [and his classes], and that's all they wanted. Some parents would just come to "Open House" [or PTO night] and just want to sit in my class and talk to me… When I'm there, I'm usually the last person to leave. The parents relate all their stories about their kids to me, how the kids talk so highly about my class.

Kofi was so successful in his teaching work that he received a lot of notes of gratitude from parents and students in appreciation of what he did for them. Even after he moved to another school, some parents from his previous school were still trying to coerce their principal to get Kofi back to coach the school's tennis team:

> I have whole files [filled with] cards, et cetera from parents and students plaques. One of my classes voted me "National Teacher of the Year." Some parents got hold of my e-mail [address]—so many e-mails—I think they sent it to other parents, even [in] the tennis team.

> The principal [from my previous school] sent me an e-mail about two weeks ago saying she's getting so much pressure from the parents of the students that she would consider having [me] back to coach tennis, because now she can't hire anybody else—because the parents are all over her that she should at least get me back [for tennis]. So I will be going back to coach tennis at [my previous school]. So that is going on too.

Form Kofi's account above, it is very apparent that international teachers could potentially become very successful in American schools if they are willing to work hard.

5.9 Knowledge Shift: International Teachers as Active Learners

Learning is something that may occur naturally and rather passively to the international traveler. For the international teacher, however, active learning should become second nature. It has been indicated that those who have had previous international or cross-cultural experiences are likely to have some rough notions about what to expect in a new country.

5.9.1 Professional development

Intentionally and inadvertently, international teachers should expect to become perpetual students. Perhaps, that is the American way, and America has a phrase for it: "life-long learning." Life-long learning is in fact, both a virtue and an expectation of the American teacher. All teachers are expected (even after obtaining a terminal degree), to continue to "refresh" their knowledge, through "professional developments." This is achieved through on-going learning activities that are normally counted in hours called

Continuing Education Units (CEUs).

Professional development activities are required in order for teachers to maintain their teaching certificates. In most states, teaching certificates are granted in five-year blocks, and are renewable only after having satisfied a required number of CEUs. As the term implies, teachers are expected to stay current of new innovations in the profession.

During the interviews with the international teachers in this book, it was observed that the theme "teacher as a learner" showed up throughout, both directly and indirectly. Such learning took place from their students—both in and outside the classroom—as has been lucidly elaborated under teacher-student relations. There was also help from ordinary people in the streets who helped them to learn about basic logistical and cultural needs for everyday living in the United States.

5.9.2 Learning from mentors

Mentors do help. Schools are places where complex human interactions occur. It is therefore helpful to have someone who can provide useful insights into the way things work in the new school environment. Official or unofficial, good mentors have the interest of those whom they mentor at heart. Although American schools are increasingly acknowledging the mentoring relationship and are creating mentoring programs, new teachers should seek out colleagues, especially in their areas of discipline, with whom to share ideas.

In the best of situations, mentors do become great social colleagues, and can help to ease support systems issues for international teachers. More importantly, they can also become a powerful instructional support system for international teachers. For example, in a specialty area as biology, a good mentor could provide information about what kinds of locally-available flowers are good for dissection, where to find specific equipment, or how to best grow bacteria under the local conditions, etc. If mentors are not available in one's subject area, then the second best choice should do. After all, in many situations, the new teacher just needs to know what needs to be done at certain times, what certain things mean, and the protocols or routines for certain occasions.

5.9.3 Mary as a learner

Mary emphasized in various ways that there was the need for her to learn in her new school, and also adequately captured the value of mentoring:

Most teachers need a mentor who can explain what the situation is, so I've been a mentor for some teachers. Some teachers in my department have mentors outside the department, and that helps.

Interviewer: Why is that necessary?

Mary: To explain the school's approach. The administration can be very supportive, if you approach it the right way, but if you tend to go it on your own, the high school principal is not going to stick [his or her] neck out to protect you. And there are school policies that have to be followed and you need to work out what they are. I think it would have been hard for me to come in as [an effective teacher] because I didn't know how things worked. I needed the year to [learn] how things work—who has the power in the school—because it never who you think it is.

5.9.4 Joe as a learner

Although he never used the term "learn" more than once throughout the interviews, Joe made allusions to the fact the he was very reflective of his teaching endeavor since he immigrated into the United States: He learned to do several things differently. From his interviews, one could decipher some of his learning activities from some of his statements. From these, he indicated that he had learned about the nature of American students, the school climate, and relevant local examples, during his lessons. Here is a sample:

Interviewer: How would you say you've grown as an educator, especially in the U.S.?

Joe: Unfortunately I have to say being in my late forties, I don't think there's much growth that goes on now as before. It's not been the growth but the fact that I've at least settled down. I can now at least relate to the area, and I can bring the easiest local examples. I can make a joke about there being more chemicals going down the [Swan Lake]; air quality.

I'm more relaxed because part of the experience of growing is getting used to the students and students getting used to me; me being comfortable in this learning environment; me being in tune with the direction the school takes; and comfortable that we have similar long-term goals.

Interviewer: To what would you attribute all this growth?

Joe: I do not want to stagnate. I want to learn as well as my students in my class. There's so much to see, do, evaluate, so I always want to push my knowledge further. I try to grow with the class. It would be so easy to say, "You know I've got the course notes set, just go and pick them out again," but no, there's a different set of students, a different set of needs. I want to go over them, change them to meet the needs of the group of students. I don't want to stagnate. I've seen that happen with teachers in the past: pulling out the same notes, with same typing error, for year after year after year. I couldn't do that; you age quickly and you lose enthusiasm, and if you lose enthusiasm, you lose the kids. If I come in all boring, monotone voice, the kids would fall fast asleep. It's got to be fun, live, pleasant learning environment.

His continued learning may be gleaned from statements such as: "I'm always on the lookout for examples that are culturally-relevant to the students that I teach. You'll find me reading weird sections of the newspaper—world section."

5.9.5 Inga as a learner

Inga provides a great prescription for what international teachers' attitudes should be in order to become more successful in American schools.

If there was one word that encapsulated the ideals of Inga, it was that of being a "learner." She either used the term "learn," or alluded to it numerous times during interviews. She was extremely conscious of her need to learn in order to become an effective teacher in America. She learned English from her students, "collected words," for inclusion into her parlance, and read her dictionary. Her reasons included the fact that

Some words only have a scientific meaning, so the students say, "I don't know that word," so I give them a definition. But sometimes you have a word where the students would say, "Yes I know what that word means," but it has a completely different meaning in a scientific context, and that's hard to figure out if you don't read your dictionary every night.

Interviewer: So you have to read your dictionary…

Inga: I read [my] English physics book, but I actually read a lot of my dictionary.

She also learned English by doing a parallel reading of German and English books:

> One of the language issues I have is that I learn words from reading. At the beginning I read parallel. I had one copy of an American textbook: I had it in German and English—and then you read the English ones, and I sometimes don't know whether this is a specific term or the students probably have a different meaning of this word in mind when you talk about this. [So I read the same passages of the book in my German copy].

She learned English by going through various exercises and drills, with determination:

> Interviewer: What would you attribute these changes that have occurred in terms of [your] language evolution?
>
> Inga: First, it's just that you use the language [daily on the job] and [so] I worked on my language. I sit down at home, where I collect words—and I can only remember words if someone writes them down for me: I'm very visual in learning, so I need to hear it and write it down, then I need to hear it again two or three times, then actually use it one day. I read, not sophisticated literature, but like mysteries or whatever I get into my hands. I consciously work on it.

Inga learned to guide her students to work with her through the language difficulty:

> Those are issues...but I trained the students. I said, "If you have no clue what I'm talking about, or if this word doesn't fit in the sentence the way I put it, then you let me know and I'll explain it to you. If it's a physics term then..."

She also learned by using all the resources that were available to her, such as computer, the Internet, and parents, as the following statements indicate:

> I completely adapted to the American [spelling] just because we use Microsoft Word and it gives you the spellings and you get used to them.

> ...Just using all the resources that I have. I have a student in ninth grade student whose parents are both professionals [who deal in] textbooks ... asking people for help, reading, but the development of the Internet is definitely a wonderful thing if you live in a different country. So I can email my professor in Germany if I have a question, and just trying to

find solutions—and if it doesn't work, just try another one: Trial and error.

5.9.6 Kofi as a learner

Kofi denoted several times that although he was a teacher, he was also a learner. He pointed out that he was a learner by the very fact that he was a teacher, and the American profession of teaching expects teachers to be learners as well. Secondly, he was a learner by the fact that he was a teacher in transition. In his teacher-student relations above, he pointed out that he was his own students' student, especially in the areas of language and culture. For Kofi, learning was not an option: it was a necessity:

> Well, I had to learn. Because we're teachers, I also consider myself as a learner, so I was quick to learn about some of the things I had to deal with on a day-to-day basis. I also learned from the old teachers who helped me through the initial shocks.

> I had a lot of support from the old faculty that helped with me things. Mike was very helpful to me my first semester.

Kofi also learned about how to use available resources. He noted that, if he had to advise new international teachers coming to teach in America,

> The other thing that I will mention is to learn to use resources. Because [in Ghana] we have lacked the resources … I'll also advise to take as many courses as possible: refresher courses, the staff development courses. Over the last four years that I have been teaching now, I have taken about twenty-eight staff development courses. That means that I have taken practically everything they have offered. I have been to almost every science teacher conference, seminar, workshop, tech courses.

> Interviewer: So they should take…

> Kofi: Everything they can lay their hands on, and also learn to use the Internet. One thing I have observed is the library—the Media Centers in the school systems are pretty well-established and pretty well-developed, and they are very good resource centers.

As a learner, Kofi emphasized an open-minded attitude as a factor for his success in his work in America. He also viewed teaching as a special calling that was to be taken seriously:

I think I've adjusted pretty well to the system, and part of that has to do with my desire to do my job well. Actually, I do not even consider teaching as a job. I considered it more of a ministry, and probably being ambitious about my calling, I try to do the very best in any area that I pursue, and that's why I think I was able to go through the early problems quicker and adjust to it and find the best means of helping my students.

In summary, Kofi would describe his learning experiences as on-going and life-long:

Everybody adapts differently to different systems. So from experience, it's taken me all of these years to try to adapt to certain things. I am still learning. So it's a life-long learning opportunity.

5.10 Pedagogical Shift: Points for Success

The teachers were asked the following summative question: "Looking back, if you had a [fellow native] teacher immigrating to teach here, what would you advise him [or her]?" To this question they reiterated certain vital factors of which international teachers need to be aware and exercise caution. These ideas are highlighted below, mostly in their own words:

- **Ask for a mentor** to help you to learn about the potential issues you may face while teaching in your new school. A good mentor will be helpful in many other areas as well.

- **Be careful with the grading** and the grading scheme. Don't let anybody bully you into changing a grade without good reasoning because that does happen sometimes. Be aware how important internal grades (or continuous assessments) are, and try to get it sorted out. Make sure you can justify the grades you're giving.

- **Don't get into confrontation with parents**. American parents do get involved in their children's education. Find convenient, but effective ways to accommodate them. (See the section on Teacher-Parent relations for ideas.)

- **Listen to your students when they talk to you,** but you must maintain discipline and courtesy in the classroom when it comes to student participation: Everybody takes their turn. Questions should be welcomed, but they have to put their hands up. Do not to be afraid of students asking lots of questions because American students do that. Let them speak, but try to learn some strategies for saying, "This isn't important: I can deal with it later." Know that this can be very difficult sometimes. You need to be consistent with them.

- **In terms of teaching relationships, there are relatively more informal situations between students and teachers**. You cannot deal with these students as you used to in your native country: Their opinions are going to count more. In certain countries, one cannot imagine a situation where a student would go and complain to the principal. That's likely to happen in American schools. That's why you have to be a bit more careful.

- **Be careful if you are using idioms or similes or analogies: Watch your language so that there are no misunderstandings.** Be careful with what you say and cut down on the sarcasm: Americans hate it because they consider it rude. Cynicism is different. Because of the nature of the American society, where racial, religious, and other rather sensitive issues abound, you have to be careful about your choice of words.

- **Maintain good instructional approaches:** Good teaching practice is good teaching practice, so best systems or practices elsewhere would likely work in America, with necessary modifications. Keep in mind that American students and administrators will expect more hands-on teaching situations.

- **Find ways to keep abreast with the current technologies in your field.** This is an expertise that is not only expected of you as a professional, but is also useful in effective instruction in the modern classroom.

- **Seize all the professional development opportunities available to you through the school system.** This will help you to achieve your learning goals as an international teacher-learner.

5.11 Summary

The transitional issues of the international teachers featured in this section may be categorized into two types: knowledge gaps, and knowledge shifts. As the terms imply, knowledge gaps and knowledge shifts suggest that there are certain differences of which international teachers should be aware, and make concerted efforts to make a "shift." These shifts are the teachers' attempts to make up for their knowledge gaps by learning and changing to suit their new teaching environments.

Systemic knowledge gaps indicate that school organization and curricula may vary in different countries, and cross-cultural teachers will therefore need to learn how education is structured in the new teaching context.

Communication issues (or gap) involved issues ranging from differences in the meaning of individual words, accents, and differences in the meanings of expressions. Textbook issues dealt with the differences in the emphasis of content, and the use of the textbooks as a workbook or a reference book.

The nature of the American high school student was viewed as initially elusive to the international teacher for several reasons. American students are relatively more aware of their rights to the democratic freedoms that America stands for. They are also aware of their rights to speech, religion, and education. They are therefore more independent both of their teachers' opinions, and even their parents.

American parents, in line with the philosophy of continuous assessment model, are more likely to keep in touch with teachers in order to keep apprised of their children's academic and behavioral progress. Owing to time pressures, teachers need to find innovative ways to manage their teacher-parent relationships. One way to manage such communication is to call parents by phone according to a schedule that works for them.

Finally and perhaps more importantly, international teachers should become perennial learners and cultivate the attitude of learners in order to succeed in their new American schools. This may be done by taking advantage of the numerous options available in most schools. These may include learning from mentors, media centers, and professional development opportunities.

Chapter #6

WHAT INTERNATIONAL TEACHERS CAN DO TO BECOME SUCCESSFUL IN AMERICAN SCHOOLS

The preceding chapters proffer that certain predictable issues are likely to arise during international teacher transitions. The argument was made that international teachers need to understand the socio-cultural, political, and physical environments in which they find themselves in order to be effective. Therefore, an understanding and orientation into the new educational environment is vital for success. Prominent differences between their familiar school organizational setups, the philosophy and nature of assessment, and communication are some of the potential issues to work through.

Other issues of interest may include the democratic nature of the American classroom (and the related issue of student behavior), urban education, and multicultural education. Figure 6-1 is a synthesis of some of the main ideas and issues which are recognized as pertinent to the international teacher. This figure shows that international teacher transitional issues can be viewed as falling into two main domains; knowledge gaps and socio-cultural issues. Each of these domains may have their related issues, some of which could be common to both domains.

To each of the above differences and potential issues for international teachers, solutions need to be found. In this chapter, some pedagogical skills useful for becoming an effective teacher in America will be discussed. This will include some of the best practices for effective instruction and classroom management. These, together with the understanding of the issues covered in the previous chapters, should help international teachers to achieve success.

It must be emphasized, however, that the ideas provided in this chapter are just brief discussions of instructional strategy issues competently treated in several available books. The information provided in this chapter is therefore meant to provide a brief review of the world of instructional issues and strategies.

**NETWORK OF POTENTIAL ISSUES CONFRONTING
INTERNATIONAL TRANSITIONAL TEACHERS**

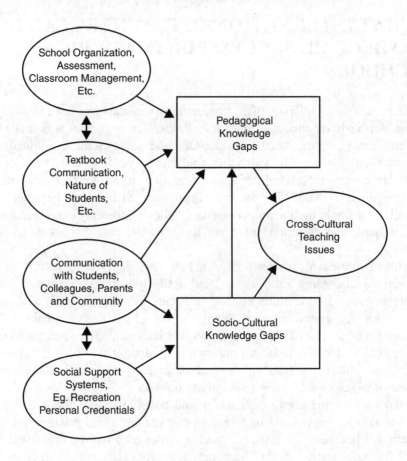

Figure 6-1

6.1   Developing a Teaching Philosophy

It is important for teachers to have a philosophy which guides their teaching professions. Although it is not a requirement in most schools, it is still useful for teachers to have a certain level of awareness of their practice. This is reminiscent of the notion of the reflective practitioner, which is currently a fundamental pursuit of several colleges of education in the Unites States. For example, the University of North Carolina at Charlotte College of Education has a conceptual framework which "seeks to develop excellent professionals who are knowledgeable, effective, reflective, responsive to equity and diversity, collaborative, and who are leaders in their profession." They emphasize that reflective practitioners have "reflective knowledge" that enables them to undertake cogent evaluation of their teaching practices, including self-appraisal. This is exactly what a teaching philosophy propels. In defining one's teaching philosophy, instructors should reflect on their beliefs about certain primary educational issues. Asking certain basic questions including the following may help:

- What is the purpose of education and schooling?
- What is the nature of the current learners in one's classes? Who are they (by age and socio-cultural characteristics)? What are they capable of learning? What are they not capable of learning?
- What is the nature of learning and cognition?
- How does an instructor therefore respond to the issues above?
- If certain previous instructional actions did not yield optimal results, what may be the reason(s), and how could they be changed to foster learning?

Periodic responses to the questions above (be it daily or weekly), constitutes the nature of the reflective teacher.

6.2   Effective Classroom Management Approaches for American Middle and High Schools

"A well-managed classroom is also a predictable environment. Both teacher and students know what to do and what is supposed to happen in the classroom." – Wong and Wong, 1998, p. 88.

Research has shown that classroom management is one of the best indicators, not only of a good teacher, but also of potentially better instruction in the classroom. Wong and Wong (1998) write: "Don't be ineffective—you and your students will pay for it." (p. 88) Even for native-born teachers in the U.S., classroom management is one of the most important issues professors of education monitor in prospective and current teachers' classes. A happy veteran teacher is likely to be one with good classroom management skills, and vice-versa. It is therefore a make-or-break factor in the life of the American teacher.

Classroom management is effectively a discipline-related issue. Discipline issues may be broadly divided according several criteria. In the context of cross-cultural teaching, it may be more illuminating to divide it according to two cultural groups: the listening cultures and conversational cultures. In listening cultures, respect for elders abounds, and the elders are seen as the custodians of knowledge, from whom such knowledge should be respectfully solicited. Children and adults socialize separately, and the axiom, "Children should be seen, but not heard" may hold true.

In such societies, students are acculturated to have the mental fortitude or discipline to listen for long periods of time. Unquestioning obedience is a natural component of such cultures. Since the discipline to listen for long periods of time translates into a more sustained cognitive presence in the students, classroom management problems are therefore less likely to arise. Teachers could therefore focus most of their class time on instruction.

In conversational societies, on the other hand, the young expect to be actively engaged by, and with adults both in activities and in conversations. In such societies, students have a need for cognitive engagement, and their attention spans may be relatively short, and may come at a high premium. Discipline issues therefore are more likely to arise. Teachers in this situation need to master the skills for constructively engaging students for learning. Class time in this environment may have to be divided between classroom management (especially student behavior management) and instruction.

For foreign teachers, classroom management will prove to be the litmus test for survival in the American classroom. Perhaps, it is worth mentioning in this regard that currently in America, it is rare to hear the word "training" associated with education. The reason may be quite simple philosophically: In America, dogs may be trained, but humans are raised. Humans need to be engaged, and accorded a lot of caring attention. Indeed, even dogs (and other animals) do have animal rights advocates. This is a clear departure from the philosophy in many other nations, where the term "training" abounds in such usage as "teacher training institutes," "child training," and the like.

Could it mean that teacher-training nations maintain the philosophy that humans could also be trained? If this is so, then the other question that arises is, How then does it affect people-management styles?

From the previous chapters, it is apparent that in nations where students have little or no voice in the classroom, teachers may be either used to, or comfortable with the authoritarian (very strict) classroom management approaches. For such teachers, coming to teach in America will mean a clear need for a change in classroom management approaches, in order to suit the American teaching context: a situation where student voice has weight.

In this section, some practical strategies for managing American classrooms are presented. Obviously, a teacher's chosen classroom management approaches will depend on several factors. These may include the natural temperament of the teacher in question, the combination of students in a particular classroom, and the kind of subject or topic being taught. One may also include the number of years on the job as a factor, since this is one area where significant progress may be expected to occur over the years.

Sparks-Langer and colleagues (2004) mention two traditions of classroom management: behavior management and humanistic/developmental models.

6.2.1 The behavioral management model

The behavioral management model, as the name implies, is based on the behaviorist theory of learning of B. F. Skinner, who believed that future human behavior is contingent on their past experiences. In this tradition therefore, the consequences of students' past behavior is expected to determine their future behavior in the classroom. In a loose sense, this is the "training" model, and international teachers may find some of the specific approaches to be familiar.

From the practitioner's point of view, Sparks-Langer and colleagues (2004) delineate the following classroom management approaches for the behavior management approach:

Contingency management. Also sometimes called the "incentive system," students are rewarded or punished for their behaviors. The reward or the severity of the punishment depends on the student's behavior.

Contracting. This is a formalized form of the contingency management system. Here, the teacher signs up a "contract" with the student, with specific details of what work needs to be done, and the rewards and punishments that go with them.

Use of praise. This is normally an immediate reward for behavior in class; a verbal form of positive reinforcement.

Non-contingent reinforcement. This is the use of rewards which are not necessarily tied to any particular positive actions. The advantage of this model is supposed to help students to generally behave better, in the hope of possibly being seen and rewarded. One may call this the "catch-me-being-good" model.

Rules/Reward-Ignore/Punish (RRIP). In American classrooms, teachers (sometimes with the help of students), may develop class rules. Students then have the freedom of "choice" either to obey the rules for positive rewards (or maintain the status quo), or ignore the rules for punishment.

In a practical sense, this is the most common approach found in most public schools. School- or class-wide rules are posted at vantage points, and students are also generally informed about such rules through various means, such as teacher syllabi, and student handbooks.

6.2.2 Humanistic/developmental approach

Sparks-Langer   and   colleagues   (2004)   observe   that   the humanistic/developmental approach has the fingerprints of clinical psychologists, school counselors, and mental health professionals. The basic tenet of this approach is to discipline with dignity, using effective communication, conflict resolution, self-control, and needs-fulfillment. They also note that in such an atmosphere, the teacher serves more as a guide than as the authority figure in the classroom.

In this approach, emphasis is placed more on student responsibility, as opposed to teacher control. It is a situation of mutual respect for humanity, viewing both teachers and students as individuals with feelings and needs. In this connection, Sparks-Langer and colleagues recognize certain factors as being helpful in easing classroom management. These factors form the topical basis for the following discussions:

Respect. Perhaps, one of the most important things a teacher can do in the American classroom, where diversity reigns, is to respect all students. It is also the law. This may include respect of their opinions, their religions, race, gender, etc. It is illegal to discriminate on any such basis, and optimally, a teacher should be perceived by his or her students as being naturally respectful of all of them, without such respect appearing contrived.

In this connection, the international teacher may need to learn to incorporate new vocabulary into their instructional language. The use of polite expressions, such as "please" and "thank you" becomes important. It is also necessary to look students in the eye, and address them by name. Veteran teachers would readily agree that this could be done very professionally, without compromising one's authority as the "leader" of the class.

Fairness. Treatment of students should be perceived by all to be fair to all—since discrimination is illegal, as mentioned above.

Humanity. Teachers may create and seize the opportunities to make human and ethical connections in lessons. This will reinforce the humanity of all, and foster the ideals of respect, fairness, and justice in the classroom.

Collaboration. Here, teachers may provide opportunities for students (and sometimes in concert with the teacher) to work together on activities.

Conversation. Teachers may take some time to talk to students during, and outside classes. Such extra-curricular activities as football and basketball game nights provide the opportunities to get to know and understand students better. Students with extra-classroom bonds with the teacher are likely to be more responsive to the teacher in class. Such connections also help to understand and better learn students' perceptions of various issues.

Empathy. This indicates a sympathetic understanding. It is an important factor that needs to be learned by the international teacher. The reason is that it may take some time for the teacher to learn and understand the nature of American adolescents and their issues. American adolescents may have peculiar issues that are appreciably different from their counterparts in many parts of the world. These may include the socio-economic status of the family, single- or two-parenthood, ethnic background, immigration status, and several others.

The socio-economic status of the family determines what they can afford. Teachers should therefore be considerate of the expenses any class projects may incur. For example, students who come from single-parent homes (which are statistically known to be relatively poorer as compared to those from two-parent, two-income families) may have difficulty affording and finding someone to assist them with their homework assignments. In this situation, teachers may decide whether or not to permit some class time to be used for assignments.

Conversely, students may come from two working-parents situations, where they may have ample income. Yet, they may have little adult supervision after school, since the parents are equally unavailable as the single parents. (Please refer to the previous discussion on "latchkey" child.) This group of students may therefore need special encouragement to do assignments, as in the case of the single-parent.

Finally if a student hails from particular racial or ethnic group, there are specific issues of educational interest. For example new immigrant parents in America who do not speak English may use the services of their children for translation after school. Therefore, such students may have little time to do their homework, and are likely to be tired as they help their parents and other English-deficient acquaintances to navigate their personal affairs.

Although the notes above do not suggest that teachers should necessarily absolve their students from their responsibilities, they do help the teacher to understand their students better, and therefore be better able to empathize with them.

Consistency and trust. Research has shown that, parents (and others in positions of authority) who are consistent in the application of their rules are more likely to succeed in their efforts (Rice & Dolgin, 2000). In the classroom, therefore, the same rule applies. For this reason, it may be necessary for the teacher not only to have effective and well thought-out rules, but also be very conversant with them—and to consistently apply them! This done, the teacher may find it easier to establish trust among the students.

Depending on the environment, teachers need to be selective in their approaches. Teachers will find the behavior modification approach to be very common, even among those who subscribe to other approaches. This may be evident in general school rules or class rules.

Kellough and Kellough (2003) suggest that effective classroom management is a process that maximizes student learning. They indicate that today's teachers share a concern for the self-esteem of their students, and may therefore select management techniques which consider such student needs. No matter what the approach may be, teachers still need to be vigilant in order to be successful. Teachers need to develop their own approaches for classroom management by working on the following practices:

- *Focus your attention on desirable student behavior and try to foster those in your classroom*: Know what kind of classroom environment and student behavioral life you want, and work to create it.

- *Attend to inappropriate behavior quickly and appropriately:* If there is student misbehavior, and two or more deviant behaviors are occurring at the same time, attend to the most serious first (not forgetting your own class rules.) Serious behaviors (which may simultaneously break school-wide rules anyway) may be referred to a school administrator or counselor. There is usually an assistant principal in charge of discipline issues. Teachers may also consider calling (preferably) or e-mailing the parents, in concert with the application of the previous discipline actions.

- *Maintain alertness to all that is happening in your classroom:* This may include the maintenance of frequent visual surveillance of the entire class, randomly calling on students to answer questions, moving around the room, and maintaining eye-contact with each student about once a minute during whole-class instruction.

- *Provide smooth transitions, keep the entire class on task, and avoid dead time during class:* Plan your lesson in such a way as to have continuity within the lesson. Have enough work to keep all students constructively busy for the given class period. (See Differentiated Instruction later this chapter for more on this). Students with nothing to do are likely to find something else to do—possibly to the teacher's displeasure.

- *Be consistent with all of the above.* All the ideas above are complementary and synergistic. Failure in one area could affect the others. (Adapted from Kellough & Kellough, 2003)

Shrigley (1985) indicated that 40% of 523 classroom disruptions were curbed when teachers applied certain coping skills. These included ignoring certain behaviors (since annoying behaviors which are not necessarily disruptive of class will often subside if ignored); using signals (including body language, such as a stern stare to indicate an unacceptable behavior); proximity control (teacher's presence near the disruptive student); and touch control (placing a hand on the student's shoulder in order to relieve tension and anger). Teachers should however use discretion when applying the last coping skill (Chiappetta & Koballa, 2002).

In brief, classroom management issues may be challenging for new teachers. Heavy-handedness may lead to student resignation and boring classes. This may in turn make in turn lead to the loss of students' interest and enthusiasm for learning. Being too easy on students may pose its own dangers of uncontrollable classes. A management plan for consideration is "the three Ms" (from business management and leadership):

1. *Mobilize:* Organize your classroom in order to induce great, fear-free, learning-inviting environment. Establish trust, fairness, confidence, respect, and goodwill in the classroom.

2. *Motivate:* Find great ideas to catch the attention of your students. This may include such instructional tools as EEEPS (Exciting Examples of Everyday Phenomena), current affairs for debate topics, great video clips, and current controversies—which are all ideas that may help to trigger the imagination of the students—and keep it going with good monitoring systems.

3. *Monitor:* Maintain surveillance (as discussed above). After a good lesson introduction, do not lose the enthusiasm generated during that introduction. Let the students know that you are interested in what they have to contribute to the topic at hand. Move around the classroom, sit with groups for a few minutes and ask questions (during cooperative activities), and then move on to another group or station, and do the same thing. Let the students know that you are interested in their mental products. Good student work may then be expected.

As with all other students anywhere, once they know the caliber of a teacher, word gets around the school, and the students behave according to the teacher's level of expectations. Research indicates that teachers with higher expectations get better behavioral performance and learning outcomes from students, as compared to those with low student expectations.

6.3   The First Week of School

According to Kellough and Kellough (2003) and Wong and Wong (1998), the first few days of school are very important in establishing how the school year will turn out. Within a few weeks, word gets around about the nature of various teachers in the school. A no-nonsense, yet fair and consistent teacher is more likely to have a better year than the lax, friendly, but inconsistent teacher. In order to have a successful year, teachers need to have a plan.

The following composite plan comprises various ideas veteran teachers have reported as effective in American classrooms:

6.3.1 Pre-day one:

- Know your classroom and your school environment.
- Make sure that you know the lesson planning format for the school, with the help of mentors or orientation or both. Plan your lesson for at least one week. (You may refer to the planning guide in Appendix One. Many schools require new teachers to produce lesson plans for at least three weeks at a time. [Again, mentors' help should be useful here.])
- Prepare your syllabus. This may include a few class rules (or such rules may be democratically created with the help of the students. Note that your rules may be used by several classes, so be very general.). Let the students understand that the rules are not intended to be punitive, but to provide the opportunities for all to derive maximum learning and fairness. Do not make more than 4-5 rules. Make them easy to both remember and apply.
- Include a time-table for covering the content through the semester as a part of your syllabus. This is your "pacing guide" for your course. In some school districts, this is provided to you by the school. Your department head should inform you if there is one. You may also opt to consult with other teachers of the same content area to compare or share notes on this.
- On your syllabus, provide a place for a parent or guardian to sign to indicate that they have read the syllabus with their child. Place this at the bottom of your syllabus. There should also be a place to write down their phone numbers and e-mail addresses. This section is to be torn off and returned to you next school day.
- Make sure that you have the required stationery for all teachers, or at least know where they are located: Class roster books, lesson planning books, detention forms, report forms, and any others that are used in that school.
- Decide on a seating chart for your classroom according to the arrangement you prefer in your class. You may decide to form a semi-circle if you expect to have more student-oriented, discussion-based classes; or blocks (also called islands) if group work will dominate instructional approach; or the conventional all-facing-the-teacher format, if teacher-led discussions will dominate.
- Draw a blank seating chart (based on your preferred format above) and make about three copies per class—since you may need to rearrange student seating later in the semester.

- Arrange your students alphabetically, using your class roster. This will help you to later remember their names easier, or you may decide to do this following a different system.
- Make sure that you have secured your class rosters—with the members of each class available.

6.3.2 Day one:

If first impressions last a long time, then this is the opportunity not to miss! On this day, students are generally coming in psychologically disadvantaged (no matter how tough they may be). A prepared teacher therefore has the upper hand to win the psychological war that may set the tone for the rest of the semester—or even the whole year.

- Stand at the door and greet the students as they enter the classroom. Many schools expect teachers to be in the hallways anyway, in order to help ease student movement. On the first day especially, many ninth graders (who are moving from the middle school to high school) and new, transfer students may need guidance to locate their new classrooms.
- Direct the students to their prescribed seats using your pre-made class roster, until all are seated. This sends to them an early signal as to who is in charge.
- Introduce yourself to the students. This may include about 3-4 minutes' talk on interesting points about your country, possibly with the help of a map. You may also provide an official website address (or URL) of your country, if available.
- Distribute your syllabus. (See Pre-Day One above for more on this.)
- Distribute textbooks. (Instructions for this are provided by the textbook managers. Usually the numbers of the textbooks need to be recorded in a class list, using a copy of each class roster. The same system would later be used to collect the books at the end of their use in your class—to verify that students have returned their exact textbooks, as confirmed by the numbers.)
- Begin formal, content-related instruction. This will depend on the length of the class period. If the class period is the normal 50 minutes, the above activities would probably take the whole class period. Formal instruction would then begin on Day Two.

6.3.3 Day two:

Wong and Wong (1998) and other veteran teachers testify to the power of constructive student engagement for preventing classroom discipline problems. They therefore propose that teachers have pre-lesson activities (sometimes called "sponges"). This is a short exercise or activity (generally taking not more than five minutes) which prevents students from initiating unproductive engagements and possible escalations into discipline problems. This should be posted on the board (or on their tables, if they are photocopies, as the case may be) before they come in. Once this is completed, the other objectives for the day may begin.

- Collect the parent- or guardian-signed material from the syllabus. Sometime during the day, make time to compile the phone numbers and e-mail addresses into a list (for each class) in alphabetical order, using a word processor (computer). When needed all you need to do is copy (Ctrl+c) and paste (Ctrl+v) into the email address area, saving a lot of time later on.
- Proceed with planned lesson activities for the day.

6.3.4 Days three to five ("testing period"):

The rest of the first week should be a period of emotional "investment." It is a time for investing initial energies and efforts for making the rest of the year productive. This should be done by knowing the class rules, and applying them consistently. Naturally, this is the time for students to test the teacher's tolerance limits, and teachers must be unyielding! To yield on the rules at this point is to set up for a miserable failure.

For the rest of the first week, and indeed the second and even third weeks, invest all your energies in the consistent application of the class rules and let the students understand that whatever they do in democratic America is a "choice" they freely make, and that leaves you no option but to apply the natural consequences of their own choices. You are just trying to be fair to all, since to make exceptions for some students is to be partial to some. Kellough and Kellough (2003), Wong and Wong (1998), and several other resources (also the Internet) are available for getting more help on such issues.

6.4   Professional Appearance:

Even for teachers who migrate from other industrialized nations, America will prove to be a nation where image rules: Americans are very concerned with their appearances, body odor and other personal hygiene-related issues. Although many schools do have professional dressing expectations, such expectations may, or may not be clearly spelt-out in their faculty handbooks which are provided at the beginning of the school year. For this reason, a good rule-of-thumb may be to observe how other teachers "professionally" dress and for what occasions.

Even if the international teacher finds that his or her school or colleagues do not dress very nicely, it is still a good idea to at least begin the school year with very good appearances, if just for the sake of classroom management. Although this may sound rather trifle, students may be more easily managed if they view the teacher as a professional. Obviously, in the Western world, and indeed all around the world, wearing a suit and tie is viewed as professional; even in the heat of tropical countries. Perhaps, there is a psychological message here; that one is serious, and is to be taken seriously. If this does not make the point, then perhaps, one should consider the saying "Clothes make the man (or the woman)." Arguably, "Clothes make the teacher." In the American society at large (as may be true of many other societies), "presentation" matters, and schools are not exempted from this value.

6.5   Effective Instructional Approaches in the American School

In this book, it has been suggested that there are two kinds of societies: listening and conversational. The American society is conversational. Classroom management is therefore an important issue to deal with. In fact, one of the most significant indicators for a teacher's success in the American classroom is the teacher's classroom management skills. International teachers will find that the American classroom necessarily demands an engaging teacher. With students' attention coming at a high premium, both teaching and learning need to be hands-on and minds-on. Teachers will therefore need to review their instructional skills in order to engage their students more constructively. Plain lectures, notes on the board, and labs; "chalk and talk," as it is sometimes called, will not do!

Although it was noted that class time should be planned with the expectation that a portion of it may needed for student behavior management, it is still possible to minimize behavioral problems in many ways, as previously discussed. Another effective avenue for managing classroom behavior is to have effective instructional approaches. In this section, some effective instructional approaches are summarized.

In general, instructional strategies may generally be seen as either teacher-centered or student-centered. Teacher-centered approaches are generally discouraged by the current ideas of constructivism, a theory discussed previously. Beyond this reason, teacher-centered approaches tend to be very labor-intensive, given the demands of the American classroom.

Student-centered instructional approaches, on the other hand, tend to tap into the energies and the enthusiasm of students for instruction. Within the limits of the curriculum expectations, teachers often define the content to be addressed by students by previous modeling. Student-centered instructional approaches should therefore not be used until the students have learned the expectations for their tasks, and have also had enough opportunities to see how the teacher does them.

The teacher may also need to complement student presentations, in cases where the content is not adequately well-explained or understood. This is because not all students are capable of understanding and explaining concepts as a teacher would. Teachers should therefore be ready to complement student information, especially in fact-driven contents.

6.5.1 Some teacher-centered instructional approaches and strategies of interest

Teacher presentations. This can be done by way of demonstrations or multimedia presentations. Multimedia presentations might feature a video tape which focuses on a particular topic relevant to classroom instruction. Video tapes are very common in America, and they can be purchased for almost any subject and topic area. The exhibition of artifacts of interest might also be used in a teacher presentation

Class discussions. This is an effective way to engage the class about a topic of interest. Here, discussion rules will be important; how to respectfully enter the conversation by raising one's hand, for example. It is also a good way to find out what students know, or if they read a particular assignment. Students may be randomly called upon for responses.

Use of analogies and anecdotes. Combined with the lecture approach, this may help students to relate stories they know in connection with the current topic. The weakness of this approach is that not all the parts of the stories may fit the current topic, and so the students may need to know where the story is deficient. It is also a good idea to have students create their own stories to fit a topic under discussion. This may help to liven up the classroom atmosphere, and may also encourage students to think more critically about the details of a topic, and where the story is deficient.

6.5.2 Some student-centered instructional approaches and strategies of interest

Student-led presentations. The term "presentations" may be broadly used to encompass anything done in class by any student (or teacher). Student-led presentations are very common in American schools—even in elementary schools. In a presentation situation, the teacher needs to provide certain clear expectations, and if possible, grade such presentations. Presentations assessment is normally done using a "rubric." Here, the teacher assigns points under categories, as he or she observes a certain degree or level of expected observations in a presentation. For example:

>   Presentation (voice, mannerism, etc): 0-10 points
>   Visuals (enhancements, technology, etc.): 0-10 points
>   Content (meeting the curriculum needs): 0-20 points
>   Evidence of mastery (during open discussion, questioning): 0-10 points

(RubiStar [http://rubistar.4teachers.org/index.php] provides excellent help for designing effective, detailed rubrics for different disciplines.)

Group or class presentations. Presentations can be made either to the whole class, or to small groups. There are several ways to do this. Although grouping students for effective leaning and instruction is almost a science in its own right, a short version of this strategy is discussed here.

It may be noted that students may be grouped either by ability levels or mixed-grouping. Grouping students by ability level or ethnic groups may have some merits. For example, a case may be made that grouping students by ability levels allows the teacher to better focus on, and help the struggling students, while providing challenging work opportunities for the gifted students. Also, in situations where immigrant students are not very fluent in English, other students from the same linguistic background may help to translate the activities within the group. This may therefore justify grouping students according to their ethnic (more justifiably linguistic) background.

Foreign teachers should be cautious with their grouping strategies, since grouping students in such a way as to either track (by ability level), or discriminate them (for example placing all students from a particular ethnic group together) is discouraged. This is sometimes so because of potential racial discrimination in America and its history. One way to avoid thi problem is to have periodic reshuffling of the groups.

A basic understanding of cooperative grouping strategies may help to group students more effectively. In the next section below, cooperative grouping strategies are discussed with the assumption that the teacher is non-discriminating in grouping students.

6.5.3 Cooperative learning strategies

Cooperative grouping is an idea that stems mainly from social constructivists, who believe that people naturally learn from their social environments. Lev Vygotsky (1896-1943), a pioneer of social constructivism, formulated the concept of the "zone of proximal development" (ZPD). This is the "distance between a child's actual developmental level and a higher level of potential development with adult guidance." (Dacey & Travers, 1996, p. 40) The idea is that children have upper limits to what they can learn on their own. However, given the proper environmental structures (such as a teacher's help), their upper "knowledge limits" could be extended; that is, personal difficulties may be reduced or eliminated, and greater learning could take place. This could be done by "scaffolding," whereby a student's previous knowledge may be used as a bridge to extend to new concepts.

Teachers naturally teach to extend the ZPDs of all the students in the class. In the classroom situation, students are surrounded by colleagues who may know more than them in different topic areas. In cooperative teaching, students in a group, unbeknownst to them, use their current gifts to extend their colleagues' ZPDs in those gifted areas. According to Hassard (2000), this may be achieved through two fundamental concepts: positive inter-dependence and individual responsibility. The result is that student team members create products that are greater than what individual team members could produce just by themselves.

Cooperative grouping can therefore be seen as the approach whereby the teacher tries to facilitate the learning process by having students effectively working together. Also sometimes called the "collaborative strategy," Hassard (2000) recognizes the following cooperative grouping strategies as very useful in the classroom:

Multiple abilities strategy. This strategy taps into the different strengths of different students in order to create a specific product. For example in a group presentation, the artistic (drawing) students would lead the production of visuals, while the linguistically-gifted may become the main spokesperson, and the kinesthetically-gifted may lead role-playing in order to demonstrate a concept.

Numbered heads together strategy. Students in the class are numbered one to four. Each student is told to remember their numbers. A problem, demonstration, or question is raised. Students put their heads together to solve the problem. After a specified time period, the teacher gives each student a certain amount of time, and reminds them that anyone could be called out for a presentation. The teacher then calls out a random number, and the student with that number in each group will present the group's findings, observations, etc. for the whole group.

Round table strategy. Here, each student completes and action and calls on another person in the group to complete another related action.

Circle of knowledge structure. This is similar to the round table strategy only that all students are required to contribute to the discussion as they reach their turn.

Think aloud pair problem-solving. In this strategy, paired students take turns working on an issue together: One student talks out loud about the problem, while the other encourages him or her. They then switch parts.

Jigsaw. As in a jigsaw puzzle, each student becomes an expert in an aspect of a problem, topic, or issue. He or she then teaches the rest of the group, or helps them to solve the general problem with his or her expertise.

6.6   Teaching Diverse Learners

As the expression suggests, differentiated instruction is an approach whereby the teacher plans his or her lessons with different kinds of students in mind, in order to respond to their learning needs more effectively. This is an approach which can be seamlessly integrated into group activities for more effective teaching and learning. The vital question in this approach is: On what basis does a teacher decide to differentiate instruction? The answer to this question is a complex one, and may depend on several factors, all contingent on the operational word: diversity.

As has been noted earlier, racial and other diversity issues in American schools are sensitive topics, and teachers need to be careful not to discriminate against students. Executed properly, differentiated instruction may help to respond to the peculiar needs of most, if not all students in a class.

6.6.1 What kinds of diversity?

The term "diversity," a synonym of "multiculturalism," was initially included in the American educational parlance in acknowledgement of the historical contributions of minority cultures to the American society. The tacit objective was to provide minority students with historical heroes, and therefore help them take some ownership of, and pride in American history.

Recently, however, the term has also come to incorporate observable differences in the nature of all students in the classroom. Some recognizable areas of diversity in American schools are ethnic and racial groups (also related to language groups for new immigrants), religious groups, class or social groups, and gender groups (which may broadly include homosexual issues).

Diversity grouping in America is rather elusive in many cases, since students generally find themselves belonging to two or more groups (Gollnick & Chinn, 2004). For example, a Latino (or Hispanic: generally Spanish-speaking) student who identifies more with middle class America will have different socio-educational issues from another Latino student who identifies more with the lower class—whereby issues of poverty then become more significant. Even within the majority white American culture, there are general language and other behavioral variations which are attributable to social classes. This is therefore an area which takes time to decipher. Some diversity-related observations may include the following:

Ethnic diversity. America is a land of many cultures and ethnic groups. Each ethnic group has its own world view, as explained in chapter three. In the classroom, as is true for the general society, knowledge is positional, and relates to the learner's values and experiences (Banks, 1993). Teaching with general cultural sensitivity therefore has its virtues, and is encouraged. On the practical level, however, the teacher meets the individual, and that goes beyond the broader cultural strokes. Teachers should therefore focus on the needs of the individual student as well (bearing in mind their ethnic backgrounds and therefore possible educational needs). (For more information on adolescents in ethnic and educational contexts, see pages 50-87 of Rice and Dolgin's book, The Adolescent: Development, Relationships, and Culture).

Language minority groups. One of the interesting issues arising from ethnic diversity in America is that of language minorities. New immigrants, especially those from non-English speaking countries may have difficulties in the classroom. Such students are normally placed into special "ESL" (English as a Second Language) classes. Once in the conventional classroom, however, teachers may use certain strategies to help such students. This may include the use of electronic translators (available for languages such as Korean, Japanese, and Chinese) and permitting more proficient students to help others in their language groups (by sitting together in the classroom or working in the same groups), etc. Teachers may use more visuals, gestures, or materials found on the Internet to help. In fact, teachers may consider the use of translating websites such as http://www.babylon.com to help some of these students.

Ability groups. Although this term is rather nebulous in meaning, and could be used in reference to the other categories, it is generally used to refer to students' abilities to satisfactorily complete different levels of school work. In the American educational system, academic tracking, whereby students are prepared for either trade schools or college is generally opposed, owing to its overt and inherent discrimination of students. In its place, however, are classes designed for students deemed to be average, above average, or below average. This tacit tracking is more obvious in several high schools, where there is the remedial curriculum at the lowest end of the pole, the basic, regular curriculum in the middle, and the honors, gifted, and advanced placement classes at the high end.

Unlike in most countries, American schools, by federal law, recognize and provide specific educational accommodations for several physical, emotional, and other disabilities or exceptionalities of students. In some school districts, separate classes are held for such students. In other school districts, however, students with certain degrees or exceptionalities are incorporated into normal classes. This is generally referred to as the "inclusion model". In these classes, specially-trained teachers help the regular classroom teachers to provide instruction to the said students.

Gender groups. In the mixed-gender classroom, girls are known to be less aggressive than boys, although they are of equal intelligence. Teachers should therefore encourage them, and also more consciously engage them in class. Adolescent girls (beginning from late middle school or junior high level through high school) may sometimes need to visit the bathrooms more frequently, especially during their menstruation periods. Male teachers especially may need to understand girls' physiological needs and provide necessary accommodations.

Religious groups. Teachers should be careful not to make disparaging or stereotypical (and largely inaccurate) religious comments, and be more accommodating. For example, Catholic, Moslem or Jewish students who are in religious observations (ex. during fasting period) may be acknowledged and accommodated by providing alternative locations for them during lunch time.

AD(H)D students: Although this is not a formal grouping category, it is still one of the issues that international teachers will have to be thoroughly familiar with, and be able to manage. American schools recognize a medical condition called Attention Deficit (Hyperactive) Disorder (AD[H]D). Students in this group have a physiological problem that causes them to have problems with attention, thus the terminology of "attention deficiency."

There are two groups of students within this category. One sub-group may be diagnosed with only the attention deficiency component of this disorder. This is the ADD classification. The other sub-group may exhibit some amount of heightened activity, and will be found to be in a relatively constant state of distracted activity, and consequently inattentiveness in class. This group is classified as, "attention deficit hyperactive," to capture their active nature.

Although many of these take medications (when so diagnosed) in order to minimize such issues, many of them sometimes forget to take their medication, or may not have been so diagnosed. They could therefore pose a serious challenge to international teachers, and are indeed a major management challenge for even veteran, American-trained teachers.

There are several strategies and accommodations for helping such students. Since the major problem is that of a lack of attention (and constant fidgeting, one idea is to let all the students in the class understand differences among people. At the beginning of the year, students may be allowed to share their strengths and weaknesses, and possibly ask others for understanding from others.

For example, AD(H)D students may explain their condition to the class, and the teacher may inform the class that such students would be allowed to stand in the back of the classroom during their episodes. Hearing-impaired students may explain how their hearing-aids work, and ask for understanding from the class. In fact, the international teacher may seize such an opportunity to ask for understanding about their own accents, and other issues as it pertains to the classroom.

A note of caution: It is important to note that student diagnoses are viewed as private information, and some students may be embarrassed to be viewed as being "deficient" in something, particularly at the middle school level. They may not want to be identified as being different from their peers. Such students' wishes should be respected. Ask them if they would like to share their issues, with their parents' permission, before you take this action.

Another strategy is to use more hands-on activities, which may help such students, since they can then legitimately move in the class. Cooperative activities are also very useful, as explained in this book. It is also helpful not to feed the sensory inputs of such students. This may be done by having cleaner classrooms with less extraneous visuals or audio signals, which all serve as distractions for such students.

Medicating students. Certainly, international teachers will find certain student diversity accommodations very foreign. This may include the fact that many American students are on some kind of medication during the school day. Two common groups may be students with AD(H)D and diabetes. Those in elementary and middle schools may be helped by the school nurse to take their medications. In the high school, however, students are likely to manage own medication issues.

From personal experience, many high school students with AD(H)D do forget to take their medications, owing to the very nature of this disorder, and teachers may need to ask them if they taken their medications, especially if they see a change in their behavior. Recent advances in pharmaceutical technologies have minimized the frequency at which such medications need to be taken, and the related class interruptions caused by students asking for permissions to go out and take their medications.

There are several other ways diversity issues may be manifested in the American school. Although it may seem a rather daunting task to know all about diversity issues in America and respond appropriately, the general rule of thumb is to be sensitive, fair, and judiciously accommodating of all students. There are several college courses and professional development programs that provide information on this issue.

6.6.2 Brain-based learning and multiple intelligences

Brain-based learning, multiple intelligences, and differentiated instruction are some of the current approaches by which diverse learners may be effectively taught.

Brain-based learning. More recently popularized by the work of Eric Jensen (1998) and several others, this approach to teaching and learning takes advantage of advances in neurological research and understandings of how the brain works. Levine (2002) for example points out that many students in schools struggle and fail needlessly because the way in which they learn is incompatible with the way they are conventionally taught. This is because students, even from the same family, may have their brains "wired" differently. Needlessly-struggling students may therefore give up on themselves, convinced that they are not brilliant. A related area of interest is multiple intelligences.

Multiple intelligences. Related to brain-based learning, this theory in its current form was proposed by Gardner (1983). He argued that there is both a biological and cultural basis for intelligence, and that there are multiple intelligences. He proposed that learning occurs as a result of the modifications in the connections among brain cells. The primary basis of this proposal is that different types of learning occur in particular areas of the brain where corresponding brain activities and transformations have occurred.

This is perhaps one of the most poplar instructional modification approaches in American classroom. Teachers may consider downloading and administering multiple intelligences surveys, freely available on the Internet, to find out the learning strengths of their students. A few examples are available at:

- http://www.mitest.com/omitest.htm
- http://snow.utoronto.ca/courses/mitest.html
- http://www.literacyworks.org/mi/assessment/findyourstrengths.html

The following is a modified summary of Gardner's eight intelligences for classroom practice, based on ideas from Meacham's (n.d.) and Special Needs Opportunity Windows Project (n.d.):

Visual/Spatial intelligence. These are people with strong visual capacity. They tend to think in pictures, and will create pictures in their minds to represent thoughts or concepts. Students in this group may enjoy the representation of information through graphs, maps, and other visual representations. During instruction, teachers should consider including activities that allow these learners to:

- see key points demonstrated or summarized with detailed or high-context graphics or visual effects, such as in a PowerPoint presentation, slides, posters, banners, objects, or transparencies
- watch a video or a filmstrip of a process or story, or a dramatic presentation that pertains to the content matter

- use flow chart, maps to arrive at a solution or destination
- interpret visual puns or metaphors that capture a key fact or concept
- use mind-mapping software (such as Inspiration) or graphic organizers to help understand or complement the solution to a problem

Verbal/Linguistic intelligence. These are people with highly developed speaking and listening skills. They often think in words, rather than in pictures. They may enjoy playing language-related games such as rhymes, pun, and poetry. During instruction, these learners will respond particularly well to activities which allow them to:

- listen to, or tell stories that illustrate key learning points on tape, watch television or live debates, discussions, etc.
- take detailed notes during a lecture (may also be recorded during classes for later listening)
- produce class presentations (which may include the use of PowerPoint); read out aloud, and interpret text
- write journals, research reports, and diaries
- have oral assessment (tests and quizzes)

Logical/Mathematical intelligence These are people with a highly developed ability in the application of reason, logic, and numbers. They tend to think by using patterns and linking concepts. These learners always like to ask a lot of "Why?" questions and expect detailed answers that help them link pieces of information together. They may benefit from learning activities such as:

- calculations or working on a spreadsheet with other learners
- conducting or analyzing an experiment and Internet scavenger hunts
- discussing or interviewing the instructor (or subject matter expert to) get the solution to a problem
- debating issues of content interest
- developing theories or conclusions based on facts in evidence
- solving a problem, puzzles, brain-teasers, etc. which may be presented though a crime or mystery, for example

Bodily/Kinesthetic intelligence. These are people with a highly developed ability to control body movements and handle physical objects. They process information by interacting with the physical space around them. It is possible to identify such students by asking them about their after-school activities. Those in sports in general, especially soccer, basketball, baseball, football, drama or dancing, for example may belong to this group. They will respond well to learning activities involving

- Role-playing, modeling (see examples in the mitosis lesson plan in Appendix 2), dramatic presentations, miming, and visuals of ideas or thoughts
- watching videos or presentations that let learners put themselves in the action simulations that let learners make decisions that affect the outcome of the story or case, or see concepts explained through gestures or dance
- hands-on activities and game-like activities that require hand-to-eye coordination
- blended solutions that let them write things out, graph or create something with their hands and share it with the rest of the class or group members through visuals

Musical/Rhythmical intelligence. These are people with a heightened ability to appreciate and produce music. They tend to think in sounds, rhythms, and patterns. They are also very sensitive to environmental sounds that might be interpreted only as background noise by other learners. Some of the following activities are therefore likely to engage these learners effectively:

- compose for them (in the lower grades), or ask them to compose a song or rhythm (including rap and poems) to summarize key points
- associate tones with different stages of a process, different eras in time (ex. louder for recent times, and much softer for distant past), or different levels of performance
- use sound effects to accentuate the key points in a presentation
- play subtle background music to enhance the desired mood (excitement, deep thought, relaxation, etc. One must however be cognizant that students with musical/rhythmical intelligence are extra sensitive to music.)
- use some ideas from verbal/linguistic intelligence, since these two intelligences are somewhat related

Interpersonal intelligence. These are learners with an advanced ability to relate to, and understand the feelings of other people. They often process information by linking it to how other people feel in a given situation (or a related story). They thrive on small group work, exhibit tact and diplomacy, and possibly take leadership roles among peers. During instruction, these learners will respond well to activities such as:

- small group discussion and other cooperative activities
- sharing different points of view (may be done in conjunction with, for example, role-playing a case or process)
- allowing friends or colleagues to quiz each other
- analyzing case studies for motivations, conflict, feelings, or intentions
- using verbal skills to build consensus or agreement

Intrapersonal intelligence. These are people who exhibit a strong sense of self-awareness. They exhibit the ability to understand and share their inner thoughts and feelings. They process information by reflecting on their own strengths and weaknesses, establishing dreams and goals, and understanding their relationships with others. Intrapersonal learning activities might include:

- letting the learner work by him or herself at least a part of the time
- surveys that focus on how the learner feels about a particular subject or fact
- role play showing their own response or emotions in a particular setting or scenario
- discussion of how the actions of others make them feel or think
- retracing how they solved a problem or learned a new skill and applying that process to a new learning situation

Naturalist intelligence. These are people with a heightened appreciation for, and understanding of the world around them. They like to experience nature: landscapes, plants, and animals. They tend to process information best by exploration. These are the students who can effortlessly name and describe the features of several plants, animals, or things around them. These learners will respond well to activities that let them:

- fix, or repair things, or find the native, intuitive solutions to problems
- create an outdoor classroom—especially in science classes—and have some classes there
- take on-campus field trips to survey the plants, animals,

landscapes, architecture, etc.

- take off-campus field trips to interview people of interest, and investigate natural phenomena, as an anthropologist would
- go on Internet scavenger hunts: visit web sites or resource documents and investigate a topic on their own.

6.7 Differentiated Instruction

Tomlinson (1997) believes that instruction could be differentiated in three ways: via content, activities, or products. She cautions that differentiated instruction is not necessarily individualized instruction, but a matching of the child's readiness level with the content. The three areas of differentiation are elaborated in this section.

6.7.1 Differentiating content: A few points of interest

- Know the curriculum: what the students are expected to understand and be able to do. The vital question in this regard is: What are the main (essential) concepts in the lesson?
- Consider the kinds of students are in the class: What do they already know? What can they do (currently)?
- Match the child's readiness level with the content. Here, the essential understanding is to be gained by all students, but students at different ability levels are appropriately challenged by the next idea.
- Present the tasks at multiple levels. Here, the teacher may consider, for example, the use of manipulatives for students cognitively operating at the concrete level. Those operating at the abstract level could work with diagrams which deal with the same concept, or possibly manipulate ideas with unpredictable outcomes.

6.7.2 Differentiating activities

- In this area, the main question to ask is: What are the students' natural gifts? (See Multiple Intelligences above). Depending on the answers, activities may be created which explain the same concept, using the natural intelligence of most of the students in the class.
- Another consideration for differentiating activities is to consider simple-to-complex activities. In this regard, the teacher may create

activity tasks which involve few to several student manipulations before arriving at the final product. For example, a teacher may pre-assemble the apparatus for a science lab for the less advanced students. For the more advanced students, the teacher may consider a more challenging situation which may involve multi-faceted, multiple manipulations before arriving at the product. In both cases, the same concept is addressed and understood. Only the means to the end have been variously modified.

- (Please see Appendix One for a sample (middle or high school level) lesson plan for differentiating instruction according to the theory of multiple intelligences.)

6.7.3 Differentiating products

In differentiating activities, a specific conceptual or cognitive product may be gained. In situations such class projects in science or fine art, product differentiation may be possible. This is normally the culminating product of a series of activities. Here again, the product may be simple to complex but illustrative of the targeted concept. The objective for using this approach is to challenge each student appropriately and optimize their learning.

6.7.4 Assessing differentiated instruction

The assessment of differentiated instruction may be easier to do with rubrics (addressed previously). This method of assessment, while being especially subjective in situations such as this one, is still reasonably specific in how points are allocated. It may therefore help students to know beforehand the exact expectations of specific class work. One advantage of the use of rubrics in connection with differentiated instruction is that even struggling students would know that passing grades are within their practical reaches, if they do their best.

In summary, differentiated instruction may be a powerful means to reach diverse students. It affords the teacher the opportunity to work more intimately with the struggling students, while the more advanced students are also appropriately challenged. By its very nature, it is simultaneously a good approach for taking care of the needs of individual students. Their learning-related issues could therefore be easily observed for more timely intervention. Having done this, teachers may possibly realize that students' behavioral problems may have been preemptively resolved.

6.8   Technology Use and Presentations

In American schools, teachers are generally expected to use some technology in their teaching. This expectation is generally a requirement for the acquisition of a teaching license. (Please see chapter two for more on this subject.) Although the Internet is a popular technology area, it is mostly used by students to research various topics. It is also a useful place to find pre-made lesson plans for various topics—all ready for use after minor revisions to suit one's instructional preferences.

During presentations, it is very common to find both teachers and students using Microsoft's PowerPoint program. This program permits teachers to scan their own diagrams or insert various diagrams. Such technology-mediated instruction may be especially useful if they teach the same subject in the future. All one needs to do is a minor revision of the lesson plan, and it is ready for use. One can then learn more to become fancier and more innovative with the program and topics over the years. It is indeed a wonderful tool.

There are many other technologies available, especially for science teachers. For example, many experiments may be done using "probes," which can be purchased from several competing companies. Such lab activities are mostly computer-mediated, and should be used in upper-level classes, probably in cooperative group situations, since most schools do not have enough computers for each student in the class. Once the equipment is available, such technology-related labs are easy to teach, and may be taught with lesson plans prepared with PowerPoint, for example.

There are several other competing companies which provide free or subscription-based services. For example, the Global Thinking Project (http://www2.gsu.edu/~wwwgtp/) provides free services, whereby several teachers around the world cooperatively work with other teachers on projects such as International Clean Air Project (ICAP), which is done every Fall or International Water Watch Project, done in the Spring. Discovery school (http://school.discovery.com) and Blackboard (http://www.blackboard.com) are both examples of services where teachers can have access to topic-specific lesson plans, lesson ideas, interesting inclusions such as puzzle-makers for quizzes, and place their tests, assignments, grades, etc. on-line. Some of these websites also provide on-line access to both parents and students. Students can therefore do their homework on-line, and parents can check their children's progress on-line.

Several schools do pay the subscription fees for all interested teachers to take advantage of such facilities. International teachers will find such websites an invaluable tool for making teaching and learning both fun and fulfilling. They are also very easy to learn and use. They should therefore not be intimidated by technology. Thanks to competition, current technologies are very user-friendly. Those which are not user-friendly are likely to lose customers and go out of business.

Any teacher planning to use the school's computer labs (normally located in the libraries which are also called Media Centers) should plan ahead and reserve the computer lab in time. In some schools, teachers may be afforded a few computers (also called "work stations") in their own classrooms for student group work.

International teachers need to seize the opportunities provided by school districts to participate in technology workshops—normally provided during professional teacher workdays, or at the school district level—which are all geared toward upgrading teacher competencies in this important area of teaching.

6.9   Teaching Large Classes

Although teachers in primary and secondary institutions may not teach larger classes beyond forty students in most cases, it is still possible to have rather large audiences in some classrooms. Many initial college course enrolments may reach over hundred students. In such situations, it is difficult—but not impossible—to teach to meet the needs of individual students. One reason is that such classes are generally held in "lecture halls," tacitly expectant of the lecture approach of instructional delivery, and cooperative activities are difficult to execute in this physical environment. Even in such situations, teachers can consider other means, including the use of technology to present their lessons so as to facilitate learning—and arguably, teaching.

Instructional presentations may be made using projection technologies. The first type may be overhead projector, which is the least expensive and most common in American classrooms. These are useful in cases where instructors may need to provide immediate feedback to students. Diagrams or other illustrations can be immediately provided to students. In classes where illustrations and problem samples may not be necessary, premeditated or prepared notes may be delivered, using PowerPoint or similar programs. There are other technologies for providing immediate feedback during instruction such as overhead LCD projectors, but these are not commonly found in American classrooms because they are much more expensive. They however, are available in a few wealthy universities and private schools.

Another useful way to organize very large classes is to consider the use of on-line format as supplementary instruction to the classroom experience. In these situations, personal, department-hosted websites, WebCT, Blackboard, or Discovery formats may be considered for organizing students into learning groups. These are very helpful for helping students who may otherwise not meet or know each other in larger classes to work cooperatively, sometimes on topics of personal interest. Students may meet each other on-line, and discuss their course content, assignments, and help each other in the process. Depending on the purpose for which this technology format is being considered, instructors may

- post their lecture, or "interactive" lecture notes (if it involves solicited responses)
- post their course schedule (or plan of activities)
- include a discussion or bulletin board for "asynchronous" class discussions (whereby students may post, read and respond to questions and each others' entries at different times in a given period of time.) It is advisable to specify the number of responses to other entries for any given time. For example, the author expects his own students to post one original entry by midnight on Wednesday, and respond to two others' by midnight on Sunday
- add a "student forum." Asynchronous class discussions may also be used as a "student forum" when it is used for students to discuss emerging issues of interest in the course
- have a chat room: a "synchronous" discussion in which all the discussants meet at the same time. In this format, it is advisable not to have more than 5-6 participants per meeting. Note that both synchronous and asynchronous group discussions can be facilitated by specified leaders, such as leaders for sub- or topical-groups of a larger group. Leadership may also be on a rotational basis
- include an e-mail for sending and receiving messages concerning the course—and students may exchange messages among themselves
- administer tests on-line—and such tests may be automatically graded (see Assessing Large Classes below for more on this)
- submit assignments

And the list goes on. Having used some of these formats for several years now, and having designed distance education courses for on-line delivery, the author is familiar with the ease with which such technologies can be adapted to large classes, and also for exclusively on-line instruction.

6.10 Assessing Large Classes

One of the most significant problems with teaching very large classes is assessment. Unlike small, seminar-type classes that can be held for classes (generally fewer that 20 students, and each student may present on a given topic per class—and essay-type assessments may be easily managed), larger classes may not lend themselves to such provisions as easily. In such cases, technology may still be available to help.

First of all, it is very easy to use the multiple-choice and true-false testing formats. Many recent textbooks now come with "test banks" for instructors (also normally available in electronic form). The tests may be easily photocopied and administered to all the students. During the administration of the tests, students can be made to use machine-specific scanning sheets (an example is one made by a company called Scantron, similar to the types used in standardized tests such as GCE and GRE examinations). By running the students' scanning sheets through the machine, it is possible to grade a 100-item test for 100 students within 10 minutes!

If such a machine is not available, it is still possible to be innovative: Create your tests as usual and print copies out. It is very important *not* to staple student copies of the test. During the administration of the test, remind students not to staple their work, but to use clips to bind them together. On the master copy (which should be printed only on one side of the paper, make about 2-3 millimeter holes exactly on the letters corresponding to the correct answers. Using a felt-tipped pen, superimpose the master on the students' copies, and mark inside the holes, page, by page. Using this technique, an instructor may grade the work in large classes easier and quicker.

The last possibility is a technology offered by formats such as WebCT, Blackboard, Discovery, and other currently emerging formats. Here, instructors may post their questions into templates within the technology, and indicate the correct answers. Students may then "log on" and take their tests, which are immediately graded by the formatting company's system. The test grades are then sent in directly to the e-mail address of the instructor, according to course sections or classes. In this way, one instructor may teach several classes, and have all the grading done by technology.

The beauty of the system discussed above is that, it is still possible to administer short-answer type of tests, which are then graded according to key words or terms.

6.11 Summary

International teachers are likely to find the nature of the American educational system different from what they are familiar with. This unfamiliarity, synergized by the nature of America students, could generate an initial challenge for them. International teachers therefore need to review certain classroom management and technology skills in order to become effective in their American schools, since plain lectures and notes on the board are likely to end in teacher failure.

Two classroom management models worthy of interest are the behavioral management model and the humanistic/developmental approach. The behavioral management model is based on the belief that future human behavior is contingent on past experience, and international teachers may find some of the specific approaches in this model to be familiar. The humanistic/developmental approach disciplines with dignity, using effective communication, conflict resolution, self-control, and need-fulfillment. Teachers coming from authoritarian (stricter), teacher-controlled environments may find a need to learn more about this model.

In general, instructional strategies may generally be seen as either teacher-centered or student-centered. Teacher-centered approaches tend to be more labor-intensive, given the demands of the American classroom. Student-centered instructional approaches, on the other hand, tend to tap into the energies and the enthusiasm of students for instruction.

In American schools, teachers are generally expected to dress professionally, and use some technology in their teaching.

The American classroom is generally diverse, especially in the larger cities where foreign teachers are likely to teach. Classroom issues related to ethnic diversity, ability, gender, religious, and other diversity groups should be considered during teaching and learning, and appropriate strategies employed to address their specific needs.

Chapter #7

IMPLICATIONS OF RESEARCH FOR EMPLOYERS

How to Help International Teachers to Succeed in American Classrooms

7.1 What International Teachers Bring to American Schools

The preceding chapters have indicated that international teachers have the potential to become great assets to their local schools. There are for several reasons for this, and school administrators may be pleased to know some of them.

7.1.1 Strong content knowledge

Throughout the study of international teachers leading to this book, knowledge of subject or content matter was never raised as a concern. This should be very interesting for relevant school administrators. In many countries such as Germany and Ghana, teacher education candidates are expected to have a full major and a minor in their content areas. Pedagogical education is taken above and beyond these content areas.

In Ghana, a science teacher education candidate, for example, would be expected to have a full major in chemistry, and a minor in botany. For this reason, it was not a surprise that Kofi, one of the featured international teachers in this book (from Ghana), was hailed as an intellectual star in his American school. He was very competent in all the science academic areas, and also in mathematics. In fact, although his major was physics (with a minor in mathematics), he had written a textbook in organic chemistry.

Similar stories could be told about Inga: a woman who was teaching physics and really enjoyed it. As most administrators know, this is rare in America, where most physics teachers (who are generally hard to find) are males. Joe taught chemistry, and had indicated that he had taught physics previously. Mary taught biology at the senior, International Baccalaureate level; a very academically-intensive program. In each of the cases in this research, the international teachers were extremely competent in their content areas. It is not a surprise that some of these teachers are receiving various awards in their American schools or school districts. (Read more about this at http://www.vifprogram.net/about/newslist.xml.

7.1.2 Global view of issues and better learning outcomes

International teachers, by the very fact that they are cross-cultural educators, means that they bring new perspectives to their schools. They become the immediately-available, international resources within their schools—both to the faculty and the students at large. As explicitly indicated by the teachers featured in this book, matters of academic interest took on new meaning when global perspectives were shed on them. It is one thing to cite the literature in order to produce examples about AIDS crisis in Africa, or the social effects of the Second World War on Germany. It is a different story to have an African teacher in person talking about the issue of AIDS in Africa, or a German teacher directly engaging the students in an academic discourse on German issues. This naturally helps to pique students' curiosity and therefore helps to foster learning. Several stories expressing this notion have been reported in some newspapers in the United States. (See http://www.vifprogram.net/about/newslist.xml.

7.1.3 Local ambassadors and authority

People who travel internationally may be expected to become the local ambassadors for their countries, and so are international teachers within their school systems. In addition to bringing new perspectives to discussions, international teachers within schools have been commonly known to act as the "go-to" people on questions pertaining to their countries. Those teaching languages, for example, may present authentic, native language proficiency to both the students and the faculty. They may also act as informal consultants to other faculty in their relevant areas of expertise or general knowledge.

7.2   Implications of Research for Employers

It has been indicated that this book is based on the research of international teachers' issues, and how to help them to become effective teachers. Several issues were uncovered in this study that had significant implications for the employers of this new, skilled workforce. The basic findings in the research are hereafter referred to in this book as the "assertions." These assertions are directly discussed in this chapter, with a view to helping new international teachers and their employers.

The first assertion, the fundamental issue in this research, indicated that certain peculiar issues arise for international teachers when they migrate to teach in a new cultural environment. This is the primary point to which all the other assertions respond. Assertion two proposes that international teachers are likely to encounter certain socio-logistical issues when they initially arrive in the U.S. Such issues are discussed in more details below.

7.2.1 Socio-cultural issues and solutions

International teachers, being new entrants into the U.S., should be expected to experience some amount of culture shock. Although "culture shock" may be variously defined, international teachers' culture shock experiences may be distinguished from the kind that tourists may experience, since tourists' experiences may be relatively more transient. People experiencing culture shock pass through a series of psychological stages, and may eventually acculturate into the new culture. (More discussion of culture shock is found in chapter one.) According to an article in The Christian Science Monitor,

> Regardless of how experienced a teacher is, it takes them at least six months to adjust to American culture ... [Foreign recruits may be] trying to find a house, rent an apartment, ... buy a car," says [an official] of the California Department of Education, which has hired more than 400 instructors temporarily over the past three years. Los Angeles also plans to hire Filipino and Canadian teachers this fall. (Cook, 2000, on-line)

Time is therefore a needed critical factor for such transplants to navigate their acculturation issues.

Administrators responsible for hiring should be aware of the fact that the first year is going to be critical for international teachers' later success and decision to continue employment in their schools. The international teachers featured in this book strongly indicated that their first years were more difficult for them, since they needed time to establish their "support systems." Such support systems included getting their driver's license, credit cards, learning about driving in the new country, the routes to work and alternatives, recreational activities, etc.

The above factors are termed "support systems" because, although they may not be directly important for teaching, they nevertheless have an impact on the emotional and psychological states of international teachers, and therefore on their effectiveness in the classroom.

Several other issues, including language and logistics, have been mentioned elsewhere in this book as being of critical importance for new, international teachers.

One clear solution to some of the issues raised in this book is to complete the hiring of international teachers early. The new hires should then be permitted to enter the country as early as possible, preferably early Summer. This is a great time for international teachers to learn about the new country, since Summer is a very active and sociable season. During this time, they would have enough opportunities to procure their support systems (both physical and emotional), and also have some time to become acculturated to the new environment.

The logistical support systems mentioned here may include driving license, bank accounts, personalized teaching materials, and proper orientation to the U.S. Compounded by culture shock, these acquisitions can be rather overwhelming for new teachers. If the new teachers arrive early enough in the U.S., they may then have enough time to begin putting to ether teaching materials they may deem necessary for their new teaching assignments, or to retrieve important items they may have left back in their native countries.

Again, during this time, they would become familiar with their way around the city or town, have opportunities to meet people, and learn the cultural and linguistic norms of the new region. Consequently, they would learn to communicate more effectively with their colleagues and students, in response to the issues raised in assertion six.

7.2.2 Knowledge gap issues and solutions

Assertion three states that, "International teachers go through 'knowledge gaps' because of the differences between their native countries' curricular and institutional setups and those of the U.S." An orientation should therefore be provided (more on this later) that includes a clear picture of the U.S. educational system, its philosophies, and practices. International teachers would then be able to differentiate between their native country's educational philosophy and that of the U.S., and use that information to shape their personal classroom practices.

A related issue is raised in assertion four, which posits that there is a difference in how different countries philosophically view the nature of assessments, and this is reflected in the way grades are assigned to students. Although this issue is best resolved only with practice, it may still be useful to provide examples of graded student work for the international teachers. This will help them to judge the "gap" between their own "estimated grade" for a sample student work and that of a veteran, successful local teacher.

The above notion is in harmony with the observations of Doran, Lawrenz, and Hegelson (1994), who noted that the term "evaluation" could be defined as "the process of making carefully determined value judgments and decisions related to the issues and concerns a given assessment has focused on e.g., student achievement, program quality." (p. 388) The idea of "value judgment" can however, be rather idiosyncratic and personal. A working knowledge of U.S. assessment criteria would eliminate, or at least mitigate numerous potential contentions between the international teacher and his or her students, parents, or school administrators.

Assertion five perhaps raises the most critical issue that the international teacher would to contend with: dealing with a different breed of students. It states that, "United States high school students have relatively higher self-esteem, and expect their teachers to be relatively more available, and to have a relationship with them, if they so desire." To note that this is the most "critical issue," is to imply that the all the issues raised in the seven assertions come to a convergence in the classroom. International teachers do not only have to deal with their students as Americans and relate to them culturally (assertion two), but they also need to know how their school operates (assertion three), and assess their students' work (assertion four). All this needs to be done—and indeed can be done only through effective communication with the students (assertion six).

The notion that U.S. students may have a relatively higher self-esteem bears concomitantly greater expectations of personal relationships with their teachers. This could potentially greet international teachers from more hierarchical societies with strife, and generate some problems in their instructional methods. This is because the "sage on stage" approach would not augur well in several U.S. classrooms: Assertion five indicates that the U.S. student may be expected to question more in class, and wants his or her voice to be heard—and it is heard—by both parents and school administrators. Implicitly, therefore, the international teacher should be forewarned about the value of student voice in American teaching and learning. Success in this area is likely to percolate several other areas of the international teachers' teaching practice. The nature of the U.S. student; their characteristics and expectations in school is therefore an area to be greatly emphasized during any international teacher orientation.

The final implication of this study is related to the final assertion, which states that, "the teaching methods used by the international teachers were determined by the issues of student behavior, time available per student, and resources available." Although international teachers may be veterans in their native countries, they should be expected to go through some induction issues, similar to new local inductees to teaching. Should this be the case, school administrators should heed the precautions of Odell (1989) and

Reinhartz (1989), who both agree that certain skills, including managerial competence and pedagogic skills are areas of concern for new teachers. Reinhartz in particular laments that despite these areas of concern for teacher inductees, schools expect them to be as competent as veteran teachers, and that this is not only unrealistic, but also unfair to new teachers.

It is traditionally known in U.S. schools that newer teachers generally are the "floaters." This means that, should there be classroom shortages, they would have to "teach from their carts," and go from classroom to classroom. They would thereby lose their precious time between classes, in transit to the next classroom.

Again, newer teachers are traditionally given several different classes, requiring more preparation time. Worse still, newer teachers may be given the classes with the most difficult students to manage. (Classroom management problems are popularly cited as a critical reason in determining the retention of new teacher recruits in U.S. schools.) Naturally, such classes are avoided by the veteran teachers, who have more clout with class planners. New teachers are therefore besieged by several issues in their initial entry into the profession, thereby discouraging them from considering teaching as a long-term career.

From this study, it was clear that all the teachers wanted more preparation time in order to function more effectively. Administrators could therefore make some efforts at minimizing any potential problem areas for their international teachers, and also to maximize their planning times. This would naturally help them to reflect more on their teaching practice, have the time to look for more relevant teaching materials, and to become familiar with existing resources. This will also allow them more time to adjust their native knowledge of the curriculum to suit their new environments, know their students and colleagues (or mentors) on a more personal basis, thereby helping them to become more effective teachers. (See Pedagogical Content Knowledge for more.)

7.3 Taking Action

In response to the assertions raised in this research, the optimal, feasible solution would be an effective orientation directed at the issues raised. Such an orientation should be tailored to two main questions. The first part of the orientation needs to address the basic question: How is life lived in the U.S., and what do I need in order to live a comfortable life? This part of the orientation should address such questions concerning cultural norms, credit cards and driver's license acquisition, where points of interest are located, local expressions, and the like. In sum, this is an orientation to life in the U.S.: a socio-cultural orientation.

The second part of the orientation should address the question: How can I become an effective teacher in the U.S.? At minimum, general educational expectations in U.S. schools should be addressed. This would include such topics as the U.S. educational system and its operations, job expectations, assessment issues and related philosophies, and student characteristics. If resources allow, pedagogical issues specifically tailored to subject areas should be addressed. This would prepare international teachers more adequately, optimally, and specifically to their discipline areas. This is important, since it is vital for new teachers to become familiar with local examples and issues of interest in order to make their lessons more realistic and relevant to their new students.

7.4   Orientations: Creating the Right Infrastructure for International Teachers

A significant portion of this book is devoted to the research and discussion of classroom issues faced by real international teachers. For the administrator, this is a section of significant interest, since the issues of student learning and learning outcomes converge there.

It has been discussed at length that it may be rather presumptuous to expect teachers who have had different pedagogical training, different content emphases, and different student characteristics to perform effectively in a new pedagogical environment. It is therefore reasonable to expect them to encounter some degree of difficulty, depending on how their previous professional experiences compare to their current assignments. Preparations should therefore be made in order to orient international teachers to the new professional climate.

7.4.1 Introduction to the community

So far, it has been strongly emphasized that one of the initial issues international teachers are likely to face is the lack of social logistics needed to live comfortably within the American society. This may include the acquisition of driver's license, bank accounts, awareness of recreational facilities, and the general knowledge of their larger surroundings. A good solution to this problem may be to organize some help to address such issues.

During the Summers, veteran teachers may be happy to help these new teachers by showing them around town; even to help them to open a bank account, get car tags, a driver's license, etc. Another good idea may be to create a welcome package, which may include maps of the area, important telephone numbers, and areas of interest. Once again, if a mentor is obtained for the new teachers, they could possibly help them with such issues, and it will be advisable to solicit such social help from the mentors as a part of mentoring.

7.4.2 Introduction to the personal classroom

One significant difference many international teachers may experience in U.S. schools is that teachers have their own classrooms, and that they remain there throughout the school day. The students, instead of having permanent seats in a classroom (as found in many countries), are rather the ones who move around the campus to the teachers' classrooms. International teachers may therefore need some help on how to plan and manage their own classrooms; keeping a poster board, electronics, science laboratories (for science teachers), ordering teaching supplies, and such issues.

International teachers should therefore be given some information on what their teaching responsibilities will entail. This may include ensuring that they have adequate knowledge concerning stationery and other instructional needs (especially for those in the sciences, where they may have to pre-order laboratory instructional materials) and plan accordingly, well in advance of classes.

7.4.3 Campus tour

One of the most confusing things about U.S. schools—especially high schools in the large metropolitan areas, where international faculty are likely to be employed—is the sheer hugeness of the campuses. From the school gymnasium on one part of the campus to the school fields; tennis and basketball courts, football and soccer fields, golfing practice area (in the more prestigious schools), new teachers can easily feel overwhelmed by the campus. It can easily become very confusing for new people to a school, if one added to the rather overwhelming campus issue, the maze of classrooms accommodating several hundred to a few thousand students.

A tour of the campus with a good map can be useful in helping new teachers to initially find their way around campus. This should be done well in advance of the first day of school, preferably during the period of orientation mentioned elsewhere in this book. One suggestion may be a bus tour of the campus, and then a walking tour of the more interesting areas, especially around the classrooms. In time, the teachers may find time to visit other areas of personal interest.

7.4.4 Technology tour

Although this may sound rather trifle, a technology tour of the campus may be critical to the effective functioning of new international faculty. It may come as a surprise to some that, although most equipment found in U.S. schools appear to be standardized, such standards (as indicated by the international teacher, Mary featured in this book), can differ across international borders. The power supplies can be different: 110-120 volts in the U.S., 220-240 volts in Europe and several other places around the world. Power plugs and adapters, and even paper sizes may be different. This implies that appliances with which they are familiar are not likely to be exactly the same in the U.S. Photocopiers may be expected to have different appearances, different buttons, and grading machines may be totally foreign to them, depending on where they come from. The use of security codes to lock or open doors, and other apparently insignificant, but potentially irritating factors should all be considered in this technology tour.

Within the classroom, the use of technology takes on a new meaning. This is something that can be introduced during the initial orientation, and more meaningfully during professional days with the school technology staff.

During an initial meeting, such tools as grade book programs, the use of the Internet to access specific, school-specific material such as the standards, and formats for lesson-planning should be emphasized.

In later technology sessions, other basic programs such as those used for writing tests can then be introduced. Although it is likely that international teachers immigrating to teach in U.S. schools are familiar with certain basic technology skills, it is still important to ensure that they have had the opportunity to become familiar with what is available in their new schools.

Once a mentor is in place, they can help out with subject-specific technology, such as probes in science laboratories, and perhaps GIS for geography.

7.4.5 Pedagogical tour

Administrators may consider showing a video of "best practices" in teaching within the school (or in a model American school) to their new international teachers. Although these teachers are probably strong in their content areas and pedagogy, they may still benefit from a good visual cue of how the best local teachers manage instruction and their students. As has been indicated elsewhere in this book, international teachers coming to America from many countries may be good managers of content, but may not necessarily be used to the management needs exacted by the nature of American students. For most international teachers, the nature of American students will likely necessitate a modification of their pedagogical repertoires in order to foster better classroom management, since the two issues are related. Video tapes and other avenues for effective instructional strategies may be useful for them

The retention of international teachers—very much like the retention issues of native, U.S.-born teachers—will be heavily contingent on how well they are able to manage their students.

7.4.6 Introduction to school staff

In many schools in the U.S., each academic year begins with the introduction of new faculty at general meetings; both at staff meetings and all-school (including students) assemblies. The agenda at this assembly sometimes includes the exhibition of the accomplishments of individual faculty to their peers (and students), and to encourage the audience to strive for similar accomplishments.

The administrator must bear in mind that the select international teachers who eventually end up in the U.S. have been hand-picked for several reasons. First of all, they possess the required credentials to work in the U.S. schools. Secondly, they include some of the more accomplished teachers available in their given countries. Such teachers have already been successful in one culture, are probably multilingual, and possess certain multicultural insights—all beyond the call of basic qualifications. Thirdly, such teachers have been hand-picked from a pool of several competitors, and are therefore the best of the lot.

For the reasons above, it is likely that many international teachers have certain peculiar traits that can be used as a part of their introduction to other staff. These traits may be important to emphasize, since they may serve as a social stimulus which may attract the interest of other faculty members in the new teachers—something that both parties may cherish and find socially and academically productive.

7.4.7 Mentoring

Mentoring should be done by a mature faculty member, preferably one with some international exposure. Mentors for international teachers who hail from developing nations should be chosen especially carefully. This is important because on rare occasions, it is very possible for local teachers attempting to joke with them to inadvertently patronize such teachers with rather pejorative comments. This may come in the form of belittling comments on their foreign names, clothes, or hairstyles, etc. Although international teachers may generally tolerate such jokes, they may not necessarily enjoy them. Administrators who hire international teachers, (especially those from developing nations), should therefore discreetly train their standing faculty to be careful with certain comments, and be sensitive to unwelcome or otherwise unproductive comments.

7.4.8 Introduction to the student body

The introduction of the new international faculty to the general student body should be conducted in a similar fashion as was suggested for their introduction to the school faculty and staff at large. Preferably, it should be done during the first all-school assembly. Here, again, the primary objective for their introduction is to create a good psychological image about them to the students. Their accomplishments should be emphasized, and some interesting, laudable comments about their native countries may be mentioned as well.

7.4.9 Introduction to other helping agencies

Depending on their countries of origin, the accents of international teachers may range from light to heavy. One way to help those with significant accents is to consider sponsoring them to attend an accent reduction course. Such courses, as mentioned earlier in this book, are sometimes available in local universities, but may be sought out. They commonly last about six weeks, (meeting for about 60-90 minutes on a specific week day, in the evening), and could be a good investment in the long run. Such meetings are often very conversational, and are attended by people with the common interest of reducing their accents. It could therefore potentially prove to be a good social outlet for new international teachers. Another idea is to introduce them to social groups such as Toastmasters and Rotary International Clubs, which all have an orientation toward international people. Recorded material (audio-visuals), are also commonly available for purchase and circulation.

7.5 Summary

Administrators responsible for hiring should be heartened to learn that international teachers bring a lot of assets into the U.S. classroom. These may include strong content knowledge, a global view of issues and better learning outcomes, and the ability to serve as local ambassadors for, and authorities on their countries or continents.

Once they have been hired, administrators should be aware of the fact that, international teachers, just like all new teachers, will experience their own peculiar induction issues. What is done for them during the initial year is likely to be critical to their later success, and also their decision to continue to work in their current schools.

The hiring of international teachers should be completed early enough, possibly two to three full months in advance of the semester, so that they may enter the country sooner. This would provide them enough time to procure their support systems—both physical and emotional—and also have some time to become acculturated to the new culture.

There are two general areas that merit the support consideration of administrators, and new teacher orientations may be good responsive solutions to them. The first part of the orientation needs to address the basic question: How is life is the U.S., and what do I need to live a comfortable life? This part of the orientation should address such questions concerning cultural norms, credit cards and driver's license acquisitions, where points of interest are located, local expressions, and the like. In sum, this is an orientation to life in the U.S.: a socio-cultural orientation.

The second part of the orientation should address the question: How can I become an effective teacher in the U.S.? At minimum, general educational expectations in U.S. schools should be addressed. This would include such topics as the U.S. educational system and its operations; job expectations; assessment issues and related philosophies; and student characteristics. During this part of the orientation, school administrators should also consider how to create the right infrastructure for their international faculty. Items on the agenda should include: introduction to the personal classroom; a campus tour; technology tour, and pedagogical tour. Introductions to the staff and student body and mentoring should also be considered. Finally, other forms of support should be considered as necessary.

Relocating into a new country is not an easy venture. Moving to teach in a new cultural context is even more challenging, yet feasible. With an open, welcoming environment such as America's, and an open mind such as the international teachers', there is a lot of learning waiting to happen. Welcome to the teacher's life in America!

Appendix

Appendix 1

Lesson Planning Considerations

Teacher_____ Subject_____ Grade level _____

a. Rationale for the Lesson (Optional in many school systems, since the curricula or pacing guides nullifies its inclusion.)

- Why is this lesson necessary, important, or useful to the students?

- Why do I want to teach it at this time in the lesson sequence? Etc.

b. Statement of Objectives/Desired Student Outcomes

- State which subject standards are addressed (For example, North Carolina Standards Course of Study. These are often provided by the departments, as a part of the pacing guide for teaching.)

- Concepts (knowledge base) to be developed (For example, characteristics of reptiles)

- Process skills to be developed (For example, how to make inferences or predictions; use instruments; or write science reports.)

- Note: Include 3-4 objectives. These may easily be crafted from the main topics in the textbook.

c. Lesson sequence (There are several available. Examples are the constructivist and conceptual change models. Many school districts have their own computer-based schemes for their teachers to follow. Find this out from the department chair or mentor.)

- What will you do and how will you do it, and for how long? State these as briefly as reasonable. Remember that this is a general guide, and deviations may occur as the real lesson proceeds.

- Using the "constructivist sequence":

    1. **Invitation Phase:** This is the introduction phase in other models, and may include a review and a "hook" or focus activity that may attract and hold students' attention. Some ideas are showing relevant video clips, demonstration, stories, etc. See chapter 6 for more of such ideas under Multiple Intelligences.

    2. **Exploration Phase** (Guided Practice and Independent Practice in other models.) In this and the next phases, teachers may refer to the instructional approaches mentioned in chapter 6 and select appropriate strategies.

    3. **Explanation Phase** (Check for Understanding in other models.) As the term implies, this is the phase during which the teacher uses different means to ensure that students understand the lesson.

    4. **Taking Action or Extension Phase** In this phase (which may possibly happen outside the classroom), teachers help students to understand the concepts by doing something related to the lesson concepts)

d. Student Accommodations (Individual Educational Plans [IEPs]) In situations such as "inclusion classes," where different kinds of students have been intentionally brought together, teachers may need to make some adaptations of their lessons to suit all learners. For example, in English as Second Language (ESL) student accommodations, one could have Spanish-speaking students seated with other bi-lingual students to facilitate translation of oral presentation. Oral assessment may be considered for ESL students. One may also use the Spanish-to-English Translation Text provided by Webster's along with textbooks and workbooks which come in

Spanish versions. AD(H)D students may be seated closer to the instructor, and be provided with color-coded worksheets. Videos and PowerPoint presentations may be considered for visual learners, and mnemonics and songs may be considered for verbally- or musically-oriented students, and the list goes on. (These kinds of accommodations have been discussed at length under Multiple Intelligences.)

e. Remedial Work: (This may be planned work for struggling or absentee students)

f. Assessment: (How will you determine that every student attained each objective?)

Criteria for Evaluating Your Lesson Plan

1. Do the objectives reflect the local school standards?

2. Can the objectives be adequately addressed in the available lesson period?

3. Is the lesson content appropriate for the grade level and cognitive development of the students?

4. Is there evidence of continuity with previous lessons?

5. Are the instructional approaches employed effective enough to help the students to achieve the expected learning outcomes?

6. Are the assessments options used effective enough to help you to know if your students met each objective?

Appendix 2

Topic: Cell Growth and Division

Rationale

Children sometimes wonder how they grow. Many believe that they are just stretching and getting bigger as they eat more food. (Alternative or misconception research deals with such studies.) With the introduction of cloning and related issues in the U.S. media, many students probably know about cells, by the fifth grade. They would understand that things could be made of basic units (stages of cognitive development). They will then begin to wonder if growth occurs though the enlargement of cells. This lesson (series), by using several teaching techniques, in conjunction with the constructivist model as the basis, could help change students' beliefs, and also introduce new information.

National Science Education Standards (Grades 5-8)

Structure and function in living systems: Cells carry on the many functions needed to sustain life. They grow and divide, thereby producing more cells.

Assessed QCC (Gwinnett County Local Schools) Standards (Grade 7)

Life Science Standard: Identifies the cell as a basic unit of life. 6.1 Describes the structure and functions of major components and organelles to include nucleus, nuclear membranes, cytoplasm, cell membrane, chromosomes, vacuoles, golgi bodies, lysosomes, endoplasmic reticulum (rough and smooth) and mitochondria. 6.2 Compares and contrasts the major structures and functions of typical plant and animal cells. 6.3 Discusses and illustrates the organization of cells into tissues, organs, and systems. 6.4 Describes and discusses the movement of materials into and out of the cell for the maintenance of homeostasis. 6.5 Describes the process of mitosis and meiosis. 6.6 Outlines the events that occur in meiosis and mitosis.

Focus Questions:

What is mitosis?

What are the phases of mitosis?

What happens during each phase of the mitotic process?

Intended Learning Outcomes

Cognitions:
Students will
- understand the process of mitosis
- know the meanings of related vocabulary terms

Cognitive Skills:
Students will be able to
- describe the process by which cells reproduce
- explain each phase of the mitotic process
- correctly define the terms associated with this lesson (vocabulary list)
- make inferences concerning how their own bodies grow

(Psycho)motor Skills:
- Students will be able to demonstrate (act out) all phases of mitosis

Affects:
Students will
- appreciate current issues in the news/media, such as cloning, and abortion
- value the place of nutrition in their lives
- respect their own bodies, and appreciate how wonderfully the body works

Procedures/Activities

Invitation Phase: 10 minutes *(Numbered Heads Together)*
1. Tell students that today's lesson is about cell growth and division. Tell the class they will jump the first "conventional" aspect of the topic (cell cycle) so that some time would be available to talk about the theory of the pedagogy. Using the *numbering-off approach,* create 5-6 groups of 4 or 5.
2. Assign four or five "offices" (of responsibility—such as materials manager, communicator, etc.) according to the numbers in each group.
3. Pose the discussion questions:
- How does a human being grow from a single fertilized cell into an individual containing billions of cells?
- Do all the cells of the body contain the same genetic information?
- How is the genetic blueprint that makes you who you are transmitted faithfully from one cell to the next?

Call out a random number (*using the numbered heads together strategy):* Take a sheet of paper, tear it into small pieces, and write the numbers 1-4 on them (or 5, depending on how many students are in each group). Roll the papers and put them into a little container, and call out a student randomly to draw a number. The number picked is used for selecting each group's representative (in step 1, above) to share with the class. This will instill the sense of responsibility in all the group members, since any could be called upon to present to the class.

Exploration Phase: 20 minutes
At this point the class should take everything off their desks and get ready for the next part of the lesson.
- Present the students with the hand-outs with the diagrams.
- Recap cell parts and the fact that the cell is at the end of the cell cycle, and is ready for nuclear division. Present the PowerPoint show of the mitotic process, emphasizing the vocabulary words.
- Present (or hand out) the instructions and materials for modeling the mitotic process.

Explanation Phase: 10 minutes
Using the modified *Jigsaw Approach (whereby a topic is sectioned into sections to be dealt with by different groups or students within the class)*, let each student group present (by acting them out, through skits) a given phase to the class. One person (other than the previous presenter—pick from the 3 rolled cards left in step 3 above) should explain to the class what is going on within the cell, especially with regard to the chromosomes and chromatids).

Taking Action/Extension: 5 minutes

Visit websites of interest (from a prescribed "hotlist") and use the information read to create a concept map, using the Inspiration program. Students may finish this work overnight as homework.

Assessment
Teacher may use the school system's unit test, or use on-line sites such as Discovery Learning, Big Chalk, etc.

Remedial Work
Assign a "buddy" to help explain difficult concepts if needed. Allow students to use their notes to correct their test papers, and present a concept map (or webbing) of the unit. Assign alternative test.

Materials and Equipment

Plastic spoons, forks, and knives (8 of each per group), scissors, yarn, grains (may use cereal, so students can eat some for fun), adhesive (edible, "gummy bears" or cellotape).

References

Atwater, M. & Riley, J. P. (1993). Multicultural science education: Perspectives, definitions, and research agenda. Science Education 77(6): 661-668. John Wiley & Sons, Inc.

Banks, J. A. (1993). Multicultural education: Development, dimensions, and challenges. In J. W. Noll (Ed.). Taking Sides: Clashing views on controversial educational issues (9th ed.). (pp. 88-103). Connecticut: Dushkin/McGraw-Hill.

Banks, J. A., & McGhee Banks, C. A. (Eds.) (1995). Handbook of Research on Multicultural Education. New York, NY: Simon & Schuster/Macmillan.

Bellah, R. N., Madsen, R., Sullivan, W. M., Swidler, A. & Tipton, S. M. (1996). Habits of the heart. Berkely and Los Angeles, CA: University of California Press.

Bodley, J. H. (1997). Cultural anthropology: Tribes, states, and the global system. Mountain View, CA: Mayfield Publishing Company.

Bowles, S. & Gintis, H. (1976). Schooling in capitalist America: Educational reform and contradictions of economic life. New York: Basic Books.

The British Council-USA. (n.d.) Education in the United States of America. Retrieved July 26, 2003, from
http://www.britishcouncil-usa.org/learning/teachers/tipd/tipdeducationusa.shtml

Bronowski, J. (1972). Science and human values. New York: Harper & Row.

Bullough R. V. & Baughman K. (1997). "First-year teacher": Eight years later: An inquiry into teacher development. New York: Teacher College Press.

Carnegie Foundation (2000). The Carnegie Classification of Insitutions of Higher Education. Retrieved on January 28, 2005, from http://www.carnegiefoundation.org/Classification/downloads/2000_Classification.pdf.

Campbell, D.E. (2004). Choosing democracy: a practical guide to multicultural education. New Jersey: Pearson/Merrill Prentice Hall.

Celente, G. (1997) Trends 2000: How to prepare for and profit from the changes of the 21st century. New York, NY: Warner Books.

Center for Educational Research and Innovation. (1994). Quality in teaching (Report). Paris: Organisation for Economic Cooperation and Development.

Chaddock, G. R., (1999). Christian Science Monitor, August 27, 1999, p. 1.

Clyne, M. 1987. Cultural differences in the organization of academic texts. In E. Kuhn, (1996). Cross-cultural stumbling block for international teachers. *College Teaching*, 44(3), 96-100.

Cobern W. W. (1991). (Ed.). Worldview theory and science education research. Manhattan, KS: NARST.

Cobern, W. W. (1993). Contextual constructivism: The impact of culture on the learning and the teaching of science. In K. Tobin (Ed.). The Practice of constructivisn in science teaching. (pp. 51-69). Hillsdale, NJ: Lawrence Erlbaum Associates.

Cochran, K. F., DeRuiter, J.A., & King, R.A. (1993). Pedagogical content knowing: An integrative model for teacher preparation. Journal of Teacher Education, 44(4), 263-272.

Cocoran, E. (1981). Transition shock: The beginning teacher's paradox. Journal of Teacher Education, 32 (3), 19-23.

Cook, S. (2000). Foreign teachers find a place in U.S. schools. Christian Science Monitor. (p. 18.) August, 22, 2000.

Cramer, J. F. & Browne, G. S. (1956). Contemporary education: A comparative study of national systems. In W. B. Spalding (Ed.). New York: Harcourt, Brace & World, Inc.

Dacey, J. S. & Travers, J. F. (1996). Human development across the lifespan. (3rd. Ed.). Dubuque: Iowa. Brown & Benchmark Publishers.

Darling-Hammond, L. (1999). Solving the dilemmas of teacher supply, demand, and standards: How we can ensure a competent, caring, and qualified teacher for every child: A report. National Commission on Teaching & America's Future.

DeBoer, G. E. (1991). A History of Ideas in science education: Implications for practice New York: Teachers College Press.

deMarrais, K. B., & LeCompte, M. D. (1995). The way schools work: A sociological analysis of education (2nd Ed.). White Plains, N.Y.: Longman.

Doran, R. L., Lawrenz, F. & Hegelson, S. (1994). Research on assessment in science. In D. Gabel (Ed.), Handbook of research of science teaching and learning (pp. 389-442). New York: Macmillan.

Driver, R., Asoko, H., Leach, J. Mortimer, E., & Scott, P. (1994) Constructing scientific knowledge in the classroom. Educational Researcher, 23(7), 5-12.

Duit, R. (1992) The Constructivist view: A both fashionable and fruitful paradigm for science education research and practice. A paper presented at the conference on Alternative Epistemologies in Education at the University of Georgia, Athens, GA, 1992.

Dzama, E. N. N. & Osborne, J. F. (1999). Poor performance in science among African students: An alternative explanation to the African worldview thesis. Journal of Research in Science Teaching, Vol. 36, no. 3, pp. 387-405.

Fleer, M. (1997). Science, technology and culture: Supporting multiple world views in curriculum design. Australian Science Teachers Journal, 43(3), 13-18.

Fortuijn, J. D. (2002). Internationalizing learning and teaching: A European experience. *Journal of Geography*, 26 (3), 263-273

Gao, L. (1998). Cultural context of school science teaching in the People's Republic of China. Science Education 82(1), 1-13.

Gardner, H. (1983). Frames of mind: The theory of multiple intelligences. In F. P. Rice, & K. G. Dolgin (2002). The adolescent learner: Development, relationships, and culture (10th Ed.) (p. 152) Boston, MA: Allyn and Bacon.

Gollnick, D., & Chinn, P. (2004). Multicultural education in a pluralistic society. (Multimedia Ed.). Upper Saddle River, NJ: Merrill Prentice Hall.

Grieder, C., Pirece, T. M. & Jordan, K. F. (1969). Public School Administration. New York: The Ronald Press.

Grissmer, D. & Kirby, S. N. (1997). Teacher turnover and teacher quality. Teachers College Record, 99(1), 45-57.

Grossman, P. (1990). The Making of a Teacher: Teacher Knowledge and Teacher Education. In J. Gess-Newsome, & N. G. Lederman, (Eds.) PCK and Science Education. The Netherlands: Kluwer Academic Publications.

Gudmundsdottir, S. (1999). Values in pedagogical content knowledge. Journal of Teacher Education 41(3), 44.

Hassard, J. (2000). Science as Inquiry. New Jersey: Good Year.

Hassard, J. (2005). The Art of Teaching Science, New York: Oxford University Press.

He, M. F. (2000) A narrative of inquiry of cross-cultural lives: lives in Canada. In He, M. F. (2002). A narrative inquiry of cross-cultural lives: Lives in the North American academy. *Journal of Curriculum Studies*, 34 (5), 513-533.

Henry, M. (1989). Multiple support: A promising strategy for teacher induction. In J. Reinhartz, (Ed.). Teacher induction (pp. 74-80). Washington, DC: National Educational Association.

Herriott, R. E. & St. John, N. Y. (1966). Social class and the urban school: The impact of pupil background on teachers and principals. New York: John Wiley & Sons, Inc.

Hillway, T. (Ed.) (1964). American Education: An introduction through readings. A collection of basic documents and literature on the American school system. Boston, MA: Houghton Mifflin Co.

Hobson (1993). In search of a rationale for multicultural science education. Science Education. 77(6): 685-711.

Huling-Austin, L. (1989) A synthesis of research on teacher induction programs and practices. In J. Reinhartz, (Ed.). Teacher Induction (pp. 13-33). Washington, DC: National Educational Association.

Hussar, W. J. (1999). Predicting the need for newly hired teachers in the United States to 2008-09 Washington, DC: U.S. Department of Education, National Center for Education Statistics. (NCES 1999-026).

Hutchison, C. B., Butler, M. B., & Fuller, S. (in press). Pedagogical Communication Issues Arising for Four Expatriate Science Teachers in America. Electronic Journal of Science Education.

Hutchison, S. B. (2005). Effects of and interventions for childhood trauma from infancy through adolescence: Pain unspeakable. New York: NY: The Haworth Maltreatment and Trauma Press.

Ingersoll, R. M. (1997). Teacher turnover and teacher quality: The recurring myth of teacher shortages. Teacher Colleges Record, 99(1), 41-44.

Interstate New Teacher Assessment and Support Consortium (n.d.) Model standards for beginning teacher licensing, assessment, and development: A for state dialogue. Retrieved October 1, 2003, from http://www.ccsso.org/content/pdfs/corestrd.pdf

Jensen, E. (1998). Teaching with the brain in mind. Alexandria, VA: Association for Supervision & Curriculum Development.

Joint Committee on Federal Funds. (n.d.) Federal Block Grants The Focus Of Joint Legislative Committee Hearings. Retrieved on November 22, 2004   from http://www.lsb.state.ok.us/SENATE/news/press_releases/press_releases_199 7/PR97Jul09.html

Kansas State University Counseling Services. (n.d.) Crossing cultures: Adjusting to your new community. Retrieved January 16, 2004 from www.k-state.edu/counseling/culture.html

Kantrowitz, B. & Wingert, P. (2000). Teachers wanted. Newsweek, October 2, 2002, pp. 37-42.

Kearney, M. (1984) World view. In W. W. Cobern (1996). Worldview theory and conceptual change in science education. Science Education, 80(5): 579-610

Kellough, R. D. & Kellough, N. G. (2003). Secondary school teaching: A Guide to methods and resources. Upper Saddle River: New Jersey. Merrill Prentice Hall.

Kuhn, E. (1996). Cross-cultural stumbling block for international teachers. College Teaching, 44(3), 96-100.

Kuhn, T. S. (1962). The structure of scientific revolutions. Chicago, IL: University of Chicago Press.

Ladd, P. & Ruby, Jr. R., 1999. Learning style and adjustment issues of international students. Journal of Education for Business, 74, 363-368.

Levine, M. D. (2002). A mind at a time. NY: Simon & Schuster.

Lindaman, L. & Ward, K. (2004) History Lessons: How Textbooks from Around the World Portray U.S. History. New York: New Press.

Liston D. P. & Zeichner, K.M. (1996). Culture and teaching: Reflective teaching and the social conditions of schooling. New Jersey: Lawrence Erlbaum Associates.

Lortie, D. (1969). The balance of control and autonomy in elementary school teaching In K.B. deMarrais, & M. D. LeCompte. The way schools work: A sociological analysis of education (2nd Ed.) (p. 128). White Plains, N.Y.: Longman.

Macionis, J. J. (1997). Sociology. New Jersey: Prentice Hall.

Mager, G.M. (1992). The place of induction in becoming a teacher. In G. P. DeBolt, (Ed.). Teacher induction and mentoring: School-based collaborative programs (pp. 3-32). New York: State University of New York Press.

Magnusson, S., Krajcik, J., & Borko, H. (1999). Nature, sources, and development of pedagogical content knowledge for science teaching. In J. Gess-Newsome, and N. G. Lederman, (Eds.) PCK and science education (pp. 95-132). The Netherlands: Kluwer Academic Publications.

Mahan, J. M. & Stachowski, L.L. (1994). The many values of international teaching and study experiences for teacher education majors. In Promoting global teacher education: Seven Reports. Reston, VA: Association of Teacher Educators.

Meacham, M. (n.d.) Using Multiple Intelligence Theory in the Virtual Classroom. Retrieved November 6, 2003, from http://www.learningcircuits.org/2003/jun2003/elearn.html

The National Commission on Teaching and America's Future and NCTAF State Partners (2002, August 20-22). Unraveling the "Teacher Shortage" Problem: Teacher Retention is the Key. Washington D.C.. Retrieved August 17, 2004 from http://www.nctaf.org/documents/nctaf/Unraveling_Shortage_Problem.doc

National Council for the Accreditation of Teacher Education (n.d.). About NCATE. Retrieved October 15, 2003 from http://www.ncate.org/ncate/m_ncate.htm

National Education Association. (November 2003 Report). Trends in Foreign Teacher Recruitment. Retrieved February 22, 2004, from http://www.nea.org/teachershortage/0306foreignteacher.html

National School Boards Association (2000, January 11). School districts cast global nets to fill teacher positions. School Board News. Retrieved October 18, 2000, from http://www.nsba.org/sbn/00-jan/011100-3.htm

Nisbett, R. E. (2003). The geography of thought: How Asians and Westerners think differently and why. New York, NY: Free Press.

Odell, S. (1989). Characteristics of beginning teachers. In J. Reinhartz (Ed.). Teacher induction (pp. 42-51). Washington, D.C: National Educational Association of the United States.

Ogawa, M. (1989). Beyond the tacit framework of "science" and "science education" among science educators. In W. W. Cobern. Worldview theory and conceptual change in science education. Science Education 80 (5): 579-610.

Orlosky, D. E. (1988). Introductory remarks in Society, schools, and teacher preparation, in D. E. Orlosky (Ed.). Society, schools, and teacher preparation: A report of the commission on the future education of teachers (Teacher Education Monograph No. 9). Washington, DC: ERIC Clearinghouse on Teacher Education.

Outlaw, Lucius. (November 19, 2003). The Moral Legacy of Slavery: A Case for Reparations. The University of North Carolina at Charlotte Center for Professional and Applied Ethics, Department of Philosophy, and the Honors College Spring 2003 Lecture.

Payne, R. K. (2001). A framework for understanding poverty, Highlands: Texas, aha! Process, Inc.

Persell, C. H. (1977). Education and inequality. New York: Free Press.

Phelan. P., Davidson, A., & Cao, H. (1991). Students from multiple worlds: Negotiating the boundaries of family, peer, and school cultures. In W. W. Cobern. Worldview theory and conceptual change in science education. Science Education 80(5), 579-610.

Pipho, C. (1988). Teacher supply and demand. In D. E. Orlosky, (Ed.) Society, schools, and teacher preparation: A report of the commission on the future education of teachers (Teacher Education Monograph No. 9). Washington, DC: ERIC Clearinghouse on Teacher Education.

Podolefsky, A. & Brown, P. J. (1997). Applying cultural anthropology: An introductory reader. Mountain View, CA: Mayfield Publishing Company.

Rakow, S. J. & Bermudez, A. B. (1993). Science is "ciencia": Meeting the needs of Hispanic American students. Science Education 77(6): 669-687.

Reinhartz, J. (1989) The teacher induction process: Preserving the old and welcoming the new: An introduction. In J. Reinhartz (Ed.). Teacher induction (pp. 4-12). Washington, D.C.: National Educational Association.

Rice, F. P. & Dolgin, K. G. (2002) The adolescent: Development, relationships, and culture. 10th Ed. Boston, MA: Allyn and Bacon.

Roth, Wolff-Michael. (1993). Construction sites: Science labs and classrooms. In K. Tobin (Ed.). The practice of constructivisn in science teaching (pp. 145-170). Hillsdale, NJ: Lawrence Erlbaum Associates.

Russo, C. J. & Cooper, B. S. (1999). Understanding urban education today. Education and Urban Society 31(2), 131-144.

Shatz, M. A. (2002).Teaching thanatology in a foreign country: Implications for death educators. Death Studies, 26: 425-430.

Shulman, L.S. (1986). Those who understand: Knowledge growth in teaching. Education Researcher, 15(2), 4-14.

Shrigley, R. L. (1985). Curbing student disruption in the classroom—teachers need intervention skills. In E. L. Chiappetta & T. R. Koballa, Jr. Science Instruction in the Middle and Secondary Schools. 5th Ed. (p. 231). Upper Saddle River: New Jersey. Merrill Prentice Hall.

Shumba, Overson. (1999). Relationship between secondary science teachers' orientation to traditional culture and beliefs concerning classroom instruction al ideology. Journal of Research in Science Teaching. 36(3), 333-355.

Southern Association of Colleges and Schools. (n.d.) Purpose and Philosophy of Accreditation. Retrieved October 1, 2003 from http://www.sacscoc.org/pdf/principles%20of%20accreditation1.pdf

Special Needs Opportunity Windows (SNOW) Project. "What are my Learning Strengths?" Retrieved December 10 2004 from http://snow.utoronto.ca/courses/mitest.html

Sparks-Langer, G. M., Starko, A. J., Pasch, M., Burke, W., Moody, C. D. & Gardner, T. G. (2004). Teaching as decision making: Successful practices for the secondary teacher. (2nd Ed.). Upper Saddle River: NJ: Pearson/Merrill Prentice Hall.

Spector, B. S. & Lederman, N. G. (1990). Science and technology as human enterprises. In B. Spector & M. Betkouski (Eds.). (p. 23). Science teaching in a changing society. Dubuque, IA: Kendall/Hint Publishing Company.

Stenlund, K. V. (1995). Teacher perceptions across cultures: The impact of students on teacher enthusiasm and discouragement in a cross-cultural context. Alberta Journal of Educational Research. 41(2), 145-161.

Tamir, P. (1988). Subject matter and related pedagogical knowledge in teacher education. In J. Gess-Newsome and N. G. Lederman (Eds.) PCK and science education. (p. 96). Dordrecht, The Netherlands: Kluwer Academic Publishers.

Teacher Advantage. (n.d.) Retrieved on October 1, 2003, from http://www.geocities.com/teacheradvantage/TA.html

Tobin, K. & Tippins, D. (1993). Constructivism as a referent for teaching and learning. In K. Tobin (Ed.) The practice of constructivisn in science teaching (pp. 3-21). Hillsdale, NJ: Lawrence Erlbaum Associates.

Tobin, K. & Tippins, D. (1996). Metaphors as seeds for conceptual change and the improvement of science teaching. Science Education 80(6): 711-730.

Tomlinson, A. (Speaker). (1997). Differentiating Instruction: Creating multiple paths for learning.   [Video]. (Available from Association for Supervision & Curriculum Development, 1703 N. Beauregard St., Alexandria, VA, 22311-1714, USA.)

Traweek, S. (1992). Border crossings: Narrative strategies in science studies among physcists in Tsukuba Science City, Japan. In Pickering, A. (Ed.), Science as practice and culture (pp. 429-465). Chicago: University of Chicago Press.

Urban, W. & Wagoner, J. Jr. (1996). American Education: A History. New York: McGraw-Hill, Inc.

U.S. Department of Education (n.d.) The Federal Role in Education. Retrieved   on   December   1,   2004,   from http://www.ed.gov/about/overview/fed/role.html

U.S. Department of Education (n.d.) The Four Pillars of NCLB. Retrieved   on   December   1,   2004,   from http://www.ed.gov/nclb/overview/intro/4pillars.html

van Driel, J. H., Verloop, N. & de Vos, W. (1998). Developing science teachers pedagogical content knowledge. Journal of Research in Science Teaching. 35(6), 673-695.

Weiss, E. M. & Weiss, S. G. (2000) Beginning teacher induction. ERIC Clearinghouse on Teaching and Teacher Education: Washington, DC. (ERIC No. ED436487)

White, G. W. (2000). Non-verbal communications: Key to improved teacher effectiveness. The Delta Kappa Gamma Bulletin, Summer 2000, 66-74.

Wong H. K. and Wong, R. T. (1998) The first days of school. Sunnyvale: CA: Harry Wong Publications, Inc.

Index

kinds of teachers
    coming to America 12
King, Martin Luther 57
knowledge gaps 139, 215, 255
knowledge shifts 139
Kuhn 1, 57, 139, 290, 293

labor movement 1
language 1, 12, 35, 57, 83, 139, 215, 255
learning
    brain-based 139
learning styles 57
lectures 83, 215
license 12, 35, 215, 255
licenses 35
licensing policy 35
lifestyle 12, 83
linguistic
    communication 57, 83, 139, 215, 255
literature 1, 12, 57, 83, 139, 255, 292
living 1, 12, 57, 83, 139
local 1, 12, 35, 57, 83, 139, 255
Locke 57
logico-structuralism 57
logistical 12, 139, 255

machines 12, 83, 255
Malcom X 57
management 35, 57, 83, 215, 255
media 12, 35, 139
mental 12, 57, 83, 139, 215
mentors 139, 215, 255
migrants 12
model 12, 35, 57, 83, 139, 215, 255, 290
modification
    behavior 215, 255
money 12
movies 12
multiculturalism 57, 215
multiple intelligences 57, 215
multiple realities 57

native language 139
neighbors 12, 83
newspapers 255
Nigeria 12, 83, 139
No Child Left Behind Act 35, 57

on-line 1, 35
opportunity 1, 12, 35, 57, 83, 139, 215, 255
organizations
    organisations 35, 83
orientation 12, 57, 139, 215, 255, 295

pacing guides
    curriculum 57
Pakistan 83
parenthood 215
parents i, 1, 12, 35, 57, 83, 139, 215, 255
parent-teacher conferences 139
passport 12
pedagogy 12, 35, 57, 83, 215, 255, 291, 293, 296, 297
perceptions 83, 215, 296
perspectives 57, 139, 255
philosophical 12, 57, 139
philosophies 57, 255
photocopiers 83
planning 12, 35, 57, 83, 139, 215, 255
pluralism
    cultural 57
poor 1, 12, 35, 57, 83, 139
Praxis Tests 35
precautions 12, 83, 139, 215
pre-lesson activities 215
presentations
    instructional strategies 35, 139, 215
Principal, See administrators
profession 1, 12, 35, 57, 83, 139, 215, 255
professional development 35, 139, 215
professional organizations 35
psychological 12, 35, 57, 83, 139, 215, 255
public education 139
punishment 83, 139, 215

qualifications 12, 83, 255

race 12, 57, 83, 215
record-keeping 139
recreational 12, 255
recruiting agencies 35
reflective 35, 139, 215
reflexive 57